C0-BXA-618

A CELTIC FLORILEGIUM

Brendan P. O Hehir, 11 April 1927 – 17 March 1991

CELTIC STUDIES PUBLICATIONS II

A Celtic Florilegium

Studies in Memory of Brendan O Hehir

edited by
**KATHRYN A. KLAR, EVE E. SWEETSER,
and CLAIRE THOMAS**

CELTIC STUDIES PUBLICATIONS
LAWRENCE, MASSACHUSETTS

First published 1996
First softcover edition 1997
© Kathryn Klar, Eve Sweetser, Claire Thomas

All rights reserved. No part of this book may be reproduced, stored in a retrieval system, or transmitted, in any form or by any means, electronic, mechanical, photocopying, recording, or otherwise, without written clearance from the Publisher

Typesetting by Celtic Studies Publications, Lawrence and Andover, Massachusetts.

Published by Celtic Studies Publications
Division of VonKamecke Corporation
Post Office Box 1178
Andover, Massachusetts 01810
USA

hardcover ISBN: 0-9642446-3-2
paperback ISBN: 0-9642446-6-7

Cover and title page design by Celtic Studies Publications. Drawing by Annalee C. Rejhon, based on a handle of an Irish bucket from the ninth-century Oseberg ship burial, Norway. The figure is reminiscent of the horned god or 'Cernunnos' of the Late La Tène cauldron from Gundestrup, Denmark.

CONTENTS

Hwn yw llyfr Brendan. ∞∞∞∞ ∞∞∞∞ ∞∞∞∞

Brendan O Hehir loved medieval Irish and Welsh texts, and he delighted in sharing that love. Many of us, who at one time or another participated in a working group in Brendan's Wheeler Hall office, experienced the puzzled or mildly suspicious glances of less fortunate passers-by; our waves of laughter over some Old Irish or Middle Welsh wordplay simply sounded too spontaneous to emanate from a serious scholarly endeavor. One of Brendan's jokes was that he just wanted one *little* book for Christmas — just the Cín Dromma Snechta, that famous "Little Book of Snowy Ridge" which contained such fascinating lost Old Irish material, if only we had it. How great was the underlying seriousness of this jesting wish, we did not need to be told. Brendan's loving and masterful connection with Old Irish texts was only too clear to us — in his published and presented work, but also in his teaching. No student could have left his class presentations on *Tochmarc Étaíne* without gaining both a new understanding of the contents and a new appreciation of philological methodology. One cannot doubt that, if he had had his "one little book", it would have been his pleasure to enjoy it and analyze it together with fellow readers — whether in CSANA sessions, in seminar groups, or in discussion over a cup of strong tea.

Here is our little book for Brendan. We began to plan it as a festschrift, and he saw the Tabula Gratulatoria early in 1991, to our happiness and his. It of course became a memorial volume shortly thereafter; but Brendan's untimely death in March 1991 did not change the fact that in editing this collection we have been celebrating his life, while mourning his loss. Every article collected here reflects some aspect of Brendan's wide-ranging interests. Some of them are almost literally continuations of conversations or debates which the authors had with him. Each of them speaks to a topic which continues to be central to the modern study of Celtic languages and literatures. Brendan would be pleased to know that his colleagues and friends continue their dialogues and disputations even in his corporeal absence. Both in its subject matter and in the communal dialogues often so clearly present in its structure, this is Brendan's book. We, and the authors, offer it to him and to our readers.

Many people helped us, nearly all of whom knew Brendan and who were always eager to do more than we asked of them. First, our thanks go to his widow, Laura Morland O Hehir, for encouragement each step of the way and for assistance whenever asked. From the beginning, the officers and membership of The Celtic Studies Association of North America have supported the project, and we owe a debt of gratitude for both their financial and intellectual contributions. The volume was originally to have been published by Pangur Press, under the editorship of Bill Mahon. Before it was ready to go to press, however, the happy circumstance of Bill's accepting a teaching post in Wales meant that a new publisher had to be found. Celtic Studies Publications, in the person of John Koch, stepped immediately into the breach and the process of preparing the manuscript proceeded with scarcely a missed beat. During the last few hectic months, John's editorial expertise has ensured that the quality of this volume would do honor to Brendan's memory.

In Berkeley, many who knew Brendan well or worked closely with him have in some way been involved. Bob Tracy has been an unfailingly genteel source of support, inspiration and assistance. Orin Gensler, a professional editor himself as well as a scholar, devoted many pains-taking hours to reading proofs, at a time when he was preparing to move overseas and could not easily spare the time. Annalee Rejhon gave freely of her talent in designing the title page for the volume. Staff members of the Departments of Scandinavian, Interdisciplinary Studies, and Linguistics provided access to photocopying and postal resources. The frequent, friendly inquiries from colleagues as to how the volume was progressing were constant motivation in the midst of hectic teaching, work and personal schedules. To the authors we can only say that we hope that the book you have in your hands does justice to the quality of your contributions and justifies the patience with which you awaited its appearance.

Finally, two of the editors (Klar and Sweetser) insist that it be noted that without our third colleague, Claire Thomas, this volume would never have appeared. She volunteered her time and expertise in text editing software at the very outset, and it quickly became apparent that her editorial acumen merited her being made a full partner in the venture.

A phopa Bhreandán, this book is yours.

Kathryn A. Klar
Eve E. Sweetser
Claire Thomas

Berkeley
May 1996

AIRNEÁN   VIGIL

Joan Keefe

UNIVERSITY OF CALIFORNIA AT BERKELEY

Go ciúin dall mar Raifteirí
    Éiríonn fairtheoirí as an lá,
    Éisteacht na gcluas acu
Le monabhair dúdhánta

Ag súil go roisfear bréid na hoíche
Á leá le saol amárach,
Aimsítear cruth na gcríoch mara
Trí chasalcheo an tráite,

Carraig Dubh, Sean-Charraig,
  Carraig Liath,
Maitín urnaitheach págánta
D'aon lámh le cling an philibín,
Mac alla chloigín Rónáin

A thionólann na bainteoirí faochan
Ag sleamhnú mar thaibhsí báite,
Is ar gnó an saoil atáid,
Ar thóir raic na móna mara.

Ligeann na tonnta osna cléibh,
Cnagann an coileach feadha,
'Sé a ghrág a scaoileann
Comhlaí le fáinne an lae.

Blind and calm as Raifteirí,
    Watchers forgo day
    Cupping their ears to catch
Murmur of night songs,

With trust that tweed of night will fray,
Ravelled by world loop
Shape of sea regions loom
Through tide's mist cloak,

Carraig Dubh, Sean-Charraig,
  Carraig Liath,
Ancient matin chant,
Echo of Ronan's holy bell
Clink of peewit,

Summons to winkle pickers
Drift of drowned ghosts,
Trailing sea-bog's wrack
To stoop to world work.

Waves heave a heart yawn,
Wood-pheasant snaps,
His rusty crakes unlock
Hatches to daybreak.

March 16, 1991

BRENDAN O HEHIR
A MEMOIR

Robert Tracy

UNIVERSITY OF CALIFORNIA AT BERKELEY

hen Brendan O Hehir arrived in Berkeley in September 1958, as Acting Instructor in English, his resumé made him sound like one of the Beat novelists then in fashion rather than a respectable young academic. Writers like Jack Kerouac, it will be remembered, typically described themselves on the dustjackets of their books as former "longshoreman, short-order cook, lumberjack, tramp, typesetter, oil rigger, racing car driver". The list presumably authenticated the novelist's knowledge of the real America. Brendan made no such claims. His list of jobs previously held was modestly intended only for the obscurity of the Department's files. But it reads rather differently from many of his colleagues' resumés, which listed schools attended, degrees earned, and academic positions held. Brendan had been an underwriter trainee for the Royal Liverpool Insurance Company, pinsetter in the bowling alley at the Chase Manhattan Bank employees' club, a counter hand at the Riis Park Howard Johnson's, a toll collector on the Triborough Bridge, a banker, a census taker. He had conducted writing courses for engineers for the Baltimore Gas and Electric Company. While most of these jobs were summer or part-time employment, Brendan spent almost five years as a full-time career banker at the Union Trust Company of Maryland in Baltimore. He rose rapidly in the Investment Section there, eventually becoming a Corporate Trust Administrator, at a salary, by the standards of 1953, that made his decision to enter graduate school a sacrifice and a genuine act of courage.

This was not the first test of Brendan's courage, nor of his ability and willingness to adapt to drastic changes in his life. He was born in New York City (11 April 1927) of Irish immigrant parents: Andrew J. O Hehir, a post office clerk, and Marie Lennon O Hehir, both originally from Westport, County Mayo. It was a home birth, and Brendan's uncle,

Michael Lennon, was quick to give the infant a spoonful of tea and a volume of Shakespeare, to ensure that he would be "both Irish and a scholar". Clearly, this "magic" took.

Brendan came to learn that the name O Hehir, originally Ó hAichir, derives from *aichear* 'bitter'. The name proved prophetic. Brendan's father fell from a New York subway platform in 1931, into the path of an oncoming train. His widowed mother, who had been a teacher in Ireland, could find little employment in Depression-era New York, and that little was menial and poorly paid. She found it necessary to send Brendan back to Ireland, to live with his grandmother, Margaret Lennon, his uncle Michael, and other members of his mother's family in Clontarf, a north Dublin suburb.

He was fortunate, however, in the Irish household that made him a welcome member. His grandmother and his Aunt Nuala (now Richardson) became in every way second mothers, and his cousin Nuala (now McCabe), a year younger and also part of the household, was like a sister. He remained close to both Nualas until the end of his life. They came from Ireland to visit and reminisce with him in Berkeley not long before he died, to his evident pleasure. His attachment to them was integral to his character. Through them, as well as through his warm relationships with other family members, he arrived at that love of Ireland, the Irish language, and Irish literature which shaped both his personality and much of his academic career.

Brendan's early schooling, at Scoil Cholmcille (also called the Central Model School) in Marlborough Street, Dublin, was conducted in the Irish language. When his mother remarried, she brought him back to New York, which involved a hazardous Atlantic crossing in wartime. At the age of thirteen he had again been uprooted, and had to find his way in a strange new environment, with a new stepfather and soon a new half-sister, Nuala. The authorities at Immaculate Conception, his new school, assumed that the sixth form he had completed in Ireland was the equivalent of the American sixth grade, and so made him repeat a year's schooling. These were further testings of Brendan's ability to adapt to new circumstances.

After a freshman year at Holy Family High, Brendan entered the demanding and prestigious Cardinal Hayes High School in the Bronx. Here many of the priest-teachers were of Irish ancestry, as were a majority of the lay teachers and students. Catholic high schools in the nineteen-forties — I write as a veteran of one — were educationally conservative places. Cardinal Hayes was for boys only, and existed to produce educated Catholic laymen, as well as candidates for the priesthood. Latin was at the center of the curriculum, partly because it was still the language of the Church, partly out of a genuine reverence for the classical tradition, and partly because daily exercises translating from Latin and composing in Latin trained students in verbal dexterity, precision, and clarity of expression. English composition was also important, history, science, and mathematics less so. There was also an emphasis on religious education, learning the doctrines and rituals of the Church. "He had taught me to pronounce Latin properly," the narrator of Joyce's "The Sister" recalls, speaking of the paralyzed Father Flynn; "he had explained to me the meaning of the different ceremonies of the Mass and of the different vestments worn by the priest . . . . Sometimes . . . asking me . . . whether such and such sins were mortal or venial or only imperfections." What the narrator learned reflects the curriculum shared by Joyce at Clongowes Wood and Belvedere, and by Brendan at Cardinal Hayes — though Father Flynn's obsession with "the duties of the priest towards the Eucharist" would have been less prominent.

Brendan had a serious bout with rheumatic fever — initially diagnosed as "growing pains" — when he was about five. A recurrence while he was at Cardinal Hayes made him miss most of his senior year, and permanently weakened his heart. He graduated in 1946, a year late, winning a New York State Scholarship to the university of his choice.

Like many of his classmates, Brendan proceeded to Fordham University, a Jesuit institution as was University College, Dublin, when Joyce studied there. Here again the student body was exclusively male, and predominantly of Irish ancestry. The curriculum, based on the *Ratio studiorum* of St. Ignatius Loyola, gave pride of place to the classical languages and to the study of scholastic philosophy. To look through the Letters and Science courses at a Jesuit university in the late forties is to encounter an educational theory that had changed little since the counter-Reformation, and had been shared with many secular universities, British and American, until about 1900. The teachings of St. Thomas Aquinas were adapted to defend traditional theories of cosmology, psychology, metaphysics, and ethics.

Brendan throve on this traditional curriculum, and was always skeptical about new educational fashions. To his high school and college years of Latin we owe his readiness with the apt Latin phrase, his ability to understand the classically trained mind of Sir John Denham, and above all *A Classical Lexicon for Finnegans Wake* (1977), compiled in collaboration with John Dillon, now Regius Professor of Greek at Trinity College, Dublin, and dedicated "to the whisky distillers of Ireland, without whose spiritual comfort it could never have been brought to completion." As a minor product, there were the many Latin exams that Brendan set and graded for aspiring graduate students over the years. I sometimes worked with him on these, and know how scrupulously he pondered a misidentified adverb or ablative, a mistaken gerund, determined that every detail of the translation be right, or clearly and provably wrong.

To those who knew him after his arrival at Berkeley, Brendan seemed always to have been destined to be a teacher and scholar. But in 1949 he left Fordham without a degree, and moved to Baltimore. At about the same time he married Irene Flynn, from his own New York neighborhood. In Baltimore he became an administrative trainee at the Union Trust Company. Brendan was serious about his banking career, attending evening classes at the American Institute of Banking. He became a successful and valued member of the Union Trust staff. But he was eager to obtain the college degree he had missed, and eager for further literary training. In 1952, while still at Union Trust, he became a part-time student at Loyola College, Baltimore's Jesuit institution. By transferring his Fordham credits, he was able to graduate from Loyola with a B.S. in English in June 1953, and entered the Johns Hopkins M.A. program in Writing, Speech and Drama that September. During the next two years, while a graduate student at Johns Hopkins, Brendan also taught a variety of courses at Loyola: eighteenth-century literature, literary criticism, the modern novel, an American literature survey, Milton.

Brendan received his M.A. with Honors in June 1954, and entered the Johns Hopkins Ph.D. program in the Aesthetics of Literature, transferring to the Department of English in December 1954. There he became particularly interested in the English eighteenth century, the period that was for many years to be his specialty. Hopkins recognized his talent and capacity for hard work with annual scholarships and with teaching fellowships; in 1957-58 a grant from the Fels Foundation of Philadelphia allowed him to carry out research at the British Museum and elsewhere in Britain. His appointment at Berkeley followed. During his first Berkeley year, he taught, as was then customary, three new courses each semester. He also completed his two-volume Johns Hopkins dissertation, "Balanced Opposites in the Poetry of Pope, and the Historical Evolution of the Concept". The dissertation, directed by Professor Earl Wasserman, traced the concept "that things are composed of balanced opposites" from the archaic Ionian "vision of the war of physical 'opposites'" through Heraclitus and Empedocles, Roman and medieval philosophers, and the Renaissance notion of a "double order . . . . In the moral order, reserved to Man . . . contraries can be combined by love; in the physical order, controlled by God, extreme oppositions are resolved by force. By breach of his own order Man becomes subject to God's order." As these brief excerpts from his dissertation abstract suggest, Brendan was examining literature both as an aesthetic and a moral order, and establishing the genealogy of that notion of the reconciliation of opposites which underlies alike the poetry of the Metaphysicals and that of the Augustan Age, as well as the art, architecture, and even landscape gardening of the latter period.

Brendan's first marriage ended early in his time at Johns Hopkins. There he later came to know a fellow graduate student, Diana Farnham Fiske, herself recently divorced. They were married in June 1957, commencing a long and mutually supportive life together. After their move to Berkeley, Diana began a distinguished career at Mills College, where she has chaired both the English Department and the Department of Drama. She has had an even more distinguished career as poet and novelist, publishing collections of verse (*Summoned* (1976), *The Power to Change Geography* (1979), *Home Free* (1988), and *Grace* (1992)); and two novels (*I Wish This War Were Over* (1984) and *The Bride Who Ran Away* (1988)); and also editing *Mothersongs* (1995), an anthology. Brendan took very seriously his stepfatherly responsibilities to Diana's son, Michael Fiske. Their own son, Andrew Willard O Hehir, was born in 1961. Those who knew Brendan only as a distinguished scholar, a committed teacher, or even as gracious host and agreeable companion may be surprised to know how enthusiastically he participated in every kind of father-and-son activity, formal or informal. Perhaps because he had hardly known his own father, perhaps because of his innate sense of responsibility, Brendan tried to be a father to both boys. He was particularly active and supportive during Andrew's Boy Scout career, organizing and attending dads' nights and troop meetings. For several summers he was the sole adult responsible for troop encampments at Camp Wolfeboro on the Stanislaus River.

After completing his studies at Johns Hopkins, Andrew O Hehir settled for a time in San Francisco, where he served as editor of a popular alternative newspaper, *S. F. Weekly*. Brendan lived to see him named "Outstanding Young Journalist of the Year" for 1990 by the Society of Professional Journalists, and knew that Andrew's one-act play, *Impeccable Hearts*, was scheduled for the production it successfully received in May 1991. A full-length play, *Cousin Martin*, about a young American discovering his family's Irish past, was performed in Berkeley in 1993 and in San Francisco in 1994. In 1995 Andrew became a freelance writer in New York.

During his first year at Berkeley, Brendan faced a potential problem, or rather suspicion, since his father-in-law, Willard Farnham, a distinguished Shakespeare scholar, was a senior member of the English Department. This situation necessitated considerable tact on the part of both men, and both rose to the necessity. Professor Farnham, who retired in 1959, carefully excluded himself from any participation in Brendan's appointment, Brendan and Diana avoiding the same topic. Despite this potential element of stress, Brendan and his father-in-law became close friends during Farnham's twenty years of retirement.

Brendan's career at Berkeley was outwardly like most successful academic careers — a matter of courses taught, articles published, papers delivered, promotions in regular order: to Assistant Professor in 1960, Associate Professor in 1965, Professor in 1970. He made several close collegial friendships, with Professors Ralph Rader, Norman Rabkin, and the late Shelley Sacks. He served on the Committee for Educational Policy (1970–72), the second year as Chair, with concurrent membership on the University Committee for Educational Policy. He received a Guggenheim Fellowship in 1965, and a Berkeley Humanities Research Fellowship in 1972. In 1981–82 the Department of English honored him by appointing him Gayley Lecturer; his lecture in that capacity, "The Cracked Looking-Glass of a Servant: Irish Writers and Irish Art", discussed the role of colonialism in creating a sense of inferiority among Irish writers, then a novel approach to problems of Irish literature.

Despite its chronological conventionality, Brendan's academic career is marked by one, possibly two, major shifts of interest. Speaking at the California Celtic Conference on the morning after Brendan's death, Professor Daniel Melia commented on his courage — that specific kind of academic courage which sometimes empowers a scholar to abandon a field in which he has become a recognized authority, and move into a very different area. In Brendan's case, that shift occurred after he had become a respected figure in neoclassic studies, where he made his mark with two related books that immediately became standard works: *Harmony from Discords* (1968), his biography of the poet and royalist Sir John Denham (1615–69), and *Expans'd Hieroglyphicks* (1969), a critical edition and study of Denham's best known poem, *Coopers Hill* (1642, revised 1655).

Rigorously scholarly, engagingly written, these works drew upon all Brendan's powers and skills: his strong sense of history; his commitment to balance and order, sometimes sorely tried in the Berkeley of the nineteen-sixties; his passion for verbal accuracy; his classical background, especially noticeable in his telling comparison of *Coopers Hill* with Virgil's first *Georgic*; his capacity for sympathy as he narrated Denham's checkered career. With characteristic ingenuity, Brendan used Moses Pengtry's 1676 Latin version of *Coopers Hill* to examine the ways in which Denham's contemporaries would have understood the poem.

Harmony from Discords and *Expans'd Hieroglyphicks* are in a sense a single book. In *Expans'd Hieroglyphicks*, Brendan looks at successive versions of *Coopers Hill* as Denham altered it over the course of his life, noting how each version was shaped by political and personal events. "Denham's public life", Brendan remarks early in *Harmony from Discords*, reveals not only a glimpse or two of the private man, but explains much about his poems . . . . Denham's character was a peculiar blend of weakness and strength which finds its correlative exactly in his poetic work. Like all his contemporaries, he lived through trying times; his reactions to the pressures of those times reveal his character, and his character reflects itself in his verse . . . .

The politic temporizing typical of Denham's career may be seen also . . . in his revisions of *Coopers Hill*. After his own initial composition of the poem he was able to absorb into the text the emblematic value of St. Paul's Cathedral thrust upon him by Waller's poem on its renovation. A decade later, the utter defeat of Royalism having rendered ludicrous the tenets of the original poem, Denham had the resilience to recast it, so that a new statement, appropriate to the change in times, arose from his warping or from his sacrifice of parts of the original. Not only did the new text comply with the times, however deleting the person of Charles I and acknowledging the outcome of the war or even speak with a new apparent universality . . . but it contained, I believe, a number of covert gibes at the new order established in the land. While outwardly complying with the state, while altering his poem in a way that seemed superficially to make it comply also . . . Denham covertly vented his discontent. (*Harmony from Discords*, pp. 1–3)

In his *Lives of the Poets*, Samuel Johnson describes Denham as the originator of "a species of composition that may be denominated local poetry, of which the fundamental subject is some particular landscape, to be poetically described, with the addition of such embellishments as may be supplied by historical retrospection or incidental meditation." *Coopers Hill* is indeed such a poem, but in *Expans'd Hieroglyphicks* Brendan shows how it is far more. The Surrey landscape Denham describes and meditates upon includes Windsor Castle and Windsor Forest, Runnymede, the Thames, and the distant London towers of old St. Paul's. In Brendan's phrase, it is a "great public manuscript . . . written in the landscape in God's hieroglyphics" summarizing England's history, a text to be read in a particular way by a royalist on the eve of the Cromwellian rebellion. For Denham, the landscape contrasted the King's residence and Puritan London:

Everything within that landscape, whether made by God or man . . . is a hieroglyph, impresa, or short emblem. The pall of cloud covering London is an accurate hieroglyph of the self-defeating busyness of the Londoners, engendered as it directly is by that very busyness . . . Windsor Hill and Windsor Castle were their "Masters Embleme" . . . St. Anne's Hill, denuded of its crowning chapel, served as a lively hieroglyph for the despoliation of the church; the Thames, flowing past Windsor, Cooper's Hill, St. Anne's Hill, and London, vividly represented all that connected those points; the flow of history, the all-encompassing constitution of the commonweal, God's design and providence, the flow of the poet's own verse. The meadow of Runnymede, a low place embraced between stream and rugged hill, was a natural hieroglyph for the great event that took place there: the meeting between King and subjects. (*Expans'd Hieroglyphicks*, p. 20)

As Denham reads it, the text endorses harmony, poetic as well as topographical, a harmony based on contraries: "The harmony of things, / As well as that of sounds from discords springs." Even methods for controlling the Thames at flood-time become metaphors for maintaining political order and controlling potentially destructive elements.

It seemed probable that Brendan would turn to another seventeenth- or eighteenth-century subject, and in fact he carried out a considerable amount of research for a book about the concept of kingship in English literature from the Age of Elizabeth to the early years of the nineteenth century. The subject developed naturally out of his concern with Denham's royalism. Royalists traditionally spoke of the King in almost godlike terms, especially in the role of maintainer of order by balancing oppositions. The book was to move from the cult of Elizabeth I as Diana or Gloriana, celebrated by Lyly and Spenser, through the central role of the King in Stuart masques and the frequent celebrations of Charles I or Charles II as Augustus by Waller, Lovelace, and Dryden. Pope's inability to see George I or George II as an Augustus becomes the mock celebration of his "To Augustus" (1737), aimed at George II: "How shall the Muse, from such a Monarch, steal / An hour, and not defraud the Public Weal?" Though Pope yearns for the power "Your Arms, your Actions, your Repose to sing!", he reminds us, and the hapless king, that "a fate attends on all I write, / That when I aim at praise, they say I bite." George III, another of the "inverted Augusti" (Brendan's phrase), is pilloried in Byron's *Vision of Judgment* (1822); George IV becomes Shelley's *Oedipus Tyrannus: or, Swellfoot the Tyrant* (1820).

But instead, Brendan turned away from neoclassic studies, though he continued for some years to offer classes in eighteenth-century literature. He sometimes described his abandonment of neoclassic studies as resulting from the sudden death, by cancer, of Miriam Lehrenbaum, whose dissertation he considered the most brilliant he had ever encountered. Though she died before achieving tenure at SUNY-Binghampton, her colleagues there shared Brendan's high opinion and instituted an annual lecture in her honor.

Brendan re-emerged as a major contributor to Joyce studies, bringing to bear upon Joyce's texts that knowledge of Irish he had acquired in his early schooling, and the knowledge of Dublin topography and folkways acquired at the same time. Few Joyce scholars were thus equipped. Brendan, who had written on Denham's "local poetry", recognized Joyce's localism. He made it his business to examine those uniquely Irish, even uniquely Dublin, elements which he was so well prepared to understand. By 1964, as he was completing his work on Denham,

Brendan had begun to publish a series of notes and comments on aspects of *Finnegans Wake* in *A Wake Newslitter* and the *James Joyce Quarterly*. These notes later became the entertaining appendices to his *Gaelic Lexicon for Finnegans Wake* (1967).

Osip Mandelstam insisted that an intellectual has no biography other than the books he has read and the books he has written. Brendan's intellectual life is indeed embodied in his books, and continues in them. We can perhaps recognize an emotional as well as an intellectual shift when he turns from neoclassic order and reason, shaped into the heroic couplets of Sir John Denham, to the controlled anarchy of *Finnegans Wake* — perhaps his response to the sixties in Berkeley, perhaps, on an even more personal level, his response to a personal crisis, his near death from a defective heart valve early in 1966. Brendan's condition was severe enough to necessitate a then new and risky operation, the implantation of a steel and silicon heart valve at Stanford Medical Center by Dr. Norman Shumway, who had recently developed this surgical technique. His own determination to live, Diana's support, and the skill of Dr. Shumway and his associates brought Brendan through this crisis and gave him an extra quarter century of life. In gratitude, he dedicated the *Gaelic Lexicon* to Shumway and his surgical team, and to Dr. A. A. Bolomey, his cardiologist at Kaiser Oakland, "because they gave me back my life", he once remarked — though one reviewer in Ireland ridiculed the dedication as revealing Americans' excessive adulation of doctors.

A glance at Brendan's bibliography suggests that his shift from neoclassic studies to Joyce studies, and even his later shifts into Old and Middle Irish and medieval Welsh studies, reveal underlying patterns. His fascination with the writer who has described Dublin most evocatively was a reminder of his own Dublin childhood. Brendan's first published scholarly article was on an Irish subject, Thomas Moore's "The Song of Fionnuala" (*Explicator*, January 1957), which he read mythically and as political allegory, but also defended as "lyric utterance" possessing "poetic seriousness". His second publication, "Structural Symbol in Joyce's 'The Dead'" (*Twentieth Century Literature* 3:1 (April 1957)), was subsequently reprinted in a case book on Joyce's story. Swift, another Dubliner, though often an unwilling one, was the subject of his third publication, "Meaning in Swift's 'Description of a City Shower'" (*ELH* 27 (1960)). Even Sir John Denham was a Dubliner by birth, though he spent most of his life in England. In his early years, Denham lived as boisterously as those Captain Fitzwaters and Sir Lucius O'Triggers who enlivened eighteenth-century English literature and serve as prototypes for the swaggering stage Irishman. Edmund Waller described Denham's literary debut, with a tragedy, *The Sophy* (1641), as breaking "out like the Irish Rebellion, threescore thousand strong, when no body was aware, or in the least suspected it." The shape of a career can never be discerned until it is ended. Brendan's reveals a sturdy inner consistency, bringing him "by a commodius vicus of recirculation back to Howth Castle and Environs."

The *Gaelic Lexicon* identified Irish words and phrases in Joyce's work. But it performed an equally valuable task, and gave a new direction to Joyce studies, by revealing to us how much Irish Joyce actually knew. Most critics had taken at face value Stephan Dedalus's impatience with Irish language enthusiasts and the "broken lights of Irish myth . . . its unwieldy tales that divided themselves as they moved down the cycles." They assumed too readily that Stephen spoke for Joyce. Thanks to Brendan, we know that the Irish language, however imperfectly learned, was a vital element in Joyce's literary development, and especially vital to the vast linguistic experiment that is *Finnegans Wake*. We know too how well-versed Joyce was in those myths that Stephen dismissed as "broken lights".

No one can seriously read *Finnegans Wake*, or indeed any of Joyce's work, without some debt to the *Gaelic Lexicon* and its successor, *A Classical Lexicon*. For many years thereafter, Brendan worked on a "Polyglossary" for *Finnegans Wake*, a page-by-page guide to the more than 250 languages — apart from English — used in the text. The dreaming sleeper in *Finnegans Wake* is Everyman, past, present, and perhaps to come, and therefore polylingual. Joyce modestly claimed to have incorporated at least a few words from every known language. Brendan, with the help of many volunteers around the globe, set out to examine this claim — to track down the Amharic and Samoan and Kwakiutl words lurking in, merging into, the work's basic English vocabulary. He was quick to recognize the value of the computer and word processor for such a task. He completed this mighty enterprise shortly before his death. All his findings, and those of his informants, are safely stored. The Polyglossary will be published electronically rather than as a conventional book; it will be available over licensed Internet sites.

Brendan's scholarly and creative work in the seventies and eighties consists of nearly forty papers, chiefly on Irish topics, read at scholarly meetings and/or published in the appropriate journals. Apart from these, he completed a splendid and witty translation, in every way worthy of the original, of *An Béal Bocht* "The Poor Mouth" (1941), a satiric novel in Irish by Myles na Gopaleen (also known as Flann O'Brien and, to the Registrar of Voters, as Brian O'Nolan). In Irish English, to be making a poor mouth is to be continually celebrating your own misery and poverty, or generally complaining. The novel is at once a sardonic commentary on Gaelic language enthusiasts, themselves usually middle class and settled comfortably in Dublin, but eager to preserve the Gaelic way of life in the remote — and poverty-stricken — Irish-speaking areas of the south and west, and on the brutal squalor endured by those remote Irish speakers in their damp cabins. In Brendan, Myles found a translator who shared his evident love for the Irish language, his scorn for some of its exploiters, and his lively sense of the ridiculous. For a time, in the early seventies, as Brendan worked on *An Béal Bocht*, his friends were privileged to receive weekly translated installments, eagerly awaited. It is hoped that a publisher will be found, so that Brendan's version can achieve the wider audience it deserves.

During the same period, that is, the seventies and eighties, Brendan increasingly turned his attention to Old and Middle Irish literature, exploring further the epic material that Joyce had drawn upon in *Finnegans Wake*, as well as other epic and saga material from the earliest periods of Irish literature. One immediate consequence of these interests was a new course, or rather two new courses, for undergraduates, offering between them a survey of Irish literature in Irish and in English from those earliest times to the present day, or, to put it more epigrammatically, from Maeldúin to Muldoon. Brendan devised a one-quarter — later one-semester — course featuring the *Lebor Gabála*, *Fled Bricrenn*, *Togail Bruidne Da Derga*, *Tóraigheacht Dhiarmada agus Ghráinne*, *Táin Bó Cúailnge*, and *Aislinge Meic Conglinne*, among others, to be read in English translation. To my great pleasure, he invited me to devise the related successor course, dealing with Irish literature written in English from 1800 to the present — that is, from approximately the time when Irish, as the generally spoken language of Ireland, gave way to English. The premise of the course was that Irish literature shows a continuity of themes and attitudes, despite the change of language by the nineteenth century. Yeats's adaptation of episodes from the *Táin* in his *On Baile's Strand* (1904), *The Only Jealousy of Emer* (1919), and *The Death of Cuchulain* (1939), or Joyce's use of Fionn mac Cumhail in *Finnegans Wake*, obviously draw upon Old Irish material deliberately. But there is also a continuity of themes when Thady Quirk's celebration of the Rackrents' recklessness and improvidence in *Castle Rackrent* (1800) ironically recalls the traditional Irish bard's celebration of his chieftain's open-handed generosity; Yeats's poems about Coole Park and those who lived there echo traditional poems in praise of a chieftain's nobility, bravery, and generosity in a more respectful way. The pedantic playfulness of Flann O'Brien's *At Swim-Two-Birds* (1939) resembles that of *Aislinge Meic Conglinne*. So do the parodic aspects of *Ulysses*. Stephen Dedalus's ornithological ancestry recalls Cuchulain's.

Initiated in winter and spring quarters 1974, the course became a regular offering of the English department, and eventually a part of the Celtic Studies Program. During our first few years of teaching the course together, always in successive terms, Brendan and I regularly attended each other's classes, I to offer brief comments on parallels yet to come, he to remind students of parallels past. I learned a great deal about Old and Middle Irish literature from his lectures. I also came to understand what a splendid teacher he was — how careful in explaining difficult material, clarifying for contemporary minds these ancient texts, with their obscurities of custom and motivations. Brendan was always eager that his students come to share his interest, and indeed his delight, in the material he revealed to them.

For many years, Brendan had generously taught Irish to anyone wishing to learn it, without any recognition of this task in terms of course credit or course relief. He was eager that I learn Irish as well, and for a ten-week quarter he set aside three hours every Friday afternoon to tutor me. I cannot claim now to remember much of the vocabulary I then slowly acquired, nor can I now master the more recondite devices of Irish grammar that he explained so well. I could never fully enter into his enthusiasm for the rules of nasalization or lenition. But I can now work my way through an Irish text, with a dictionary, well enough at least to be skeptical about translations. What chiefly remains is a sense of the power of the language, its role in shaping English as it is now spoken in Ireland — that, and Brendan's evident love of Irish, and of sharing that love.

Since he was now regularly teaching Old and Middle Irish literature, Brendan began to look for better translations of some of the material. Apart from Thomas Kinsella's version of the *Táin*, which he warmly welcomed, most of the available translations of early Irish literature dated from the nineteenth or early twentieth century. They were stilted in their diction, and later linguistic or archeological research had clarified much that was obscure to earlier translators and scholars. In some cases, a combination of Victorian prudery and Irish nationalism had suppressed some of the heroes' gaudier exploits, especially their sexual exploits: Brendan would disdainfully quote Lady Gregory dedicating her *Cuchulain of Muirthemne* (1902) to "the People of Kiltartan": "I left out a good deal I thought you would not care about for one reason or another . . . ."

Brendan sensibly decided to translate the necessary texts himself, and produced a photocopied course reader, "Six Old Irish Tales", which gradually became "Ten", "Twelve", and finally "Twenty-Four Old Irish Tales". The translations clarify without simplifying their difficult originals. Brendan developed an on-going seminar, regularly attended by those with enough Irish to collaborate with him in elucidating these often baffling stories, full as they are of archaic concepts and terms that were sometimes unintelligible even to the medieval scribes who copied from earlier manuscripts. These tales, with explanatory notes, also await publication.

Brendan was a founding member of the Celtic Studies Association of North America (1978), and, with Annalee Rejhon and Professor Dan Melia of Berkeley, and Professor Patrick Ford (then of UCLA), he was a founder of the University of California Celtic Conference (1979), which meets annually, alternating between Berkeley and UCLA. In 1980 he began the study of medieval Welsh with a Berkeley colleague, Kathryn Klar, and soon began to publish on Welsh as well as Irish literature.

In Kathryn Klar's class, Brendan, Eve Sweetser, and Klar first read together the body of medieval Welsh poetry known as the *Gododdin* (also called *Canu Aneirin*, after Sir Ifor Williams's 1938 edition). The result was a decade of collaboration, often of weekly meetings, as they worked to re-evaluate both the poems and the poetics shaping them. Beginning with a joint presentation at the 1981 U.C. Celtic Conference and making an international debut in 1983 at the International Congress of Celtic Studies at Oxford, "Y Tîm" ("the Team", as Welsh colleagues christened them), Klar, O Hehir, and Sweetser gradually worked toward a re-edition of the *Gododdin* poems, as part of a monograph on Welsh poetics, which Klar and Sweetser are currently preparing for publication. The trio's work has already provoked considerable discussion in Welsh scholarly circles, notably during their joint special exchange with Welsh scholars at the Aberystwyth Colloquium ar yr Hengerdd in 1984.

Brendan's work as a member of "Y Tîm" was characteristic of his teaching and his collegial relationships. With his characteristic immersion in a text and its problems, and the scholarly humility that such immersion often brings, he brought his immense knowledge of Celtic poetic tradition to bear on each poem. His collaborators found him a constant source of brilliant analyses, as well as an enthusiastic and supportive listener as they developed their own ideas. This Welsh project continued and extended Brendan's earlier interests, especially in issues of literacy and orality, and in early Celtic metrics.

In 1983 Brendan met Laura Morland, then a graduate student in the Berkeley Department of English, a medievalist who shared his interest in the Celtic areas of northern Europe. They were married on March 22, 1987, in a joyous Faculty Club ceremony, exchanging a portion of their marriage vows in the language, and indeed the very words, of the legendary lovers in the ninth-century *Tochmarc Étaíne*. Brendan's great happiness was evident as they began what was to be a strong and affectionate marriage, though shadowed by ill health. Cancer of the colon, in the summer of 1987, necessitated two operations and a lengthy hospital stay. Later cancer was to return in the form of the brain tumor which brought about his death. Through this period of recurrent illness, Laura encouraged, cheered, and sustained him. She became his nurse, his secretary, his research assistant, his advocate with doctors and nurses. Their brief marriage was an intensely happy one. Laura enabled him to die at home with dignity. Later she carried out his last wish, that his ashes be carried to Ireland and scattered in Blasket Sound, joining lost Armada sailors and drowned Kerry fishermen in sight of the Blasket Islands. There the Irish language he loved had survived until the forced evacuation of the Great Blasket in 1953, flowering in a remarkable trio of writers, Peig Sayers, Tomás Ó Criomhtháin, and Muiris Ó Suilleabhán, who gave us, in E. M. Forster's phrase, "an account of neolithic civilization from the inside . . . itself become vocal, and address[ing] modernity."

Also in the eighties, Brendan was working to fulfill a long-cherished dream, the establishment of a Celtic Studies Program at Berkeley. Together with Daniel Melia of the Department of Rhetoric, Robert Tracy of English, and Eve Sweetser and Gary Holland of Linguistics, he planned and organized an undergraduate major that emphasized the learning of Celtic languages, especially Welsh and Irish, and also offered courses in the Celtic literatures. Celtic Studies formally began operation in spring semester of 1989, with Brendan, all too briefly, as the Program's first Chair. It was fitting that when the President of Ireland, Mary Robinson, visited the University on 18 October 1991, she paid a special tribute to Brendan's work in establishing Irish studies at Berkeley. He was also remembered — and commended — at the Celtic Program's first graduation exercises, in May 1992.

Brendan often visited family and friends in Ireland during the seventies and eighties. On his last trip, in the summer of 1990, he also spent time with Dr. Joan Keefe's Irish class from Berkeley, then in residence at Ballyferriter in the Kerry Gaeltacht. It was clear that his health was failing, though he continued to work as hard as any two colleagues, administering Celtic Studies, teaching, and writing. On November 26, 1990, he was diagnosed as suffering from a metastatic brain tumor, and by early January 1991 it was evident that the end was near. He continued to see students at home, to invite friends to visit, to listen to music, and, like Pangur Ban's master, to take pleasure in the activities of Angie, his one-eyed tabby.

He helped plan the Celtic Conference scheduled for mid-March of 1991 in Berkeley, in conjunction with the annual meeting of the Celtic Studies Association of North America (CSANA). "Y Tîm" continued to meet. Brendan described the *Gododdin* project as the work he was most eager to complete, and his two collaborators presented at the Conference a paper on *Gwarchan Maeldderw*, a section of the *Gododdin* corpus, based on their recent findings. He and Laura hoped that one session, the CSANA text seminar on the *Gododdin*, could take place in their living room, so that Brendan could participate as an international group of scholars discussed and responded to the Team's work.

But on the scheduled day — 16 March — Brendan was dying. He had asked Laura to continue in her role as Chair of the Conference. His son

Andrew was with him all day. By one last effort of will, a brave and loving gesture, he lived until Laura returned in the early evening, then made his farewells to them both. Laura was able to send word to the Conference banquet, where participants rose for a moment of commemorative and sorrowful silence. Many of his close friends and colleagues then went to the house, to commence an impromptu wake that lasted well into the morning. Since it was already St. Patrick's Day in Ireland, and even in New York, it was generally agreed that March 17 would be Brendan's official date of death.

Brendan had ceased to be a practicing Catholic as a young man. When he planned his memorial service, many years before his death, he envisioned a secular Faculty Club gathering, and chose music with that setting in mind. However, due partly to the encouragement of his visiting Irish family, he rejoined the Church a month before he died. This meant that he would have a funeral mass in his parish church. The pastor generously agreed that some of Brendan's musical choices be retained, and so the recessional to the mass was a pagan hero's farewell: Siegfried's funeral march from *Götterdämmerung*.

BRENDAN P. O HEHIR
WRITINGS AND LECTURES

1957

"Moore's 'The Song of Fionnuala'", *Explicator* 15:4 (January), item 23.

"Structural Symbol in Joyce's 'The Dead'", *Twentieth Century Literature* 3:1 (April), pp. 3–13. Revised and reprinted in *Joyce's The Dead* (a casebook), William T. Moynihan, ed. (Boston: Allyn & Bacon, 1960), pp. 120–32.

1960

"Meaning in Swift's 'Description of a City Shower'", *Journal of English Literary History* 27:3 (September), pp. 194–207.

"Virtue and Passion: the Dialectic of *'Eloisa to Abelard'*", *Texas Studies in Literature and Language* 2:2 (summer 1960), pp. 219–32. Revised and reprinted in *Essential Articles for the Study of Alexander Pope*, Maynard Mack, ed. (Hamden, CT: Archon Books, 1964), pp. 310–26.

1963

"Vergil's First *Georgic* and Denham's *Cooper's Hill*", *Philological Quarterly* 42:4 (October), pp. 542–47.

1964

"Denham's *Cooper's Hill* and Poole's *English Parnassus*", *Modern Philology* 61:4 (May), pp. 253–60.

"'Lost', 'Authorized' and 'Pirated' Editions of John Denham's *Cooper's Hill*", *PMLA* 79:3 (June), pp. 242–53.

"The Humptyhillhead of Mulachy our Kingable Khan, according to Dinny Finneen", *A Wake Newslitter* 1:4 (August), pp. 3–4.

"The Names of Shem and Shaun: 1. The Names of Shaun", *A Wake Newslitter* 1:5 (October), pp. 1–6.

1965

"Anna Livia Plurabelle's Gaelic Ancestry", *James Joyce Quarterly* 2:3 (spring), pp. 158–66.

1966

"The Early Acquaintance of Denham and Waller", *Notes and Queries*, New Series 13:1 (vol. 211 of Continuous Series) (January), pp. 19–23.

"The Names of Shem and Shaun: 2. The Names of Shem", *A Wake Newslitter* 3:5 (October), pp. 91–93.

"The Name of Humphrey", *A Wake Newslitter* 3:5 (October), pp. 93–96.

"That Cute Old Speckled Church", *A Wake Newslitter* 3:6 (December), pp. 124–25.

"A Correction and Addition Corrected and Added To", *A Wake Newslitter*, 3:6 (December), pp. 129–30.

1967

A Gaelic Lexicon for Finnegans Wake *and Glossary for Joyce's Other Works* (Berkeley and Los Angeles: University of California Press) [monograph].

"O'Cannochar, O Conchobhair, Conchobhar", *A Wake Newslitter* 4:4 (August), pp. 67–72.

1968

Harmony from Discords: A Life of Sir John Denham (Berkeley and Los Angeles: University of California Press) [monograph].

"An Unnoticed Textual Crux in *Ulysses*", *James Joyce Quarterly*, 5:4 (summer), pp. 297–98.

"Whines, Whiskey, Life, Death, in Polyglutteral", *A Wake Newslitter*, New Series, 5:5 (December), p. 74.

"The family of Denham of Egham", *The Surrey Archaeological Collections* 65, pp. 71–85.

1969

Expans'd Hieroglyphicks: A Study of Sir John Denham's "Coopers Hill," with a Critical Edition of the Poem (Berkeley and Los Angeles: University of California Press) [monograph].

1970

"*The Poetry of Limitation: A Study of Edmund Waller*. By Warren L. Chernaik", *Modern Philology* 68:1 (August), pp. 100-105 [review].

1972

"Who is to be Master?: Linguistic Autarchy in the 'Cyclops' Chapter of *Ulysses*". Paper read at MLA Convention (New York).

1974

"Some Problems in the Decipherment of Ogam, and a Few Tentative Solutions". Lecture presented to Irish Literary and Historical Society (San Francisco).

1975

"The Origins of the Celtic Nations". Lecture presented at International House (Berkeley).

"Sir John Denham (1615-1669)". Bibliographical note. In *Crowell's Handbook of Elizabethan and Stuart Literature*. James E. Ruott, ed. (New York: Thomas Y. Crowell Company) 108-9.

1977

A Classical Lexicon for Finnigans Wake: *A Glossary of the Greek and Latin in the Major Works of Joyce* (with John Dillon) (Berkeley, Los Angeles, and London: University of California Press) [monograph].

"A Crux within a 'Retoiric' in *Tochmarc Étaíne*, and some suggestions about 'Retoirics'". Paper read at Kentucky Foreign Language Conference (Lexington, Kentucky).

1978

"Adaline Glasheen, '*A Third Census of* Finnegans Wake'; Roland McHugh, *The Sigla of Finnegans Wake*; Margot Norris, *The Decentered Universe of* Finnegans Wake", *Novel* 12 (fall), pp. 78-85 [review].

1979

"Máirtín Ó Cadhain, *An tSraith Tógtha*", *World Literature Today* 53 (winter), p. 167 [review].

"*Paddy No More: Modern Irish Short Stories*", *World Literature Today* 53 (summer), pp. 544-45 [review].

"Seán Sheáin Í Chearnaigh, *Iarbhlascaodach ina Dheorai*", *World Literature Today* 53 (autumn), pp. 729-30 [review].

"Nioclás Tóibin, *Duanaire Déiseach*", *World Literature Today* 53 (autumn), p. 730 [review].

"Re-Grafting a Severed Tongue: Reviving Irish". Paper delivered to a panel on Reviving Languages, MLA Convention in December (San Francisco). Published in *World Literature Today* 54 (1980).

1980

"Flann O'Brien, *A Flann O'Brien Reader*, Stephen Jones, ed.", *World Literature Today* 54 (winter), p. 155 [review].

"Breandán Ó hEithir, *Lead Us Into Temptation*, Breandán Ó hEithir, tr.", *World Literature Today* 54 (winter), pp. 155-56 [review].

"Re-Grafting a Severed Tongue: The Pains (and Politics) of Reviving Irish", *World Literature Today* 54 (spring), pp. 213-17.

"Seán Ó Faoláin, *And Again?*", *World Literature Today* 54 (autumn), pp. 682-83 [review].

"Yeats and the Irish Language". Paper presented to PAPC Conference in November (Berkeley). Revised and printed as "Kickshaws and Wheelchairs: Yeats and the Irish Language", *Yeats* I, pp. 92-103.

1981

"Seán Ó Luing, *Ó Donnabháin Rosa* II", *World Literature Today* 55 (winter), pp. 159-60 [review].

"Fallon & Golden eds. *Soft Day: A Miscellany of Contemporary Irish Writing*; Bradley, ed. *Contemporary Irish Poetry: An Anthology*", *World Literature Today* 55 (summer), pp. 514-15 [review]

"Ireland Before Saint Patrick". Illustrated lecture, Oakland Public Library in March.

"The Meters of the *Gododdin* Re-examined". Paper presented to Celtic Studies Association of North America (CSANA) Conference in April (Lexington, Kentucky).

"The Poetics of the *Gododdin*". Paper delivered to California Celtic Conference in May (Berkeley).

"Art of Ireland: Joyce's Environment". Lecture at a James Joyce Marathon in November (Berkeley).

1982

"The Corpus of the *Gododdin*". Paper delivered to Berkeley Celtic Colloquium in February.

"The Cracked Looking-Glass of a Servant: Irish Writers and Irish Art". Presented to English Department and Center for Study of Folklore and Mythology, UCLA, in March. Also presented in April as the Gayley Lecture (English Department, University of California at Berkeley).

"Cardiff Ms. Welsh I, Called *Llyfr Aneirin*: The Make-up of the Book and the Corpus of the *Gododdin*". Paper presented to CSANA Conference in May (UCLA).

"Joyce and Irish Art". Paper presented at VIII James Joyce Symposium Centenary in June (Dublin).

1983

"Is *o* a Graph for *w* in Older Welsh?" Paper presented to CSANA Conference in April (University of Chicago).

"Welsh Metrics in the Indo-European Tradition: the Case of the Book of Aneirin" (with Kathryn Klar and Eve E. Sweetser). Paper delivered at the VII International Congress of Celtic Studies in July (Oxford University).

"The Christian Revision of *Eachtra Airt meic Cuind ocus Tochmarc Delbchaime Ingine Morgain*" in *Celtic Folklore and Christianity, Studies in the Memory of William W. Heist*, Patrick K. Ford, ed. (Santa Barbara: McNally & Loftin and Los Angeles: Center the Study of Comparative Folklore and Mythology, UCLA), pp. 159–79.

1983–1984

"Welsh Poetics in the Indo-European Tradition" (with Kathryn Klar and Eve E. Sweetser). *Studia Celtica* XVIII–XIX, pp. 30–51.

1984

"Traces of Lost Welsh Myth in the Book of Aneirin". Paper presented to CSANA Conference in April (Queens College, New York).

"Too Many Dogs in Ayrshire: What is *Aeron*?" Paper presented to California Celtic Conference in May (UCLA).

"What Is the *Gododdin*?". Paper presented at *Colloquium ar yr Hengerdd*, National Library of Wales in June (Aberystwyth). Published in *Early Welsh Poetry — Studies in the Book of Aneirin* (1988).

"Flann O'Brien and the Big World". Paper delivered at the Interim Congress of the International Association for the Study of Ango-Irish Literature, in July (Graz, Austria). Published in *Literary Interrelations: Ireland, England and the World*, vol. 3: *National Images and Stereotypes*, Wolfgang Zach, Heinz Kosok, eds. (Tubingen: G. Narr Verlag, 1986), pp. 207-16.

1985

"The Components of Cardiff MS Welsh I, *Llyfr Aneirin*" (with Kathryn A. Klar and Eve Sweetser), *Bwletin y Bwrdd Gwybodau Celtaidd/The Bulletin of the Board of Celtic Studies* XXXII, pp. 38-49.

1986

"Foinse Bréagach Miotais a bhí ag Yeats" (in Irish). Invited paper North American Congress of Celtic Studies (Ottawa). Published in *Proceedings of the First North American Congress of Celtic Studies, Ottawa 1986* (1988). English version presented at South Atlantic Modern Language Association Convention in 1987. Revised and expanded in *Yeats: An Annual of Critical and Textual Studies*, vol. 6 (1988).

"Manuscript Sources of the *Gododdin*". Paper presented at North American Congress of Celtic Studies (Ottawa). Revised and published in *Proceedings of the First North American Congress of Celtic Studies, Ottawa 1986* (1988) 1-529.

"Traces of Orality in *Tóraíocht Dhiarmada agus Ghráinne*". Paper presented to Old English Colloquium in November (Berkeley).

1987

"*Ticfa Tálcenn* Reconsidered". Paper presented to CSANA Conference in March (Cincinnati).

1988

"The Irish Origins of the Tristan and Iseult Story". Paper delivered at the Celtic session of the MLA. Revised and published in *De Gustibus: Essays for Alain Renoir* (1992).

"The Passing of the Shee: After Reading a Book about Yeats and the Tribes of Danu", *Yeats: An Annual of Critical and Textual Studies*, vol. 6, pp. 245-65 [essay review of Peter Alderson Smith, *W. B. Yeats and the Tribes of Danu: Three Views of Ireland's Fairies*].

"Yeats's Sources for the *Matter of Ireland*: I. Edain and Aengus", *Yeats: An Annual of Critical and Textual Studies*, Richard J. Finneran, ed., vol. 6 (Ann Arbor: University of Michigan Press), pp. 76-89. Expanded from "Foinse Bréagach a bhí ag Yeats" (1986).

"What Is the *Gododdin*?" in *Early Welsh Poetry — Studies in the Book of Aneirin*, Brynley F. Roberts, ed. (Aberystwyth: National Library of Wales, 1988), pp. 57-95.

"Foinse Bréagach Miotais a bhí ag Yeats" in *Proceedings of the First North American Congress of Celtic Studies, Ottawa 1986*, Gordon W. MacLennan, ed. (Ottawa: University of Ottawa, 1988), pp. 357-64.

"Manuscript Sources of the *Gododdin*" in *Proceedings of the First North American Congress of Celtic Studies, Ottawa 1986*, Gordon W. Mac-Lennon, ed. (Ottawa: University of Ottawa, 1988), pp. 521-529.

Talk delivered to the American Rock Art Research Association Symposium, in May (Ridgecrest, California).[1]

1989

"Frank Kinahan, Yeats, Folklore & Occultism: Contexts of the Early Work and Thought", *Yeats: An Annual of Critical and Textual Studies*, vol. 7, p. 236 [review].

"Nera and the Devil's Child". Paper delivered to the Eleventh Annual California Celtic Conference in April.

1992

"Traces of Orality in an Irish Literary Text". In *De Gustibus: Essays for Alain Renoir*, John Miles Foley, ed. New York: Garland Publishing, Inc., pp. 378-387. Published version of "The Irish Origins of the Tristan and Iseult Story" (1988).

---

1   This talk is mentioned in O Hehir's unpublished 113-page typescript entitled "Barry Fell's West Virginia Fraud".

TABULA GRATULATORIA

Professor Anders Ahlqvist, Department of Old and Middle Irish, Room 512, Tower 1, Unversity College, Galway, Ireland

Dr. John K. Bollard, Florence, Massachusetts

Professor Dorothy A. Bray, Department of English, McGill University, 853 Sherbrooke Street West, Montreal, PQ, H3A 2T6, Canada

David K. Broadwell, MD, 197 Eighth Street, Flagship Wharf No. 802, Charlestown, MA 02129-4234

Karen E. Burgess, 411 W. Sierra Madre Boulevard, Apt. No. 4, Sierra Madre, CA 91024

Dr. John Carey, Department of Early and Medieval Irish, University College, Cork, Ireland

Professor Irmengard Rauch Carr, 862 Camden Court, Benicia, CA 94510

Dr. Thomas Owen Clancy, Department of Celtic, University of Glasgow, Glasgow G12 8QQ, Scotland

Professor Linda K. Coleman (University of Maryland), 8903 Woodburn Court, Lanham, MD 20706

J. Michael Collier, 1510 Virginia, Berkeley, CA 94703

Professor Frederick C. Crews, 636 Vincente Avenue, Berkeley, CA 94707

Professor David N. Dumville, Girton College, Cambridge CB3 OJG, England

Dr. Vincent A. Dunn, 1012 Keith Avenue, Berkeley, CA 94708

Edinburgh University Library, George Square, Edinburgh EH8 9LJ, Scotland

Professor D. Ellis Evans, Jesus College, Oxford OX1 3DW, England

Professor Patrick K. Ford, Department of Celtic Languages and Literatures, Harvard University, 61 Kirkland Street, Cambridge, MA 02138

Dr. Philip M. Freeman, Boston University, The Castle, Bay State Road, Boston, MA 02215

Dr. Orin Gensler, c/o Linguistics Department, University of California at Berkeley, Berkeley, CA 94720

Professor Toby D. Griffen, Department of Foreign Languages and Literatures, University of Southern Illinois, Edwardsville, IL 62026-1432

Professor R. Geraint Gruffydd, Centre for Advanced Welsh and Celtic Studies, University of Wales, Aberystwyth

Professor Eric. P. Hamp, Emeritus, Department of Linguistics, The University of Chicago, Classics Building, 1010 East 59th Street, Chicago, IL 60637

Harvard College Library, Cambridge, MA 02138

Dr. Marged Haycock, Department of Welsh, The Old College, King Street, Aberystwyth, Dyfed SY23 2AX, Wales

Professor Sarah L. Higley, English Department, University of Rochester, Rochester, NY 14627

Professor Gary Holland, Department of Linguistics, 2337 Dwinelle Hall, University of California, Berkeley, CA 94720-2650

Pamela S. Hopkins, Department of Celtic Languages and Literatures, Harvard University, 61 Kirkland Street, Cambridge, MA 02138

Dr. Colin Ireland, Beaver College C. E. A., 6 Clare Street, Dublin 2, Ireland

Dr. Nicolas Jacobs, Jesus College, Oxford OX1 3DW, England

Jesus College, Oxford

Jan Johnson, Department of Linguistics, Dwinelle Hall, University of California, Berkeley, CA 94720-2650

Dr. Joan Trodden Keefe, Celtic Studies Program, Dwinelle Hall, University of California, Berkeley, CA 94720

Kennys Bookshop, High Street, Galway, Ireland

Dr. Kathryn A. Klar, Celtic Studies Program, Dwinelle Hall, University of California, Berkeley, CA 94720-2690

Professor John T. Koch, Slavic, Lyons 210, Boston College, Chestnut Hill, MA 02167

Professor Pierre-Yves Lambert, C.N.R.S, 212 rue de Vaugirard, 75015 Paris, France

Professor John Lindow, Department of Scandinavian Languages and Literature, University of California, Berkeley, CA 94720-2690

Dr. Katharine T. Loesch, 2129 North Sedgwick, Chicago, IL 60614

Llyfrgell Hugh Owen, Prifysgol Cymru, Aberystwyth

Professor Proinsias Mac Cana, Dublin Institute for Advanced Studies, 10 Burlington Road, Dublin 4, Ireland

Kevin A. McCarthy, 132 Fifth Avenue, Kings Park, NY 11754-4317 [pd]

Professor Catherine McKenna, City University of New York Graduate School, Medieval Studies Program, 33 West 42nd Street, New York, NY 10036

Margaret McKenzie, P. O. Box 4652, Berkeley, CA 94704-06522

Professor Yakov Malkiel, Emeritus, Department of Linguistics, University of California, 2321 Dwinelle Hall, Berkeley, CA 94720-2650

Laurance Maney, Department of Celtic Languages and Literatures, Harvard University, 61 Kirkland Street, Cambridge, MA 02138

Professor Ann T. E. Matonis, 7312 Emlen Street, Philadelphia, PA 19119

Professor Daniel F. Melia, Celtic Studies Program, Dwinelle Hall, University of California, Berkeley, CA 94720-2690

Maija Murphy, 208 Reichling Avenue, Pacifica, CA 94044

Professor Joseph Falaky Nagy, Department of English, University of California, Los Angeles, CA 90024-1525

National Library of Ireland, Kildare Street, Dublin 2, Ireland

Professor Mary Niepokuj, Department of English, Purdue University, West Lafayette, Indiana

Professor John D. Niles, 124 Hearst Avenue, Berkeley, CA 94703

Professor Tomás Ó Cathasaigh, Department of Celtic Languages and Literatures, Harvard University, 61 Kirkland Street, Cambridge, MA 02138

Der Präsident, Philipps-Universität Marburg, Universitätkasse, Postfach 582, 3550 Marburg, Germany

Vgl. Sprachwissenschaft, FB 11, Univ. Marburg, Wilhelm-Röpke-Str. 6 E, D-35032 Marburg, Germany

Professor Dr. Erich Poppe, Philipps-Universität Marburg, Fachgebiet Vergleichende Sprachwissenschaft, Wilhelm-Röpke-Str. 6 E, D-35032 Marburg, Germany

Professor Ralph W. Rader, 127 Lakeshore Court, Richmond, CA 94804

Professor Jo Radner, Department of Literature, Arts and Sciences, The American University, Washington, D. C. 20016

Professor John Henry Raleigh, 1020 Keeler Avenue, Berkeley, CA 94708

Professor Alain Renoir, 913 Kingston, Piedmont, CA 95611

Dr. Annalee Rejhon, Celtic Studies Program, Dwinelle Hall, University of California, Berkeley, CA 94720

Professor Dr. Michael Richter, FG Geschichte, Universität, D-7750 Konstanz, Germany

Dr. Paul Russell, Radley College, Abingdon, Oxfordshire OX1 2HU, England

Professor Patrick Sims-Williams, Department of Welsh, Old College, King Street, Aberystwyth, Dyfed SY23 2AX, Wales

Professor Edgar M. Slotkin, Department of English and Comparative Literature, M. L. 69, University of Cincinnati, Cincinnati, OH 45221

Professor Robin Chapman Stacey, Department of History, D. P.–20, University of Washington, Seattle, WA 98195

Professor Claude Sterckx, Institut des Hautes Études de Belgique, 21 Avenue Pierre Curie, 1050 Bruxelles, Belgium

Ned Sturzer, 7013 Genoa Drive, Chattanooga, TN 37421

Professor Eve E. Sweetser, Department of Linguistics and Celtic Studies Program, University of California, Berkeley, CA 94720–2650

Claire Thomas, 1442A Walnut Street, no. 170, Berkeley, CA 94709

Elizabeth Thomas, 275 Virginia Street, Salt Lake City, UT 84103

Kathleen Thomas, 162 West Avila Place, Salt Lake City, UT 84103

Professor Leonora Timm, Linguistics Program, University of California, Davis, CA 95616

Count Nikolai Tolstoy, Southmoor, nr. Abingdon, Berkshire, England

Professor Robert Tracy, Emeritus, Department of English, University of California, Berkeley

Professor Dr. Hildegard L. C. Tristram, Waldhofstrasse 50, D-79117 Freiburg, Germany

Professor Maria Tymoczko (University of Massachusetts), 28 Pomeroy Terrace, Northampton, MA 01060

Dr. Thomas Walsh (Occidental College), 1470 Campus Road, Los Angeles, CA 90042

Kirsten J. Walstedt, Department of Linguistics, Cornell University, Ithaca, NY

Professor Calvert Watkins, Department of Linguistics, Harvard University, Cambridge, MA 02138

Professor J. E. Caerwyn Williams, Centre for Advanced Welsh and Celtic Studies, University of Wales, Aberystwyth

Donna I. Wong, Department of Celtic Languages and Literatures, Harvard University, 61 Kirkland Street, Cambridge, MA 02138

ST. PATRICK IN CORNWALL?
THE ORIGIN AND TRANSMISSION OF
VITA TERTIA S. PATRICII

David N. Dumville

GIRTON COLLEGE, CAMBRIDGE

The most popular Life of St. Patrick in medieval Europe was that which John Colgan published in 1647 as *Vita III S. Patricii*.[1] New editions were published by J. B. Bury in 1903[2] and Ludwig Bieler in 1971.[3] Bieler was able to establish that the work was composed in Ireland and by an Irishman.[4] As to its date, however, his conclusions were very much less satisfactory.[5]

Bieler took over from Bury the deduction that St. Patrick's second petition (§85), *ut alienigenae in hac insula non habitarent usque in diem iudicii*, refers to the vikings and that the text could therefore hardly antedate the 790s.[6] Not only is this argument feeble in itself,[7] but it runs into the difficulty that in the Book of Armagh (one of whose scribes was at work in 807) a section of text allegedly supplementary to Tírechán's *Collectanea* records his second petition as *ne barbarae gentes dominentur nobis in sempiternum*[8] and that in the Cambro-Latin *Historia Brittonum* (written in A.D. 829–30) we read in the same context *ne a barbaris*

---

1 *Triadis thaumaturgae seu diuorum Patricii, Columbae, et Brigidae . . . communium patronorum acta*, John Colgan, ed. (Leuven, 1647).

2 "A Life of St. Patrick (Colgan's Tertia Vita)", Bury, ed., *Transactions of the Royal Irish Academy* 32 C (1902–4), pp. 199–262.

3 *Four Latin Lives of St. Patrick. Colgan's* Vita Secunda, Quarta, Tertia, *and* Quinta, Ludwig Bieler, ed. (Dublin, 1971).

4 Ibid., p. 25.

5 Ibid., pp. 25–26.

6 "A Life of St. Patrick", J. B. Bury, ed., p. 218.

7 In the *Vita tripartita* the English fulfil this role: '*Fail,*' ol Pátraic, '*Saxain náró trebat Héirinn ar áiss nách ar éicin céin mbéo-sa for nim*': *Bethu Phátraic. The Tripartite Life of Patrick*, Kathleen Mulchrone, ed. (Dublin, 1939), p. 73.

8 Tírechán, *Collectanea*, §52: *The Patrician Texts in the Book of Armagh*, Ludwig Bieler & Fergus Kelly, ed. and trans. (Dublin, 1979), pp. 164–65.

consumentur in aeternum.[9] Only if we can be certain both that the Book of Armagh's account was not taken over from its exemplar, and that there was rapid transmission of new Patriciana from Armagh to Wales between 807 and 829, can Bury's argument stand. Of course, we can be sure of neither. What is more, we have only to recall the stir made by the Northumbrian expedition to Meath in 684 to remind ourselves that another specific context is possible,[10] if indeed such specificity is needed at all.

As to the *terminus ante quem* of *Vita Tertia*, Bieler argued that it must have been written before 1135.[11] His evidence was that William of Malmesbury referred to his own Life of Patrick in a work written not later than that date, and that examination of that Life shows it to have depended on *Vita Tertia*. Neither conclusion can still stand, as I show elsewhere.[12] It would be better to say that the visible manuscript tradition begins, in a number of different locations in central Europe, in the second half of the twelfth century. The work can therefore hardly be later than the first half of that century. Moreover, the text makes its appearance in two recensions: a version which seems to have circulated exclusively in England [Π] (in manuscripts of *ca.* A.D. 1200 and later) is in general textually superior to that found in central Europe [Γ].[13]

Bieler was able to show convincingly that the archetype was written in Insular script.[14] Indeed, it is striking that one twelfth-century German manuscript transmits some paleographical features deriving from an Insular manuscript.[15] Bieler perhaps made less of the evidence than he might have done. There is also a fair presumption that the archetype contained a number of errors.[16] In other words, the textual history is far from complete: we cannot see far enough back in the tradition of *Vita Tertia* to get a view of a clean text. The paleographical and text-historical

---

9   *Nennii Historia Britonum*, Joseph Stevenson, ed. (London, 1838), p. 46 (= Harl. §48).

10 Cf. *Críth Gablach*, D. A. Binchy, ed. (Dublin, 1941), pp. xiv, 20–21 (§38), 37; see H. Moisl, 'The Bernician Royal Dynasty and the Irish', *Peritia* 2 (1983), pp. 103–26 at pp. 120–24, for discussion of other sources.

11 *Four Latin Lives*, Bieler, ed., p. 25.

12 See David N. Dumville et al., *Saint Patrick, A.D. 493–1993* (Woodbridge, 1993), pp. 265–71.

13 For all this information, cf. *Four Latin Lives*, Bieler, ed., pp. 13–39. His MS. O (p. 21) is usually thought to have been written at the Fenland abbey of Ramsey. His MS. C (Cambridge, Corpus Christi College, MS. 66A + Cambridge, University Library, MS. Ff.1.27 [1160], pp. 253–642 and 41–72) was written at Bury St. Edmunds (Suffolk) in the first half of the fourteenth century; for a further Patrician dimension of its history, see *The Historia Brittonum*, III, David N. Dumville, ed. (Cambridge, 1985), and Dumville et al., *Saint Patrick*, pp. 221–32, at pp. 225–28.

14 *Four Latin Lives*, Bieler, ed., p. 26.

15 Ibid. (MS. E).

16 Ibid., pp. 26–27.

evidence about the archetype might suggest that, chronologically, it is not necessary to look far behind the earliest manuscripts. There are two apparently complicating factors, however.

The Insular features displayed or attested by the extant twelfth-century and later manuscripts include the following. I begin with the evidence presented by the "English" (Π) text:

(a) a row of suprascript hooks stands above an Irish word in MS. O;

(b) the abbreviation *etī* for *etiam* stood in the hyparchetype of the Π-recension;

(c) the Insular compendium for *autem* stood in the exemplar of MS. D.

These three items seem to suggest that the recension (called Π by Bieler) which we see circulating in England in the thirteenth and fourteenth centuries was dependent on an Insular source-manuscript. The two abbreviations would do nothing to disturb an assertion that that could have been, say, an eleventh- or twelfth-century Irish manuscript.[17] But how long the habit of writing apices above vernacular words continued is another question: Bieler did not offer examples later than the Book of Armagh.[18] Kenneth Jackson, however, drew attention to the existence of some later examples from Wales and argued that the practice was still current in the first half of the twelfth century when the Gaelic charters were written at Deer (Aberdeenshire) in the pocket-gospelbook now Cambridge, University Library, MS. Ii.6.32.[19] The matter will need more precise discussion before any certainty can be achieved, but an eleventh-century Welsh or twelfth-century Gaelic source-manuscript for the "English" recension of *Vita Tertia* need not be ruled out at this stage. A fourth Insular feature occurs in all manuscripts of the "Continental" (Γ) recension:

---

17 Doris Bains, *A Supplement to 'Notae Latinae'* (Cambridge, 1936), pp. 3, 15. For the circulation of Irish ecclesiastics and Hiberno-Latin texts in England in that period, see D. Bethell, "English Monks and Irish Reforms in the Eleventh and Twelfth Centuries", *Historical Studies* [Irish Conference of Historians] 8 (1969), pp. 111–35, and David N. Dumville, *Histories and Pseudo-histories of the Insular Middle Ages* (Aldershot, 1990), chapter XI.

18 *Four Latin Lives*, p. 26 and n.2, and *Studies on the Life and Legend of St Patrick* (London, 1986), chapter XIII, p. 91, n.7, and p. 97.

19 *The Gaelic Notes in the Book of Deer*, Kenneth Jackson, ed. and trans. (Cambridge, 1972), pp. 17–18. However, for disagreement with Jackson's interpretation of this feature in the Book of Deer itself, see the reviews by R. B[lack], *Celtica* 10 (1973), pp. 264–67, and B. Ó Cuív, *Éigse* 14 (1971/2), pp. 341–46 (at pp. 345–46).

(d)   the misreading *deos* for *celos* (correct in Π) seems to point
       to the use of a Late Celtic abbreviation in the archetype.[20]

A fifth Insular feature is found in one manuscript of the "Continental"
recension (Γ) of *Vita Tertia*:

(e)   a ligature of **m** with subscript **a** is found three times in MS.
       E, written at Tegernsee in the second half of the twelfth
       century.[21]

This archaic practice, which goes back to the origins of Insular minuscule
script, is still found in eleventh-century Welsh manuscripts but may already have been eliminated from Irish usage in the tenth century.

The archetype contained two Old Brittonic phrases — in §§83 and 88.

§83 (Π):[22] Quadam autem die dixit angelus Patricio iuxta fontem qui
       dicitur *tipra Phátric* in latere Ardmache: 'Curabis duodecim uiros
       cach   sathairn   et   quatuor   uiros   **pop   iou**   ab   omnibus
       infirmitatibus et doloribus suis'.

In the "Continental" (Γ) text, one witness reads *popicu* for *pop iou*,[23] but
in all the others corruption has gone one step further, to *popicii*. It is
noteworthy that the "English" recension retains Gaelic phrases untrans-
lated while the "Continental" recension disposes of them in favor of
accurate Latin renderings. On the other hand, the Brittonic phrase *pop
iou*, 'every Thursday',[24] while making perfectly good sense in itself and
indeed being apparently necessary to complete the meaning of the
passage, could not be rendered into Latin in the Γ-recension.

§88:[25] Dixit autem angelus: 'Noli contristari, quia ordinatio gratie tue in
       Ardmache fiet, dum illum locum diligis; et alia multa bona
       donabit tibi Deus. Primo, quod Díchu cum omni sua progenie et
       gente uitam eternam possidere fecisti. Secundo, quia usque ad
       diem iudicii septem[26] uiros (**do**)[27] **pop saturn**[28] de uiris Hyber-
       niensium liberabis et deduces eos ex igne inferni.

---

20 *Four Latin Lives*, Bieler, ed., p. 26; for the text, see p. 153 (line 1); for Bieler's
   commentary, see pp. 223–24.
21 Ibid., p. 26.
22 Ibid., p. 179.
23 MS. B: *saec.* xii²; provenance Biburg.
24 See *Geiriadur Prifysgol Cymru. A Dictionary of the Welsh Language*, R. J.
   Thomas et al., ed. (Cardiff, 1950–), II.2002, s.n. *Iau*. This appears to be the
   earliest attestation in any of the Brittonic languages.
25 *Four Latin Lives*, Bieler, ed., p. 184.
26 *quatuor* Γ.
27 *de* Γ.
28 O; *saturnn* C; *saturnus* D; *saturan* Γ.

Here the Brittonic phrase could make sense in context. If *do/de* were to be retained, *do* could be Breton or Cornish but not Welsh (where *di* would be used);[29] but it is hard to see the sense in which the preposition might be intended here. That *pop saturn*, 'every Saturday',[30] is meant here is made clear by the Irish Tripartite Life of St. Patrick: *'Fail,' ol int aingel, 'mórfeiser cech Sathairn do thabairt a píanaib hiffrind co bráth'.*[31]

What seems likely to have happened in these instances is that when the Irish ancestor of the archetype — which now appears of necessity to have been a British manuscript of the period *ca.* 850 × *ca.* 1100 if Welsh or *ca.* 850 × *ca.* 950 if Cornish (no Breton manuscript can be hypothesized which would meet the paleographical conditions)[32] — was resident in a Brittonic-speaking country, it acquired two Old Brittonic glosses to probably Irish phrases.[33] In the words *Iou, pop*, and *Saturn* there is a lack of evidence for establishing dialect. When the text was copied, these glosses displaced their lemmata. The *uita* travelled on to England (spawning the Π–recension) whence it found its way to central Europe.[34] There it was copied by an Irish speaker who eliminated most of the Irish phrases but updated the spelling of some Irish name-forms: the descendants of this reviser's copy constitute the Γ-group.[35] A great deal of useful work remains to be done on explaining the development of this text and reconstructing an archetypal version.

It was suggested by J. B. Bury that the text contains some other evidence for the British interlude in its history.[36] §§19–20 tell us that after his Irish captivity (two such in this text!) Patrick returned to his parents' home, where in due course he had the vision which called him

---

29 J. Loth, *Vocabulaire vieux-breton* (Paris, 1884), pp. 99, 108.

30 Kenneth Jackson, *Language and History in Early Britain* (Edinburgh, 1953), p. 289.

31 *Bethu Phátraic*, Mulchrone, ed., p. 73 (lines 1324–25); cf. *The Patrician Texts*, Bieler & Kelly, ed. and trans., pp. 233–34, on Tírechán, *Collectanea*, §52 (cf. p. 1, above).

32 For the last attested specimens (mid-tenth century) of Cornish Insular script, see W. M. Lindsay, *Early Welsh Script* (Oxford, 1912), pp. 26–32 and plates XIV–XV. For the demise of Insular writing in Brittany by *ca.* 850, see W. M. Lindsay, "Breton Scriptoria: Their Latin Abbreviation-symbols", *Zentralblatt für Bibliothekswesen* 29 (1912), pp. 264–72, and Bernhard Bischoff, *Latin Palaeography: Antiquity and the Middle Ages* (Cambridge, 1990), pp. 89–90, 117.

33 For Irish words and phrases in this text see *Four Latin Lives*, Bieler, ed., p. 25 and n.3. We may note *cach sathairn*, 'every Saturday', in §83 (quoted above, p. 4).

34 For Continental evidence of a text of *Vita III* nearer to the archetype than to either of the surviving recensions, see ibid., pp. 24–25 (MS. Gr, a late fifteenth-century abridgment) and 27. Bieler's account of the place of the exemplar behind MS. Gr in the textual history of the whole involves geographical difficulties which remain unresolved.

35 Cf. the discussion of §83 (above, p. 4).

36 "A Life of St. Patrick", pp. 212–15.

back to Ireland. §21 tells us that this provoked him to wish to learn and understand Holy Writ so that he could then teach it to the Irish. As a result he travelled to Gaul and in particular went to see Bishop Germanus at Auxerre, where he remained for forty years. In §22 we then read:[37]

> Et postea uenit ad Martinum et mansit quadraginta dies secum. Et angelus ad Martinum dixit, ut iret Patricius ad Tamerensem[38] insulam. Transactis autem ibi quadraginta annis, uoluit Patricius uisitare Romam, caput uidelicet omnium aecclesiarum, ad quam christiani ab omnibus mundi partibus conueniebant; et hoc placuit sancto Germano. Misitque sanctus Germanus seniorem cum illo, hoc est Segitium presbiterum, ut testem haberet idoneum.

In other words, Patrick spent forty years with Germanus at Auxerre, forty days with St. Martin, and then forty more years at *Tamerensis insula*, after which with Germanus's approval he set out for Rome. The island-sojourn derives ultimately from §1 of Tírechán's *Collectanea* — a stay of thirty years on *insula Aralanensis in mari Terreno*, presumably intended to be Lérins.[39]

Bury allowed himself to be persuaded that the name-form which appears here — *Tamarensem/Tamerensem/Temerensem* — represented what Bieler has called an interpolation but is in fact a substitution for a pre-archetypal name-form such as that in Tírechán's text. On the argument adopted by Bury the island has the name of the River Tamar in Cornwall and was substituted by someone who thought that the island was, should be, or might as well be St. Nicholas's Island at the mouth of the Tamar.[40]

I find myself less than enthusiastic about this theory and feel very hesitant about joining Bieler in describing it as "plausible".[41] In other words, I should wish to be persuaded that the change from *Aralanensis* (which may itself be a corrupted reading — for it derives uniquely from a manuscript at a century's remove, or more, from the author) to *Tamerensis* (or the like) is beyond the normal range of mutation of name-forms in the corpus of *uitae Patricianae*. At any rate, the notion that the Tamar belongs here is absurd in the context of the story. The argument is one of a number in which scholars have sought to provide

---

37 *Four Latin Lives*, Bieler, ed., pp. 130–31.
38 *Tamarensem* R, *Temerensem* αD.
39 I say Lérins in spite of Bieler's strictures: *The Patrician Texts*, Bieler & Kelly, ed. and trans., p. 216. Unlike Bieler, I make no assumption that statements in the Patrician *uitae* may transmit information about the saint's actual life and therefore require to be judged accordingly.
40 Bury, "A Life of St. Patrick", pp. 212–15; *Four Latin Lives*, Bieler, ed., pp. 26–27.
41 Ibid.

favored local identities for places named in the Patrician story. René Louis's identification of *Aralanensis insula* as a place near Auxerre is of a similar sort:[42] it defies what is required in the context of the story but feeds a pre-existing theory about a source-text.

If *Tamarensis* or the like does indeed derive from a British episode in the history of the text, and if it does refer (indirectly) to the River Tamar, the presumption would be that that British phase was a Cornish one. If so, it should presumably (on the paleographical evidence) have occurred by *ca.* 950. This is, however, an exceedingly conditional conclusion.

Vita III S. Patricii was in origin a Hiberno-Latin text containing some admixture of Irish vernacular phrases. It is unlikely to have been written earlier than the eighth century or later than the eleventh. Closer study of the vernacular material which it contains may help that 400-year dating range to be narrowed, as may closer attention to the place of the text in the continuum of Patrician hagiography. It was transmitted to the Brittonic-speaking world where its visible, direct textual history begins. From there the later medieval English and Continental circulation ramifies.

---

42 R. Louis, "St. Patrick's Sojourn in Auxerre and the Problem of the Insula Aralanensis", *Seanchas Ardmhacha*, Special Issue (1961/2), pp. 37–44 (a version of an argument first published in French in 1951); cf. D. A. Binchy, "Patrick and His Biographers, Ancient and Modern", *Studia Hibernica* 2 (1962), pp. 7–173, at pp. 84–85, 89–90 (Louis was renamed "Dubois" by Binchy, ibid., p. 84).

DUCATS, DAUGHTERS, AND THE PURSUIT OF CATTLE

Vincent A. Dunn

In a recent study, I identified some formal characteristics of a traditional narrative pattern that enjoyed currency in Western Europe over the course of many centuries and that found expression in a significant number of oral and literary contexts.[1] Focusing principally on narratives set to writing in the European Middle Ages — a time when this particular story type was especially popular — the study tested the extent to which the constituent features of the story might remain intact, despite considerable superficial change, as it found expression in markedly different cultural and generic environments. Taking two Old Irish story types as my principal models, I identified their structural equivalent, replicated many times over, in two different but contemporaneous genres in Old French. I then examined two instances in Middle English, one in which the story was borrowed from a foreign source and another in which the transmission can be attributed to legitimate traditional paths. To illustrate the remarkable tenacity of the story in question, I concluded my investigation with a discussion of two eighteenth-century British ballads which strongly suggested that, even centuries after the Medieval "heyday" of the pattern, it was capable of reasserting itself with its constituent structure essentially unchanged.

In a footnote to the latter remarks, I alluded briefly to the fact that certain plays of Shakespeare's bear witness to the pattern under discussion, and I lightly sketched out the principal arguments. At that time, however, I did not elaborate on the matter, for fear that it would constitute too great a digression. My goal in the present brief note will be to

---

1 *Cattle-raids and Courtships: Medieval Narrative Genres in a Traditional Context.* (= Garland Monographs in Medieval Literature, 2; New York and London: Garland, 1989).

return to the question long enough to explore this one point. To do so, however, requires that I recapitulate enough of the previous argument to provide a context. To the reader who may already be familiar with the previous study I apologize in advance for this repetition, and to the many more who will not have read the monograph, I apologize for putting the case so hurriedly and without proper development.

At its core, the story is an initiation narrative, akin in its basic terms to the narratives and practices of many cultures around the world — particularly those that might be labeled "primitive" today. Such stories and rituals re-enact the culturally and mythically significant journey of a young representative of society, wrenched from protected innocence and obliged to undergo a traumatic and danger-fraught transition into adulthood. Among so-called primitive peoples, the initiation of each successive generation of eligible adolescents, instigated and overseen by older males in the society, follows culturally prescribed behavior that can be both instructive and terrifying. The initiates' journey separates them from a world characterized by irresponsibility, and ultimately it leads to a confrontation with death, represented in a variety of symbolic fashions. Reborn as a recognized and fully-fledged member of society, often marked with some scar as token of the ceremony, the initiate returns to assume new responsibilities in his society. Anthropologists argue that such rituals serve an important social and cultural function, recreating with every enactment of the initiation ritual the culture and its values.[2] Mythologists identify the same potential in traditional narrative.

Resonant with social and mythic overtones, the initiation story as it takes shape in the context of Indo-European narrative has the definitive characteristic that it conflates two rites of passage: a young man's coming of age and his subsequent acquisition of a wife from a territory outside of his own. A further point of distinction is the fact that, historically, wherever and whenever it came to the surface within the general matrix of cognate European cultures, the story assumed two structurally similar but discrete modes of expression. Where one turned up in a culture's repertoire of narratives, the other could be expected to exist as well, offering a complementary perspective on the same social phenomenon.

The points that distinguish the two members of this matched pair from one another are in some respects quite subtle. In no case is there an overt internal indication to link the one to the other, nor, indeed, do the paired stories always occur in the same generic class. Yet the basic story, stripped of both its superficial characteristics and its generic markers, is

---

2 Particularly instructive is Mircea Eliade's *Rites and Symbols of Initiation: The Mysteries of Birth and Rebirth*, Willard Trask, trans. (New York: Harper & Row, 1958).

quite the same in both. It tells of a young man who goes outside of his immediate territory or kinship group to perform a deed of bravery that will elevate him from the status of untested youth to that of adult. In some contexts, the idea of "making his name" is particularly operative. Invariably linked to this action is his encounter with the daughter of the man against whom he must perform his aggressive deed. She is kindly disposed to his purpose, but her father is hostile and opposes the young man. The young man's eventual success in his mission results in the acquisition of the young woman as his wife, and he returns with her to his own people.

The rich but idiosyncratic corpus of Old Irish narrative provides readily discernible examples of the initiation story. Indeed, this body of archaic and highly conservative material offers an important but still relatively unexploited perspective on the development of better known, cognate literatures within the same linguistic group. Like the Irish language itself, which for years defied inclusion in the Indo-European family, Irish story types stand apart from the genres known in more "mainstream" environments. Standard fare for Irish storytellers were tales labeled destructions, feasts, cattle-raids, courtships, frenzies, visions, slaughters, and loves, to name only some. Virtually no contemporary information about these tale types is available, and we must deduce what we can from internal evidence.

Two story types, ostensibly unrelated, stand out as having much in common, and together they address a central event in the social and mythic life of the culture, offering complementary perspectives. One focuses on a young man's coming of age with an emphasis on the broad social implications of such an event. The second gives a more personal perspective, focusing on the concerns of the individuals involved.

The appointed deed of heroism that the young man of the initiation story must perform is culture specific, and in the Irish instances it is a *táin bó*, a raiding of cattle. This act has deep roots among Indo-European peoples as a ritual gesture often associated with the assertion of a leader's sovereignty. Cattle, of course, were a principal unit of exchange in the culture. Some half-dozen examples of cattle-raid stories are still extant. Perhaps best known of all stories bearing this label is the major Irish epic *Táin Bó Cúailnge,* the *Cattle-raid of Cooley,* but for a variety of reasons this long and somewhat unwieldy narrative does not provide the most straightforward example of the type. More serviceable models are the short and unadorned stories such as *Táin Bó Regamain* or *Táin Bó Dartada.* In composite form, the cattle-raid presents the following elements.

A young man is summoned by figures in authority over him and told that he must leave his territory and perform a raid against a powerful man in distant lands. He leaves under duress, expressing his own in-adequacy for the task and fearing the strength of the forces he must face. On his journey he is often accompanied by a group of his peers. Once in the territory of the enemy, he somehow makes contact with the daughter of the man whose cows he must steal. In some cases the young man and woman are said to have already loved one another from afar, but in any event the woman quickly decides to side with the young man and to assist him in his task of stealing the cattle. When the father learns of the invasion of his land, he meets the raid with martial force. In most cases, the conflict results in heavy losses on both sides and the successful abduction of the cattle.

Interestingly, however, in *Táin Bó Regamain*, a truce is reached and the father agrees to give over some of his cows to accompany his daughters. This ending gives a clue to what may have been the under-lying point of the encounter. Arguably, the stories are a reflection — and reinforcement — of a practice of marriage outside of the kinship group and a statement of the appropriateness of bringing moveable property back to the young man's territory. In this one instance, the resolution suggests the symbolic nature of the hostilities and recognizes the pecuni-ary exchange that traditionally accompanies marriage.

The second type of story, the *tochmarc*, or "courtship", again re-counts the adventures of a young man who is under some obligation to prove himself, and to do so, he must go off far from home and face impossible odds in the process. Interwoven with the need to prove him-self is the necessity of acquiring a bride. One chief area of difference between the cattle-raids and the courtships is that in the latter, the nature of the young man's task is less martial and more oriented towards successive proofs of worth on the part of the individual. Although martial prowess may figure among the skills that the young man is expected to demonstrate, the emphasis is more on his worthiness as a person and as a mate. Of note, too, is the fact that although the young woman is wholly in sympathy with the young man's goal, she refrains from the kind of overt alliance against her father that characterizes the behavior of the women in the cattle-raids. Instead, she assumes some of the responsibility for obliging him to prove himself by accomplishing a series of tasks. Thus, the young woman will sometimes engage the young man in verbal contests such as a riddling dialogue. We see this, for example, in the *Courtship of Emer*.

Beyond the superficial differences in plot, other more salient points distinguish the cattle-raids from the courtships. Chief among these is the orientation of the narrative as a whole. As has already been suggested above, the cattle-raids give a social perspective and the courtships an individual one. With these distinguishing traits go other more subtle ones. The cattle-raids are rooted in the contiguous world. Their ethos is heroic and martial in nature. By contrast, the courtships are predicated on mythic premises. In *Tochmarc Emire*, "The Courtship of Emer", for example, Cú Chulainn goes in search of his bride in *Luglochta Logo*, the Gardens of Lugh, a locale that plainly betokens the Otherworld. His quest eventually leads him to a series of trials also set overtly in the Otherworld. Here, for example, he encounters Scáthach, a woman whose name means "phantom" or "shadowy". Even more Otherworldly in its context and premises is *Tochmarc Étaíne*, "The Courtship of Étaín", in which some tasks involve accomplishing a series of superhuman feats all within a single night. In the Welsh *Culhwch ac Olwen*, which fits into the same pattern as the courtships, the hero, assisted by a band of Arthurian warriors, each with his own special talent, satisfies the impossible demands put upon him by Olwen's hostile father.

The two story types, each offering its own view of the same socially relevant phenomenon, may be seen to form a matching and complementary pair, all within a common cultural context. One is firmly tied to the real world and concerned with issues that affect the life of the community. This type of story is well suited to matter-of-fact, horizontal interpretation. By contrast, the second type of story is pointedly mythic, often defying easy interpretation. Where the first is direct and linear, the second is subtle, building upon a vertical accumulation of episodes to convey its message. Stories in the courtship mode have an associative and metaphoric relationship to the world of the audience, allowing for a more imaginative and affective response to the subject. Borrowing language from the structuralists, I have found it useful to characterize the cattle-raids and courtships, respectively, as "syntagmatic" and "paradigmatic".

In the case of the Irish narratives, both the cattle-raids and the courtships, though classed differently, may be understood to be similar in kind, in the sense that each was considered a *prímscél* ('main story') and part of the repertoire of the *filid,* or master poets. In the later career of this paired set of narratives, as they emerged in one cognate literary context after another, this generic kinship sometimes became quite remote. In Medieval France, the syntagmatic narrative found expression in the epic environment of the *chansons de geste*. In this cultural environment, the requisite deed of bravery performed by the young man striving to make his name as a warrior was not the theft of cattle but the capture of a Saracen town. The encounter with death is entirely real in this martial context and the incursion into foreign territory reflects the polarized realities of the world as it was understood by Medieval Christian France.

In keeping with the story's ability to adapt its superficial characteristics while still preserving its constituent parts, the young woman in the

French stories is a Saracen princess, a perennial character in the French epic. The young woman's conversion to Christianity, her vehement rejection of her father, and her return with the French hero to his own territory all take the root matter of exogamous marriage and the appropriate commodity exchange, as witnessed in the Irish cattle-raids, into a new register of social and political relevance. This adaptation is consistent both with the syntagmatic narrative's manner of focusing on the social dimensions of the story and with the pattern's general proclivity for adapting itself to a generic environment to remain viable.

The paradigmatic version of the initiation story is well attested in Medieval French narrative as well, but not in the *chansons de geste*. It is in the fictitious and subtly mythic world of Chrétien de Troyes's Arthurian romances that the version of the story corresponding to the Irish courtships appears. In keeping with the pattern, these romances focus on the adventures of an individual whose good name has been called into question, most often because of some transgression he has committed. However, the perceived fault for which the young man must atone is not so much a matter of social concern as it is a personal one. Only when he has regained favor in the young woman's eyes can the young man's personal and social reintegration be achieved.

The final segment of my study examined the emergence of the two-part pattern in the narratives of Medieval England. Superficially, the pattern seemed to be present in the Middle English metrical romances, where the story is, in fact, quite common. Upon closer examination, however, the division into two discrete perspectives failed to materialize in this genre with its constituent features intact. This I attributed to the fact that these romances were, unlike the stories considered elsewhere in the study, derivative. Following the Norman conquest, the importation of foreign narrative put *chanson de geste* and courtly romance alike into the hands of people who had no native sensitivity to the subtleties that distinguished them. As this new genre evolved, it conflated many sources and, as a result, failed to preserve something as intuitive and culturally dependent as the dual perspectives on initiation.

Yet this large body of derivative material does not account for the entirety of Middle English narrative, and I argued that the pattern emerged, at least partially, elsewhere in the native tradition of English narrative. Although no clear examples of the syntagmatic version of the story were in evidence, I found that the paradigmatic side of the story can be witnessed, fully developed and entirely sensitive to the nuances of the pattern, in the fourteenth-century masterpiece *Sir Gawain and the Green Knight*. Belonging to the alliterative tradition that predated the invasion, this work reflects a "grassroots" awareness of traditional narrative motifs from which the pattern was able to draw its strength and keep its integrity over many centuries.

In tracing the pattern through cognate cultures, I sought to argue that the pattern is deeply rooted in a shared tradition. Analogous to the cognate linguistic forms found in languages that have evolved separately, traditional narratives, superficially dissimilar by virtue of years of independent life, can be shown to have close kinship upon comparative examination. Such is the case, I believe, with the initiation narrative. Making the point that grassroots conservatism kept the initiation pattern and other such encapsulations of folk wisdom intact even when their heyday as popular genres had long since passed, I cited in conclusion the examples of the Child ballads in which separate songs preserved the discrete strands of the pattern.

This brings me, finally and with reiterated apologies for the long and largely unargued summary I have had to offer, to the observations I wish to make concerning the occurrence of the initiation motif in two of Shakespeare's plays. In approaching the subject, I should make it clear that my intention is not in any way to argue for presumed Celtic origins for these plays. Shakespeare certainly had no Celtic sources, as such, to work from. Indeed, he might well have expressed astonishment at the thought that the "rough rugheaded kerns" had so rich a narrative tradition and even more so at the idea that this tradition was cousin to the great literatures of the Medieval and Renaissance authors from whom he borrowed so freely.

Nevertheless, in two of Shakespeare's plays, we find an interesting survival of the two-part initiation narrative with many of the constituent features very much intact. I have made the point earlier that the two parts of the pattern sometimes found expression in the same generic category, as in the case of the Irish stories, and sometimes in completely different but contemporaneous genres, as in the case of the French examples. In the present instance, although the two versions of the story appear in the canon of a single author, it should be noted that they fall into somewhat different categories of drama. The syntagmatic story emerges in the subplot of the tragi-comedy of *The Merchant of Venice*. Interestingly, the main plot of the same play may also be construed as a partially developed instance of the paradigmatic story pattern. The paradigmatic version of the story finds a home, full-blown, in Shakespeare's last and finest romance, *The Tempest*.

Looking first at the straightforward and relatively unadorned subplot in *The Merchant of Venice*, we find some of the basic characteristics of the cattle-raid pattern. The story involves the stratagem of Lorenzo to elope with Jessica, the daughter of Shylock, and, in the process, to steal his money as well. Let us recall that the composite view of stories of this type calls for an aggressive action, taken against someone outside of the young man's kinship group. The young woman in such stories offers little resistance and usually helps the young man accomplish his objective.

The world in which *The Merchant of Venice* is set is every bit as polarized as the Saracen vs. Christian world of the French epics, except that the incarnation of all that is, by definition, foreign and hated and suspect happens in this instance to be Shylock the Jew. Critics note the social mores of the times and cite popular literary antecedents (such as Marlowe's *Jew of Malta* or another work no longer extant[3]) upon which Shakespeare may have drawn, and they point to topical matters such as the notorious case of Dr. Roderigo Lopez, a Jewish physician executed for high treason a year before the play was written. Such a political and social climate is easily adapted to the traditional pattern's need for a context of opposites.

Though not martial in character, Lorenzo and Jessica's behavior is overtly hostile to Shylock. Jessica's role is very much in character with that of her counterpart in the Irish and French examples. She dispatches her betrayal of her father in a few lines:

> Alack, what heinous sin it is in me
> To be ashamed to be my father's child!
> But though I am daughter to his blood,
> I am not to his manners. O Lorenzo,
> If thou keep promise, I shall end this strife,
> Become a Christian, and thy loving wife. (II,iii,16–21)

The promise of conversion makes the exogamous character of her behavior all the more evident. Lorenzo elaborates on her active complicity:

> She hath directed
> How I shall take her from her father's house,
> What gold and jewels she is furnished with,
> What page's suit she hath in readiness. (II,iv,32–35)

Shylock himself ties together the motifs of theft of property, betrayal, and conversion in his tortured lament:

---

3   A play called *The Jew*, alluded to obliquely in Stephen Gosson's *School of Abuse* (1579), is supposed by some to have been a model upon which Shakespeare may have drawn.

My daughter! Oh, my ducats! Oh my daughter!
Fled with a Christian! Oh, my Christian ducats! (II,viii,15–16)

It may be objected, quite legitimately, that there is nothing in Lorenzo's actions that qualifies as an initiation, and yet both in the subplot and in the main plot the prevailing condition is one of young men in loosely related groups, striving against difficult odds (whether in commerce, in stealth, or in the courts) to improve their condition and even save their lives within a context tightly constrained by fortune and the law. This effort is interwoven with the general replication of the marriage motif: Bassanio weds Portia and Gratiano weds Nerissa in a kind of ripple effect. What happens in the main plot is echoed at all levels.

The courtship of Portia, as that portion of the plot might be called, has many of the characteristics of the paradigmatic narrative pattern. Portia's father is not physically present, but his hostility to his daughter's suitors lives on in the caskets. Although she feels oppressed by her father's injunctions, Portia, like the young women in the courtship stories, obeys them faithfully. Even when the right man comes along, she will do nothing overt to help him choose correctly. The riddles of the caskets, of course, are entirely consistent with the non-martial nature of the trials imposed on the young man in stories like this. The risk, however, is not trivial, as suitors who guess incorrectly learn. In the syntagmatic story, emphasis is placed on the fact that marriage is taking place outside of the kinship group. In the courtship stories, we are meant to focus instead on the appropriateness of the match. Fearing rejection on the grounds that he is too different, Morocco bids Portia, "Mislike me not for my complexion" (II,i,1). She answers him fairly, but when he chooses the wrong casket, she sighs in relief, "Let all of his complexion choose me so" (II,vii,79).

The main plot of the play is concerned with measuring individuals' worth, and much attention is paid to contracts, promises, the letter of the law, and interpretation. In this respect, too, the plot has much in common with other examples of the paradigmatic narrative pattern. Although such matters may have strong social implications, the emphasis here is on the interpersonal understandings involved. Portia plays a pivotal role. In her capacity as judge and as lover, she must exercise a balance of severity and compassion, whether in the court or in her testing of Bassanio's faithfulness with the device of the ring.

In its locale, the "courtship of Portia" part of the play reflects the paradigmatic mode described in the Irish courtships and the Arthurian romances. It steps outside of Venice and the world of commerce, usury and daily strife and brings us to an exotic sanctuary visited by the Princes of Morocco and Aragon, who must stake their entire future on one guess.

The two worlds in which Portia must function are constantly commenting on one another, and what transpires is marked by a mood of dissembling and disguise. In such a world, women can be taken for men and, as the caskets tell us, appearances can be deceiving.

It is particularly striking that this one play written in the late sixteenth century should yoke together both the paradigmatic and the syntagmatic initiation patterns. Although I do not wish to suggest that this pairing betrays an explicit awareness of ancient traditional narrative, it is likely that in Shakespeare's mind and in the minds of his coevals, it was somehow appropriate.

It is in *The Tempest* that the paradigmatic initiation narrative assumes its most fully developed form outside of the Medieval period. *The Tempest* is a story of testing and measuring. It compresses the real-world themes of rebellion, treason, freedom, slavery, social contracts, punishment, love, and forgiveness into the metaphoric and stylized concerns of a small group of characters on a magical island.

Certainly the locale itself is as Otherworldly as anything found in the Irish or French stories cited. Prospero's island is populated by creatures and spirits well outside of our own experience. Yet, as in other stories of this kind, much of what happens on the island speaks to our intuitive experience and understanding, and concepts such as sea change resonate for us at an emotional level. What is important in achieving this effect is that there be just enough distance to gain perspective. Miranda reminds us of the fact that exoticism and wonder can be relative concepts when she first beholds the full assembly of those who were washed ashore by the storm:

> Oh, brave new world,
> That has such people in't. (V,i,183–84)

The pattern calls for a hostile father, a dutiful daughter, and a suitor who is willing to endure great trials for her sake. On one level, it can be argued that Prospero's hostility is more a sham than a reality, for, indeed, the entire plot to bring Miranda and Ferdinand together is a thing of his creation. Yet, on another level, we can see Prospero fitting very legitimately into that role. Human in spite of all his magical skills, Prospero still bears hostility towards the powers that conspired to exile him, and his testing of Ferdinand to determine his innate goodness is very real. An exchange with Caliban reveals yet another dimension to Prospero's role as the hostile father guarding his daughter against suitors:

Caliban:　　And here you sty me
　　In this hard rock whiles you do keep from me
　　The rest o' th' island.

Prospero:　　Thou most lying slave,
　　Whom stripes may move, not kindness. I have used thee,
　　Filth as thou art, with human care, and lodged thee
　　In mine own cell till thou didst seek to violate
　　The honor of my child.

Caliban: Oh ho, oh ho! Would't had been done!
　　Thou didst prevent me. I had peopled else
　　This isle with Calibans.　(I,ii,342-51)

Both Miranda and Ferdinand fulfill their roles as dictated by the pattern. She is wholly in sympathy with the young man's suit, but she does nothing to defy her father's will, beyond making an occasional mild protest, inadvertently breaking his command not to reveal her name, and showing an unselfish willingness to help her suitor in his task of carrying wood. Though Miranda is quite passive in her dealings with her father, ultimately it is for her sake and with the goal of restoring her birthright that Prospero's entire stratagem is set in motion.

In this version of the story, we see a young man prematurely thrust into adulthood by the sudden death of his father (or so it seems). Believing his father lost at sea, he identifies himself as "the best of them that speak this speech" (I,ii,429). Coupled with this upheaval of his life and social status is his sudden exposure to the sexual dimensions of adulthood. The young man's pursuit of the hostile father's daughter in this type of narrative often results in the overthrow — and sometimes death — of the father. Ferdinand accepts Prospero's tasks without complaint and only in his own thoughts does he acknowledge the old man to be "composed of harshness". Nevertheless, the inevitable conclusion to the story is that Prospero, here by his own choice, will lose his power over his daughter and all his other powers once the "revels" of the play are ended.

I have indicated that the initiation pattern has always exhibited extraordinary powers of adaptability and that, whenever it took form in a culture or time period, it did so in a medium that maximized its ability to communicate the underlying message that the pattern encapsulated. It is noteworthy, therefore, that in the present case the pattern should have emerged simultaneously in tragi-comedy and romance environments.

For Shakespeare, comedy is quintessentially a medium that describes social processes. Its characters, who are more likely to function as a group of replicated couples than as individuals, are caught up in large, commonly experienced imperatives over which they ultimately seem to have little control, the chief of these being to marry. Unlike the tragedies or histories, in which human actions have perceptible consequences, characters in the comedies are swept along often ignorant of what is really happening to them. Comedy is the medium which creates and reinforces in us the expectation that, as Puck puts it in *A Midsummer Night's Dream*,

> Jack shall have Jill
> Nought shall go ill. (III,ii,461–62)

To be sure, *The Merchant of Venice* is not a comedy of the same ilk as *A Midsummer Night's Dream*. Nevertheless, we see in this play characters moving on parallel courses towards a common resolution in which, ultimately, nought does go ill.

A similar imperative is being articulated in Shakespeare's romances, but the medium in which the joining of the young man and the young woman will take place is considerably more subtle and personal. We are not distracted by multiple pairs of lovers in *The Tempest*, nor is there any question of confusing one set of lovers with another, as is the case with Helena, Hermia, Lysander, and Demetrius in *A Midsummer Night's Dream*. We are asked to look at human relationships as timeless and deeply significant bonds rather than as a spontaneous and collective response to seasonal and cyclical rhythms of life. It was the genius of Shakespeare to be able to portray both perspectives with sympathy.

Throughout the Medieval period, we find evidence that the initiation narrative pattern enjoyed a dynamic interaction with the genres in which it found expression, sometimes exerting influence on their development and evolution. By the time the pattern found its way into the works of Shakespeare, it had certainly ceased to have any such formative influence. Nevertheless, the degree to which the two parts of the pattern were able to maintain their constituent characteristics, particularly in the hands of a single author, suggests that in Shakespeare's time, and even afterwards, the pattern still had something of value to impart to new audiences.

RE-READING
DAFYDD AP GWILYM

Patrick K. Ford

DEPARTMENT OF CELTIC LANGUAGES AND LITERATURES
HARVARD UNIVERSITY

In a paper published in 1958,[1] Eurys Rowlands declared that it is a great pleasure to read Dafydd ap Gwilym's *cywydd* to the month of May for the first time, but he insisted that the more one re-reads it the more that pleasure increases and the more magnificent the poetry appears. It is that sense that is intended by the title of the present paper — reading and then reading again — and not some revisionist approach to the great poet's work. Even so, it is implicit in this paper that we might give more attention to Dafydd's *text* than to his *context*.

It has long been rued by Welsh scholars and partisans that Dafydd is so little known outside Wales and the small international community of Welsh scholars. Had he written in some other language, say English or French or Italian, some have argued, he would be recognized as one of the greatest poets of the Middle Ages. Translations of Dafydd abound, to be sure. But reading almost any of them, at random, makes it easy to understand why Dafydd is an underrated poet outside of Wales and outside of Welsh scholarship: it is simply impossible to translate anything but his images, his themes, and the arguments of his poems, and those only partially. And the choices we make in translating necessarily deprive us of all of the other meanings possible while encouraging new and probably unintended meanings that derive from the switch of code. As Rachel Bromwich has said, "This difficulty [of adequately translating] arises from the sheer virtuosity of Dafydd's elaborate artistry, in which

---

1 "Cywydd Dafydd ap Gwilym i Fis Mai", *Llên Cymru* 5 (1958), pp. 1–25. An earlier version of the present paper was prepared to be read at Berkeley at the 1991 annual meeting of the Celtic Studies Association of North America in the high hopes that Brendan, with his fine ear for poetry and his assiduous attention to detail, would hear it. Alas, he didn't; if he had, the present version would have profited from his comments and criticisms. If it contributes aught to his memory, then that is due to the inspiration of his own efforts in the field of early Irish and Welsh studies.

he deployed all the resources of the linguistic and metrical media which had come to him as the legatee of an ancient and elaborate poetic tradition. . . ."[2]

As a consequence of this difficulty, scholars who write about Dafydd in English (and some of those who write about him in Welsh!) often resort to discussing Dafydd in the context of the literary tradition of Wales or of Europe. The early studies of Th. Chotzen pioneered the study of Dafydd in relation to the troubadour poetry of the Continent, and those studies have been enlarged and enriched by the numerous writings of Rachel Bromwich. Dr. Bromwich, like other Welsh scholars, has stressed the Continental heritage (innovation) as well as the native heritage (tradition), showing the poetic development and indebtedness of Dafydd to a tradition that begins with the earliest Welsh poetry of Aneirin and Taliesin in the sixth century and extends to the so-called *gogynfeirdd* or poets of the princes in the twelfth and thirteenth centuries. She singles out the themes of nature and love and traces their development in the antecedent tradition culminating in the flowering of those themes in the poetry of Dafydd ap Gwilym. Historical criticism of that sort is most useful to the reader who has a rather thoroughgoing knowledge of the antecedent traditions. A recent book by Helen Fulton[3] presents a fine study of the social contexts of medieval European poetry and an analysis of Dafydd's corpus in terms of the analogous social context of Wales after the loss of Welsh independence and the fall of the native aristocracy, as it were, at the end of the thirteenth century. It is yet another kind of historical criticism that situates Dafydd's poetry in yet another context.

The historical approach tends to hang heavily on the poet's work, often obscuring it, at best, or trivializing it, at worst. Scholars have shed much ink in attempting to sketch the history of this "father of Welsh poetry", but the final result thus far is summed up neatly in *The Oxford Companion to the Literature of Wales*: "Of Dafydd's life virtually nothing is known beyond the little to be deduced from his poetry."[4] A good example of the difficulties inherent in trying to deduce biography from the poetry is the case of the two young women Dafydd mentions in so many of his love poems: Dyddgu and Morfudd. Sir Ifor Williams maintained that these were fictional names, sobriquets, as it were, for the current object of Dafydd's affection. But pedigrees have, tentatively, been provided for both.[5] The *Companion* is unequivocal about Dyddgu,

---

2 *Aspects of the Poetry of Dafydd ap Gwilym* (Cardiff, 1982), p. 8.
3 *Dafydd ap Gwilym and the European Context* (Cardiff, 1989).
4 Meic Stephens, ed. (Oxford University Press, 1986), p. 120.
5 See Bromwich, *Aspects*, pp. 28–29, for a discussion.

calling her "the dark-haired woman who is the subject of nine *cywyddau* by Dafydd. . . . Dyddgu was aristocratic, remote and virginal, and remained the unattainable object of the poet's affections." In contrast to the nine lines accorded Dyddgu, the even more tenuous reality of Morfudd rates one and a third columns in the *Companion*. Nevertheless, it begins honestly enough: "Morfudd: the principal sweetheart of Dafydd ap Gwilym, if the evidence of his poems is accepted."

I rehearse all this because it shows how criticism has tended to focus on the biographical, as if our appreciation of the literature depended primarily upon our intimate knowledge of the life and times of the literary figure. There is no question — in my mind at least — but that the life and times of an author are an important ingredient in the works that are the unique linguistic expressions of that author. But what are we to do when the times are only dimly visible to us and the life not at all (outside of what can be gleaned from the works). Combing literary works for historical facts raises serious methodological questions. It brings to mind what the Chaucer scholar Derek Pearsall once called "the 'Did Shakespeare Like Dogs' school of criticism".[6] This school, as Professor Pearsall put it, goes through the corpus of Shakespeare's works collecting references to dogs, and then shows on balance that the bard either did or did not like dogs.

Historical and biographical approaches can help us little in understanding the greatness of Dafydd's artistic achievement. For present purposes, let us grant the facts that Dafydd is both a product of the poetic tradition of Wales stretching back to the sixth century, and a product of social forces at work in fourteenth-century Wales, including changing literary tastes influenced by Norman and Continental elements and the changed political status of the Welsh nobility. (How could he not be?) But all of the historical criticism we have cannot lead us into the world of poems left to us under Dafydd's name; for that there is only one avenue of access: their language. And so what I propose to do here is to suggest ways of exploring that language with you, and to champion the non-historical, non-contextual approaches to Dafydd's poetry.

I begin with Stanley Greenfield's *caveat lector* in discussing Old English poems, that, "syntactic features cannot be ignored if we are to perceive the full complement of meaning in a poem." And then he goes on to quote Winifred Nowottny (*The Language Poets Use*),

> however little it is noted by the reader, [syntax] is the groundwork of the poet's art. Often it supports a poetic edifice elaborated by many other poetic means and the reader is content to believe that these other means are the cause

6 Unpublished paper, UCLA, April 26, 1991.

of his pleasure, but when a passage relies chiefly on its especially compelling and artful syntax to make its effect, the reader and the critics, who never expect syntax to be more than 'a harmless, necessary drudge' holding open the door while the pageantry of words sweeps through, will be at a loss to understand why the passage affects them as it does and at a loss to do critical justice to its art.[7]

Some critics have, in fact, attempted to show how syntax, especially the use of *sangiad*, enhances or interacts with the argument of Dafydd's poetry. David Johnston, in discussing the poem "Y Ffenestr", says, "The sense of frustration which the lovers feel is effectively expressed by the long sentence from lines 32 to 38, the reference to the kiss itself being delayed by asides (*sangiadau*) and subordinate clauses, giving the impression of futile straining."[8] One could advance a similar argument in the case of "Trafferth mewn Tafarn".

At the phonological level, some critics have signalled the importance of the effect of *cynghanedd*, the system of alliteration and rhyme raised to such exotic levels in Dafydd's poetry, on meaning. Thomas Parry, in "Dafydd ap Gwilym a'r Cyfriadur",[9] calls the poem "Dagrau Serch" ('Tears of Love') a masterful example of Dafydd's work, and he wonders whether part of its excellence might be the frequency of two types of *cynghanedd* — *croes* and *traws* — in the poem. In other words, *cynghanedd*, far from being a device to be admired apart, complements or enhances the meaning of the poem. For one thing, these two types of *cynghanedd* have distinct elements of complementarity: in *croes*, the line is divided into two with the consonants in the two parts echoing one another; in *traws*, the line falls into three parts, with the consonants in the first and last parts echoing one another. In "Dagrau Serch", each line of the poem begins with the letter *D*, and the poem has to do with Dafydd's love for Dyddgu, each of whom is named once in the poem, and the *dagrau* or 'tears' of love. Even our untrained ears can hear the echoes of half lines, suggesting the pair of lovers, Dyddgu and Dafydd.

> **Dydd**gu liw **dydd g**oleuaf,
> **Dy n**awdd, er Unmab Duw Naf,
> **Deurudd** Mair o di**redd** Mael,
> **D**uon **l**ygaid a **dwy**ael

---

7   Quoted in *The Interpretation of Old English Poems* (Routledge and Kegan Paul, 1972), p. III.

8   "The Serenade and the Image of the House in the Poems of Dafydd ap Gwilym", *Cambridge Medieval Celtic Studies* 5 (1983), pp. 1–19.

9   *Ysgrifau Beirniadol* 13 (1985), pp. 114–22.

But to my knowledge, there are few detailed studies of this kind, looking precisely at the metrics and the language (syntax, morphology, phonology) as significant elements of meaning in Dafydd's poetry, although we are often enough told that that is where we must look. To quote Rachel Bromwich again,

> By intricate innuendo, and frequently by an intentional ambiguity attained by a complex play upon the richly varied nuances both of his traditional vocabulary and of the new words which were at his disposal, Dafydd evolved for himself a poetic medium of a degree of complexity which had never previously been envisaged in Welsh, and which at times by its very nature defies all attempts at adequate transposition into another language. . . . The degree of one's comprehension of Dafydd's poetry is directly commensurate with the degree of one's knowledge of the sum-total of his linguistic resources. . . .[10]

Although her comments indicate she is thinking primarily of Dafydd's dexterity at the lexical level, her reference to his linguistic resources urges us to go beyond the merely lexical.

Above all, and regardless of themes and images, Dafydd is a consummate linguist. As a professionally trained poet, he was surely well acquainted with the *Gramadegau'r Penceirddiaid*,[11] which, as has been shown, was an evolving textbook for use in bardic schools.[12] The Welsh triads state that poets were required to "give accompt for every word and sillable" of their compositions.[13] And when we remember that the patrons of the poets of Dafydd's time "formed a knowledgeable audience, and that they and the bards shared a common tradition of learning,"[14] then we can feel certain that close readings of this poetry based on linguistic subtleties will not fall too short of the poet's intentions or his audience's perceptions.

Eurys Rowlands's analysis of "Mis Mai" is a model essay for uncovering the layers of meaning to be found in Dafydd's poems. He begins by showing that *geiriau mwys* (= *geiriau amwys*) 'ambiguous words, puns, homonyms' were an acceptable and expected part of the *gordderchgerdd* 'love poems' of the *teuluwr*, even if such ambiguity was frowned upon in the higher grade of poets.[15] And granting the influence of the *teuluwyr* on Dafydd, Rowlands agrees with Thomas Parry that the *gair mwys* was an important part of Dafydd's artistry. He then goes on to

10 Op. cit., p. 9.
11 See Rachel Bromwich, "Dafydd ap Gwilym and the Bardic Grammar", chap. 4 of *Aspects of the Poetry of Dafydd ap Gwilym*.
12 Eurys Rowlands, *Poems of the Cywyddwyr* (= Mediaeval and Modern Welsh Series VIII; Dublin: Institute for Advanced Studies, 1976), p. xiv.
13 Quoted in Rowlands, op. cit., p. xviii.
14 Rowlands, op. cit., p. xvi.
15 The reference is to *Gramadegau'r Pencerddiaid*; v. Rowlands, "Cywydd Dafydd ap Gwilym", pp. 1–2.

take the poem apart, line by line, couplet by couplet, paragraph by paragraph, to show how not only lexical ambiguity but sentential or syntactical ambiguity enriches the poem. This is what he says about the first couplet, which reads,

> Duw gwyddiad mai da y gweddai
> Dechreuad mwyn dyfiad Mai.

First he points to the possible *geiriau mwys: Duw, mai, gweddai, mwyn.*

Duw:	God; day
mai:	that; May
gweddai:	became, befitted; submitted, obeyed
mwyn:	tender; riches

Duw as subject of the verb *gwyddiad* surely means 'God', but, reading vertically,[16] we have *duw dechreuad*, and *duw dechreuad Mai* is an acceptable expression for 'the first of May' on the model of *duw calan Mai*, which in fact occurs in line 4.

As Rowlands points out, in MW *mai* 'that' is spelled *mae*, but given the kind of *cynghanedd* in the line that leaves *mai* without stress, and considering the emphasis on *Mai* in the poem, it is safe to conclude that the word is ambiguous.[17] Therefore, the opening words may mean

> God knew that . . .

or

> God knew May . . . .

We would have no trouble in reading,

> God knew May; a rich growth well suited the beginning of May.

But the ambiguity is preserved, for the alternative reading is equally valid:

---

16 Compare lines 37–40 of the poem, which begin *Paun . . . , Pa un . . ., Pa . . . ,* and *Un . . .* respectively (the last two are as emended by Rowlands).

17 He also calls our attention to Simwnt Fychan's pun in *Pum Llyfr Kerddwriaeth (Gramadegau*, p. 126) on *ardderchawg*, which ordinarily means 'noble, dignified' but if the man is a philanderer then it means *ordderchawg* 'fornicator'. It would be a mistake for us to deny Middle Welsh the right to make bad puns, a right we so much enjoy and exploit today ourselves.

God knew that a gentle beginning well befitted the start of May.

The point is that the poet has succeeded in introducing his subject well in advance of the final rhyme at the end of the second line of the first couplet by a simple syntactic stratagem, one that requires the use of *mai* in place of *bod* when an element of the following clause is topicalized; that is, a syntactic rule has catapulted the very homonym of the poem's subject into the crucial position in the type of *cynghanedd* with which the poem opens.

The ambiguity of *mai* then opens the door for taking the last four words of the first line as *sangiad* or aside: "well did May submit" (e.g., to God's plan). In that reading, the main sentence is "God knew the beginning of riches", e.g., with *dyfiad Mai* in apposition to *mwyn*.

If the first line is taken as a complete sentence, "God knew that well did it fit", then the second line may be taken as a nominal construction in two or more ways:

> the tender/rich growth of May is a beginning

or

> the beginning of tender/rich growth is May.

The mutation rules do not help us in sorting out these ambiguities, because the rests, caesuras, required by *cynghanedd* obviate the normal rules of mutation.[18] Thus, we could take *mai* in the first line to be the month and the object of *gwyddiad* without worrying about the lack of mutation of the object.[19]

I have not exhausted the possibilities suggested by Rowlands for this opening couplet, but I think I have said enough to indicate his method for elaborating the resonances of the poem. Rowlands does not pretend to be exhaustive in his reading of "Mis Mai". Quite the opposite, he goes to some pains to make it clear that he is trying to open up the poem by identifying some possible *geiriau mwys* and *brawddegau mwys*: lexical and syntactical ambiguities. And he supposes (p. 21) that he has failed to see enough of them rather than having seen too many.

I think he supposes correctly, for at this distance in time we cannot hope to recover all the nuances in Dafydd's skillful manipulation of his language. I would suggest that also crucial to the dramatic opening of the

---

18 See T. J. Morgan, *Y Treigladau a'u Cystrawen* (Cardiff, 1952), e.g., p. 196.
19 Ibid., p. 215.

poem is the fact that the force of *mai* — ambiguous with respect to meaning but clearly announcing the subject of this poem — is not diluted by the preceding imperfect verb form, for unlike the remainder of the imperfect verbs in the poem, it does not have the characteristic *-ai* ending.

"Mis Mai" is one of two poems in which Dafydd uses a single rhyme throughout. In a note on the poem, Rachel Bromwich says, "The poet's necessity to find a series of di-syllabic words to rhyme with Mai is responsible for the sequence of verbs ending in 3 sg. imperfect in *-ai*."[20] I think Dr. Bromwich might have framed these remarks in a more positive way. It is not so much that Dafydd is constrained by his decision to retain the monorhyme in *-ai*; rather, he perceived the dramatic possibilities inherent in the fact that the word for May rhymed with the morpheme denoting imperfect or past habitual and thus evoked a sense of reflection and longing, of *hiraeth*, as it were, for the month that belongs to lovers. I think he perceived it, therefore, as his month, his as the poet of love and lovers. It is worth quoting the words of Eleanor Knott, writing about medieval Irish bardic poetry: "With a skilled and intelligent craftsman this attention to ornament can accompany genuine feeling and even be quickened by it. It need not be a bar to expression and is often a stimulus. The true artist is served by the difficulties of his medium, and the Irish poet, even in his most rigidly patterned quatrains, can express a mood, serious, tender or humorous."[21] Of another famous monorhyming poem in the language, the lament for Llywelyn ap Gruffudd by Gruffudd ab yr Ynad Goch, D. Myrddin Lloyd wrote, "[it] is the most powerful expression in the language of dismay and unrelieved black despair. It is at the same time a miracle of art. The one main rhyme, *-aw, -aw, -aw*, like an unending wail occurs ninety-four times."[22]

Most of the words rhyming with *Mai* are verbs in the imperfect third singular. There are four exceptions. The poet speaks of May as having come in "yesterday", and he professes to be vexed that it did not last forever; he wishes that winter would never come. The passing of spring did not bother him, but now he worries that the start of summer has trammeled May, and that brings tears, for it belongs to him as poet of

20 *Selected Poems of Dafydd ap Gwilym* (Harmondsworth: Penguin, 1985), p. 18. Compare Margaret Goldsmith's statement about the Beowulf poet: "It is rather obvious that the rhythmic, alliterative, and syntactic frames within which the Anglo-Saxon poet has to work inhibit precise utterances." Quoted in Greenfield, op. cit., p. 133.
21 *Irish Classical Poetry* (Dublin, 1960), p. 18.
22 *A Guide to Welsh Literature*, I (Swansea, 1976), pp. 186–87.

love and nature. *Mai* thus evokes what may have been a close homonym in *mau*: the independent 1st sg. possessive pronoun 'mine'.

It is not just that these rhymes are fortuitous, but that the poet, by choosing to use but a single rhyme throughout, accomplishes the following: reinforces the association of May with something that belongs to Dafydd (*mau*); creates a constant anticipation of topicalization or focus (*mai*) that rivets our attention; reflects a melancholic past (imperfect -*ai*). Because *Mai* does not occur in its mutated form in the poem, it cannot be confused with *bai* 'fault, blemish'; it is therefore faultless, as the poet says in line 23: *Mab bedydd Dofydd difai*, translated by Bromwich, "faultless god-child of the Lord" (Bromwich has "a god-child of the perfect Lord"). But even in this line, note the punning on *Dafydd/Dofydd*, whereby Dafydd himself, the *mab bedydd*, is the faultless *dofydd* 'tamer' who tamed a girl, as he says in line 19: *dofais ferch*, and also the 'lord' or 'governor' of the wooded bower.[23]

The other poem that maintains a single rhyme throughout is the poem to "Summer", where each couplet ends with the word for 'summer', *haf*. The poem is spoken in the first person, and is loaded with superlative adjectives. Rachel Bromwich notes that "the monorhyme in *haf* . . . is responsible for the numerous 1 sg. pres. indic. endings in -*af* and superlative adjs. in -*(h)af*."[24] Here too, it is not so much a matter of "responsibility" or that Dafydd is constrained by the monorhyme in -*af*; rather, the fact that the word for 'summer' is identical with the morpheme for 'superlative' and the first person ending of verbs quickens the poem and provides the poet with essential meaning. The self-consciousness of his decision is reinforced when we remember that final -*f* began to disappear early in the spoken language and in the fourteenth century was "freely dropped after any vowel".[25] There are plenty of examples in Dafydd's own poetry of first person singular verbs and superlative adjectives rhyming with final -*a*. As Morris Jones says, "The word is treated in every way as a word ending in a vowel . . . ", although when necessary the -*f* can be restored as needed. In the poem "Rhagoriaeth ei Gariad", we see both possibilities:

23 The richness of this poem is magnified by its very genre. Poems celebrating May are common not only in early Irish and Welsh but in the medieval poetry of Europe generally. Furthermore, in each of these literatures, the common theme of nature poetry is played with, with considerable artistic dexterity. As R. Geraint Gruffydd has so skillfully shown, the poet of "Cyntefin Ceinaf Amser" appropriates the nature genre to his own spiritual purposes, but in so doing he is imitating a common practice of Continental poets of the period. For them summer could be a sad time when it brought memories of love lost, just as winter could be a time of joy when warmth was provided by a lover. See "Cyntefin Ceinaf Amser o Lyfr Du Caerfyrddin", *Ysgrifau Beirniadol* 4 (1969), pp. 12–26.

24 P. 21.

25 John Morris Jones, *A Welsh Grammar* (Oxford, 1913), p. 180.

Policsena ferch Bria,
Gwaisg o grair yn gwisgo gra.
A'r ail fu Ddiodemaf,
Gwiwbryd goleudraul haul haf.[26]

In the first line cited, Dafydd secures the rhyme with *gra* by leaving off the final *-f* of Priam's name. In the next couplet, he adds an inorganic *-f* to Deidamea's name to get the rhyme with *haf*.

Dafydd's close identification with summer may be seen in the fact that one-third of the words that rhyme with *haf* are 1st person singulars (*-af*). The frequency of superlatives (five) as rhymes with summer reinforces Dafydd's argument that summer is the most splendid time. And note the self-consciousness with which he calls attention to this link:

Dyn Ofydd, hirddydd harddaf (*GDG* 24.29)

Pwy ni chwardd pan fo hardd haf? (*GDG* 24.16)

Ovid's man, most splendid long days
Who wouldn't laugh when summer is so fine?

so that both *hardd-af* and *hardd haf* occur. Certainly, re-reading this poem would reveal a wealth of ambiguities along these and other lines.

*

*   *

*   *   *

Earlier, I explored Thomas Parry's judgment that the excellence of the poem "Dagrau Serch" might depend in part on the frequency of a particular kind of *cynghanedd*. In *cynghanedd groes*, we might say that the poet uses the same consonants to say different things. That is, the line falls into two parts and the consonants in the second half of the line echo those in the first half — in precisely the same order. Thus, with the exception of the vowels, the two half-lines are identical, and their meanings are drawn inexorably to each other.

26 Thomas Parry, *Gwaith Dafydd ap Gwilym* (Cardiff, 1952), 51.7–10. Note that in *GDG* 83.50, Dafydd uses the form *Adda* to rhyme with *da*; in our poem, *Addaf* in the first line rhymes with *haf*.

The well-known poem "Yr Wylan" or 'The Seagull' begins as follows:

Yr wylan deg   ar lanw dioer.

Here we have the consonants *r-l-n-d* of the first half of the line repeated in the second half. The two halves, in translation, say:

The lovely seagull   on a hospitable tide (or 'on the tide; God knows').

In Welsh, however, the seagull, whom we see to be bobbing on the waves, is really at one with the welcoming tide because of the *cynghanedd*: the consonants announcing the seagull are precisely those that describe its situation. It works in Welsh, but not in English. We would have to abandon the Welsh text altogether to arrive at something close, like

Beautiful bird on briny bobbing,

where the alliteration pulls all the elements together reasonably well, but not absolutely as in the Welsh. The second line of the poem is:

Unlliw   ag eiry   neu wenlloer

The color   of snow or   a bright (white) moon.

Here, the line falls into three parts, and it is the consonants *n-ll* of part one and part three that echo one another. The brilliance of this line is that *unlliw* 'identical in color' is followed by snow, and then by the compound bright moon. It is unnecessary to repeat 'identical in color' before 'bright moon' because, in Welsh, and by the rules of *cynghanedd, unlliw* contains the identical consonantal sequence as *wenlloer*. Literally, *unlliw* is already present in *wenlloer*. Furthermore, because in the couplet form which Dafydd is using couplets rhyme, this line is attracted to the preceding line. Thus we have both vertical and horizontal movement.

Meaning in these poems thus evolves from the constant interplay of phonological, syntactical, and morphological elements, as well as from the semantic mobility of the lexicon. Like the constant piling up of images, which happens at the contextual level in the poem, the burden of the poem's linguistic detail compels the listener (reader) to focus on the grammar of the text, to understand *that* as the primary thrust of the artistic enterprise. Though the content of Dafydd's poetry helps us to situate him in the literary history of his own country and in the literary milieu of the fourteenth century, it is his language that sets him apart from the poets who preceded him and who came after him, and that continues to give pleasure in re-reading him.

THE *ENGLYNION*
IN *LLYFR ANEIRIN*

(*Canu Aneirin*, lines 535-37, 1209-11)

R. Geraint Gruffydd

CENTRE FOR ADVANCED WELSH AND CELTIC STUDIES
THE UNIVERSITY OF WALES

Brendan O Hehir's trenchant and important critique of the received view of the *Gododdin* did not address itself to the question of those fragments of verse which have become known as interpolations. He and his partners were after bigger fish than that! (Klar, O Hehir and Sweetser 1983–84; Klar, O Hehir and Sweetser 1985; O Hehir 1988, 57–95). I have already ventured to comment briefly on two of these interpolations (Gruffydd 1990, 261–66; Gruffydd 1992) and would now like to consider, as briefly, a third. I regret that what follows is so slight a tribute to the memory of a man and scholar for whom, in common with all his friends, I had the profoundest respect and admiration.

The interpolation, or rather interpolations, I would like to consider are the two *englynion* (three-line stanzas) that occur in the *Gododdin*. In a sense, everything I say is a work of supererogation because the whole matter has been exhaustively considered by Dr. Jenny Rowland in her magisterial edition of the complete corpus of saga *englynion* (Rowland 1990). Indeed, the notes that follow can best be regarded as a summary of Dr. Rowland's findings, with some additional comment, and as such they may have a certain utility.

I

The first *englyn*, written as one and a half lines by Hand A, occurs on p. 12 of *Llyfr Aneirin* (Cardiff, South Glamorgan Library MS. 2.81; Huws 1989). It is given below as found in the manuscript, but arranged into lines (a). There follows a version in Modern Welsh orthography, with punctuation added (b). Finally a literal translation is appended (c). In all that follows knowledge is assumed of the fundamental work of Sir Ifor Williams (Williams 1938), Professor Kenneth Jackson (Jackson 1969), and Professor A. O. H. Jarman (Jarman 1988). Dr. Rowland also provides a text and translation (Rowland 1990, 413, 472, 534–35). I should add that the translation I offer differs slightly from all of these.

a.   Ket bei cann wr en vn ty
     atwen ovalon keny.
     penn gwyr tal being a dely.

b.   Cyd bai cannwr yn un tŷ —
     Adwen ofalon Cyny —
     Pen gwŷr tâl baing a ddyly.

c.   Although there were an hundred warriors in the one house —
     I discern the anxieties of Cyny —
     The chief of warriors deserves the head of the bench.

Metrically the stanza is a regular *englyn milwr*. A few points call for comment.

Line

1   *cann wr*: The equivalent in Modern Welsh orthography, *cannwr*, is misleading because the accent was undoubtedly on the final syllable.

2   *atwen*: Jarman (1988, 151) points out that this form could be either 1st person or 3rd person singular present indicative of the verb *adnabot*, thus making possible, if the second alternative were adopted, a translation such as "Cyny knows cares". Rowland (1990, 534), on the other hand, argues for "an original preterite meaning" and translates accordingly.

3   *penn gwyr*: For discussion of this phrase and its equivalent in the corresponding *englyn* in the Llywarch Hen cycle, considered below, see Hamp (1976, 349–51) and Koch (1991, 114). It should be added that after *penn* in the manuscript there is inserted what appears to be a highly irregular *punctus elevatus*.

    being: A loan word from Old English *benc*.

As has been already alluded to in the note on *penn gwyr* in line 3, the *englyn* "*Ket bei . . .* " is generally assumed to be a stray from the Llywarch Hen cycle of saga *englynion* — "a stray sheep from Llywarch

Hen's flock" in Sir Ifor Williams's picturesque phrase (Williams 1938, 203). A similar *englyn* does indeed occur in that cycle:

> Atwen leveryd kyni.
> pan disgynnei yg kyfyrdy.
> penn gwyr pan gwin a dyly.

which Dr. Rowland translates thus (1990, 413, 472, 534–35):

> I knew the speech of Cyni
> When he would drop into the drinking hall.
> The chief of men deserves a cup of wine.

The assumption is that *"Ket bei . . . "* was attracted into the *Gododdin*'s orbit from its proper sphere by the inclusion nearby in the longer poem of an eight-line *awdl* celebrating the rescue of the poet from prison by a hero named *Keneu vab Llywarch*; this clearly forms part of the incipient "Legend of Aneirin" discussed by Ms. Morfydd Owen (1978, 123–50). Indeed, so convinced was Sir Ifor Williams that the two *englynion* belonged together and to the Llywarch Hen cycle that he proposed emending *leueryd* in line 1 above to *leuenyd* 'joy' so as to provide a contrast with the *govalon* 'cares, anxieties' in line 2 of *"Ket bei . . ."* (Williams 1935, 99). As recent editors of the Llywarch Hen cycle have pointed out, however, there are difficulties about the "stray sheep" theory. No *Cyny* (or *Cenau*, for that matter) is attested as a son of Llywarch Hen either in the saga *englynion* about Llywarch or in the earlier genealogical tracts. Professor Patrick Ford, in his highly stimulating *Poetry of Llywarch Hen*, thinks *"Ket bei . . . "* is simply part of the *Gododdin* (Ford 1974, 47 n. 78). Dr. Rowland is more cautious but makes an intriguing suggestion which demands quotation in full (Rowland 1990, 58–59):

> . . . the narrator in the stanzas to Cyni is inappropriate for Llywarch who is never presented as being extraordinarily or even moderately sensitive to the feelings of his sons. The ability to pick one voice out of a hundred and to know the hearts of another in a situation which does not allow for intimate discussion is an attribute of lovers rather than a proud, but basically uncaring parent. Could these two verses be a snatch of love song spoken by a woman (*Frauenlied*) such as are found elsewhere in the early Middle Ages, often in marginal notations? The two stanzas even in their isolation have an appealing directness, but no firm conclusion can be made concerning their content.

Notwithstanding this suggestion, however, at other points in her discussion Dr. Rowland abides, albeit reluctantly, by the view put forward by Sir Ifor (Rowland 1990, 302 n. 78, 394).

II

The second *englyn*, written by Hand B and occupying nearly two lines, occurs on p. 35 of *Llyfr Aneirin*. The orthography, as would be expected of Hand B, is distinctly more archaic than is the case with "*Ket bei . . .* " I reproduce the second *englyn* using the same method as that adopted for the first.

a.   Tra merin iodeo trileo yg caat
tri guaid fraut fraidus leo
bubon a guoreu bar deo.

b.   Tra Merin Iddew trylew — yng nghad,
Tri gwaeth ffrawdd ffrawddus lew,
Bubon a worau, bar dew.

c.   Beyond the Sea of Iddew, most bold in battle,
Three times worse as regards ferocity than a fierce lion,
Bubon, with intense wrath, took action.

Metrically the stanza would be a regular *englyn penfyr* if it could be supposed that the double *a* in *caat* has the value of two syllables; there is, however, no link that I can discern between the *gair cyrch* and the second line. Not unexpectedly, this *englyn* poses many more difficulties of interpretation than the first.

Line

1   *merin iodeo*: Almost certainly the Firth of Forth (Jackson 1981). In his translation of the *Gododdin*, Jackson renders the phrase as "[From] over the sea of Iuddew . . . " and comments, "Bubon would therefore either be a Pict or could be from the northern part of Manaw across the Forth" (Jackson 1969, 108). Jarman also has "From beyond the sea of Iddew . . . " and quotes Jackson's comment in his notes (Jarman 1988, 62, 147). *Tra*, however, does not, as far as I know, mean 'from over' but simply 'over, beyond' and the line almost certainly refers to Bubon's exploits in enemy territory north of the Forth.

2   *bubon*: Although the consensus established by Sir Ifor Williams and followed by Professors Jackson and Jarman has been adopted in translating this *englyn* (see (c) above), it must be confessed that its adoption presents many difficulties. Apart from the fact that the translation as presented calls for a number of assumptions which

may or may not be justified, the personal name *Bubon* is difficult to account for. There is a possibility that at some stage in the manuscript tradition *G - g* (or *C - c*) was mistaken for *B - b* and that the hero's true name was *Gwgon* (cf. Williams 1938, 14 [line 358], 40 [line 1002]), although such a mistake is difficult to account for paleographically. Assuming that it happened, however, it becomes immediately tempting to look for two other names in the same line, matching such triplets as are found, for example, in the sequence "*Enwey meibon*" in the Llywarch Hen cycle (Rowland 1990, 413–14, 473). *Guoreu* would present no difficulties (Lloyd-Jones 1931–63, 563), but some ingenuity would be needed to deal with *bar deo*, although **Gwardew* 'the thick–necked one' suggests itself as a remote possibility (Lloyd-Jones 1931–63, 622). Such a revised reading of the last line would force a reinterpretation of the first two lines as well, yielding a translation somewhat as follows:

> Across the Firth of Forth three lions in battle,
> Three [that were] worse as regards ferocity than a fierce lion:
> Gwgon, Gorau and Gwardew.

It is striking that no commentator before Dr. Rowland has remarked upon the anomalous nature of this *englyn*. All have seemingly accepted it as an integral part of the *Gododdin*. Dr. Rowland is more cautious and concludes as follows (Rowland 1990, 302; cf. ibid., 39–95):

Northern origin is indeed likely for the *englyn* whether or not it was part of Aneirin's poem, and this is an important point for the history of the metre. The *englyn*, especially if an original part of *The Gododdin*, could testify to early use of the metre for bardic eulogy, but it could be a stray from a northern saga poem.

III

I would finally like to sum up the possibilities regarding the two *englynion*, beginning with the first, "*Ket bei . . .*".

1. It could be, as Professor Ford has argued, part of the *Gododdin*. "*Atwen leueryd . . .*", the corresponding *englyn* in the Llywarch Hen cycle, would then be a replica designed to enhance the prestige of the Llywarch Hen story through the inclusion of a *Gododdin* hero.

2. Alternatively, both "*Ket bei . . .*" and "*Atwen leueryd . . .*" could be fragments from a verse saga featuring a hero named *Cyny*, perhaps, as

Dr. Rowland suggests, spoken by a woman narrator; such a saga could have been composed either in the North or in Wales.

3. Thirdly, "*Ket bei . . .*" could indeed be, as Sir Ifor Williams argued and as has been generally accepted, a "stray sheep" from the Llywarch Hen cycle, notwithstanding the difficulties implicit in this view. Even Dr. Rowland inclines towards this position, and the occurrence in "*Ket bei . . .*" of the loan word *being* from Old English *benc* is certainly a powerful argument against positing for the *englyn* a very early date.

The possibilities for the second *englyn*, "*Tra merin . . .*", are even more numerous.

1. It could be praise poetry in an *englyn* meter for a hero of the kingdom of Gododdin (assuming for the present that it is for one warrior only), but unconnected with the Battle of Catraeth.

2. It could be, as has been generally assumed, praise poetry in an *englyn* meter and part of the *Gododdin*. Bubon's exploits *Tra merin iodeo* would then be proof of his fitness, as it were, to take part in the Battle of Catraeth.

3. It could be part of a saga about a Northern hero which was composed in the North. Dr. Rowland tends towards the view that the Urien Rheged cycle of saga *englynion* is exclusively located in the North and may indeed have been composed there (Rowland 1990, 75-119). "*Tra merin . . .*" could be a fragment of a similar Northern saga.

4. It could, however, be part of a saga about a Northern hero which was composed in Wales but which was somehow attracted to the text of the *Gododdin* during the course of that poem's transmission. The Llywarch Hen cycle of saga *englynion* likewise has a Northern "hero" and was composed in Wales, but that cycle was also largely relocated in Wales.

At present, as we have seen, the leading authority on the *englynion* corpus inclines to the third of the views stated regarding "*Ket bei . . .*" and to the second or third regarding "*Tra merin . . .*". If she is right about "*Tra merin . . .*", in particular, the implications are large either for the history of the *englyn* meters (option 2) or for the textual history of the *Gododdin* (option 3). The question, however, can hardly be regarded as closed. Dr. Rowland herself has spoken of the *Gododdin*'s "complex and difficult . . . textual history" (Rowland 1990, 394), and it is only by intensive work on individual words, lines, and stanzas that that history can be unravelled — to the extent that it can be unravelled at all. I myself believe that the synthesis proposed by Sir Ifor Williams in 1938 will prove difficult to controvert in its main outlines, but fresh work of the kind done by Brendan O Hehir and his partners, questioning old certainties and putting forward new initiatives, can only be of benefit in the awesome task of probing the mysteries of this fascinating and baffling poem which still in parts, after fourteen centuries (or more, or less), has the power to speak to us with the unmistakeable resonance of great poetry.

REFERENCES

Ford, P. K., ed. 1974. *The Poetry of Llywarch Hen*. Berkeley and Los Angeles: University of California Press.

Gruffydd, R. G. 1990. Where Was *Rhaeadr Derwenydd* (*Canu Aneirin* Line 1114)? In Matonis, A. T. E. and D. F. Melia, eds. *Celtic Language, Celtic Culture: A Festschrift for Eric P. Hamp*, 261-66. Van Nuys, California: Ford & Bailie.

———, 1996. The Strathcarron Interpolation (*Canu Aneirin*, lines 966–77). *Scottish Gaelic Studies* (forthcoming).

Hamp, E. P. 1976. Why Syntax Needs Phonology. *Papers from the Parasession on Diachronic Syntax*, 348-64. Chicago: Chicago Linguistic Society.

Huws, D., ed. 1989. *Llyfr Aneirin: A Facsimile*. Cardiff and Aberystwyth: South Glamorgan County Council and the National Library of Wales.

Jackson, K. H. 1969. *The Gododdin*. Edinburgh: Edinburgh University Press.

——— 1981. *Varia*: I. Bede's *Urbs Guidi*: Stirling or Cramond? *Cambridge Medieval Celtic Studies* 2: 1–7.

Jarman, A. O. H. 1988. *Aneirin: Y Gododdin*. Llandysul: The Gomer Press.

Klar, K. A., B. O Hehir and E. E. Sweetser. 1983-84. Welsh Poetics in the Indo-European Tradition. *Studia Celtica* 18-19: 30-51.

——— 1985. The Components of Cardiff MS. Welsh 1, *Llyfr Aneirin*. *Bulletin of the Board of Celtic Studies* 32: 38-49.

Koch, J. T. 1991. Gleanings from the *Gododdin* and other Early Welsh Texts. *The Bulletin of the Board of Celtic Studies* 38: 111-18.

Lloyd–Jones, J. 1931-63. *Geirfa Barddoniaeth Gynnar Gymraeg*. Caerdydd: Gwasg Prifysgol Cymru.

O Hehir, B. 1988. What is the *Gododdin*? In Roberts, B. F., ed. *Early Welsh Poetry: Studies in the Book of Aneirin*, 57–95. Aberystwyth: National Library of Wales.

Owen, M. E. 1978. Hwn yw e Gododin. Aneirin ae Cant. In Bromwich, R. and R. B. Jones, eds. *Astudiaethau ar yr Hengerdd*, 123–50. Caerdydd: Gwasg Prifysgol Cymru.

Rowland, J. 1990. *Early Welsh Saga Poetry: A Study and Edition of the* Englynion. Cambridge: D. S. Brewer.

Williams, I. 1938. *Canu Aneirin*. Caerdydd: Gwasg Prifysgol Cymru.

—— 1935. *Canu Llywarch Hen*. Caerdydd: Gwasg Prifysgol Cymru.

CLAS:
LUCUS A NON LUCENDO

Eric P. Hamp

EMERITUS PROFESSOR, UNIVERSITY OF CHICAGO

The only reasonable derivation of *clas* 'ditch, trench, pit, grave, groove' is **klassā* < **klad-tā* (: *claidid* 'digs'), i.e. 'what is dug'. The apparent feminine may well be an old collective ("neuter plural") **klad-to-H_a*. But *clas* also has the meaning 'fence'; see Dermot C. Twohig,[1] *PRIA* 90, C, 1 (1990), p. 27, on banks of soil with revetted faces or toppings of thorn hedge or paling, and textual references there cited from *Bretha Comaithchesa*. We thus see vividly from the informative excavations of the pre-fort field systems antedating the ring-forts at Lisduggan North, County Cork, that by the same action of digging a ditch or trench a bank of soil can be thrown up to form a field bank or fence.

Thus, 'what is dug' is both the earth which constitutes the fence and the void of the ditch whence the earth came.

We find exactly the same situation for another lexeme, a near synonym, *clad* m. 'ditch, trench; dyke, earthen rampart' *DIL* C-1 (1968), p. 206. This noun must go back to **klad-o-s*, a formation of the type τόμος. For this, *DIL* comments: "the former [i.e. the meaning 'ditch'] is probably the earlier meaning. When associated with múr or doé the clad is the ditch from which the earth of the múr or doé has been excavated." While the last sentence is perfectly justified by reasoning and now by archeology, we see that this semantic sequence is not at all necessary. A single action produces two material results.

The verb *claidid* is matched by Welsh *claddu claddaf* 'dig, burrow, bury; stab'; *clad* is the apparent equivalent of Welsh *cladd* 'pit, ditch, trench, grave', while the sense 'fall of rock in a quarry' is a manifestation by accident of the same material effect we have identified in the Irish

---

[1] I recall with this note the memory of Dermot Twohig, whose death 13 February 1989 prevented him from seeing his lastingly useful paper.

meaning 'dyke, rampart'. Welsh *claddfa* is simply a well known compound derivative of the last, as is *claddle* 'graveyard', and *claddiad* 'burial, digging' and *claddwr* 'digger, burier' are productive derivatives.

Replying to the Welsh, we find Med. Breton *claza* 'couper la terre, faire une tranchée', Vann. *claouein, claouatt* 'creuser'; Med. Bret. *claz* 'l'endroit . . . où l'on cesse de bêcher, ce qui fait une fosse ou crevasse'. On this basis by our normal principles we have no alternative but to entertain a Celtic pre-form **klad-o-s* 'what is dug'.

However, British Celtic gives us further information. The richest testimony is Welsh *clawdd* m. 'mound, wall made of earth, dyke, earthwork, boundary; hedge, fence; ditch, gutter, trench, pit, quarry, moat, fosse', attested from the twelfth and fourteenth centuries in these senses. Med. Breton replies with *cleuz* 'fossé'. If we accept the relation to Lat. *clādēs* 'disaster' and κλαδαρός 'fragile', we see here **kloH$_a$d-o-s > *klādo-s²* and we must now recognize in this the true equivalent formation of the τόμος class. In that light **klado-s* appears to be a fresh Celtic morphological formation with levelled vocalism.

We may further see in Welsh *clais* 'bruise, wound; groove, rut, ditch, rivulet, lee' < **klassi̯-* a development of an old verbal noun **klad-ti- < *klH$_a$d-ti-*. This would not, in fact, be an equivalent of OIr. *clas*, as has been claimed. The latter must be a nominalization of the old verbal adjective.

Thus, to summarize, we have morphologically:

$$\text{*klóH}_a\text{d-o-s 'what is dug'} \rightarrow$$

$$\text{*klH}_a\text{do-s = *klədo-s > *klado-s;}$$

$$\text{*klH}_a\text{d-tó-H}_a \text{ 'what is dug' > *klətst-ā;}$$

$$\text{*klH}_a\text{d-tí- 'a digging' > *klətsti- > *klassi̯-.}$$

In each case what is dug is both the earthwork wall and the ditch.

This situation calls to mind another which I have discussed in *BBCS* 25 (1974), pp. 388–91, and *Norwegian Journal of Linguistics* 28 (1974), pp. 1–7, where the single formations **ad + kan-* in Celtic and *gogan-* in Welsh each can mean both 'satirize, insult' and 'praise' in their attested history. The fact that the same formation and original lexeme can have two diametrically opposite meanings is explained by their derivation from a single activity of the traditional court poet whose unitary function was to support his lord. The discriminating factor was pragmatic, situational, external.

---

2 In fact, we cannot tell which **H$_a$* we have here. The second (> Hittite *ḫ*) would give **ā*, while the fourth (> Hittite zero, Albanian *h-*) would give **ō*; but each of these presumably yielded Celtic **ā*.

A lexeme in the course of such a development is seen in Latin *precēs* 'prayer', but also 'curse, imprecation', and Welsh *rhegu* 'curse'; see my detailed account *KZ* 91 (1977), pp. 242–43.

To grasp the meanings of texts and situations we must understand language. But over and over again we see that we cannot correctly and adequately understand language without comprehending its cultural context and situational setting. In this way many a paradox dissolves.

In the tragic death of a valued and beloved scholar we are justified in greeting eternal life. But our bitter grief finds no present joy in losing the first of our little CSANA family.

THE SPOILS OF ANNWN: TALIESIN AND MATERIAL POETRY[1]

Sarah Lynn Higley

UNIVERSITY OF ROCHESTER, NEW YORK

*All connexion with thought seems
to have been studiously avoided.*

So wrote Sharon Turner[2] of the Middle Welsh text which has perhaps inspired more controversy than any other poem in the under-
examined and undertranslated *Book of Taliesin*.[3] "Preideu Annwn"
is a labyrinth of contradiction and alternative meanings (see translation
below). Jet is mingled with water; monks howl (or 'pack together') like
wolves; warriors (or 'readers') are cowardly; a prisoner sings before the
spoils (or 'the cattle') of *Annwfyn*, which can mean both 'un-world' and
'very deep'; and in a hauntingly beautiful refrain that is repeated six
times, seven heroes associated with Arthur rise up from a submerged
fortress that has eight mysterious names.

One could spend decades combing the poem for analogues.[4] It has
tantalizing connections with Old Irish narrative, particularly the Ulster
tale of the "Tragic Death of Cú Roí mac Dáiri" about a siege made upon

---

1 Early versions of this essay were delivered at the 1983 meeting of the Celtic
  Studies Association of North America at Berkeley and a mini-colloquium on
  "Preideu Annwn" at Jesus College, Oxford, in 1984. I was delighted by the
  indebtedness expressed by Marged Haycock for my own and others' criticisms of
  her paper ("'Preideu Annwn' and the Figure of Taliesin", *Studia Celtica* 18/19
  (1983–84), p. 58, n.1), also an outcome of that same conference, and here wish to
  return the favor.
2 *History of the Anglo-Saxons*, vol. III (London, 1828), pp. 634, 636.
3 J. Gwenogvryn Evans, *Facsimile and Edition* (Llanbedrog, 1910), pp. 54–56.
4 For sources and analogues, see Roger Sherman Loomis, "The Spoils of Annwn:
  An Early Welsh Poem", *Wales and the Arthurian Legend* (Cardiff: University of
  Wales Press, 1956), pp. 131–78.

an overseas fortress where a cauldron is carried off.[5] This text refers to a poem in the *Lebor na Huidre* called "Dún Scáith" ('Fortress of Shadow'), in a story about the shade of Cú Chulainn,[6] which has in common with "Preideu Annwn" a sea voyage, a raid upon a stronghold with iron doors and a subterranean chamber, magic cattle, a cauldron which they filled with drink, an escape. Our poem has achieved renown largely for its evocative references to Arthur, not its implications for medieval textuality — much less how or why it is pleasurable to twentieth- as well as fourteenth-century readers. Scholars have shied away from interpretive or aesthetic studies not only because its language is impossible in places, but also because of the seductions it offers to dabblers.[7] It has been marginalized and amputated by more cautious scholars, and subjected to editorial foregrounding.[8] Marged Haycock takes interpretation in a new direction by stressing the identity of the imagined speaker and the agonistic aspects of the persona of Taliesin as

5   See Patrick Sims-Williams, "The Evidence for Vernacular Irish Literary Influence on Early Mediaeval Welsh Literature", in Dorothy Whitelock, Rosamund McKitterick, David Dumville, eds., *Ireland in Early Medieval Europe: Studies in Memory of Kathleen Hughes* (Cambridge: University Press, 1982), pp. 235-57. Sims-Williams translates and discusses the *Marwnat Corroi m. Dayry* in *BT*: 66.18-67.8, the clearest evidence that the tale of Cú Roí was known to the redactor(s) of *The Book of Taliesin* (pp. 248-55).

6   "Siaburcharpat Conchulaind" ("Cu Chulainn's Phantom Chariot"), *Lebor na Huidre: Book of the Dun Cow*, R. I. Best and Osborn Bergin, eds. (Dublin: Royal Irish Academy), pp. 281-87.

7   Robert Graves's mistranslation in *The White Goddess* (New York: Farrar, Straus and Giroux, 1966), p. 107-8, along with his misspelling "The Spoils of Annwm", have led many a dilettante Celticist astray. Desire not to reproduce anything of either antiquarian enthusiasm or Gravesian feminism has made "serious" scholars overcareful.

8   Interested only in the "historical" poems of the Bard of Urien, Ifor Williams and J. E. Caerwyn Williams give passing mention to the text, which they associate with the "mythological" Taliesin in their excised edition (*The Poems of Taliesin* (Dublin: Institute for Advanced Studies, 1968), pp. xiv-xvii); Kenneth Jackson translates those stanzas that deal with Arthur ("Arthur in Early Welsh Verse", in R. S. Loomis, ed., *Arthurian Literature in the Middle Ages* (Oxford: Clarendon Press, 1959), p. 16) and ignores the last stanzas about monks which D. W. Nash looks upon as interpolations (*The Book of Taliesin, or The Bards and Druids of Britain* (London: John Russell Smith, 1858), p. 212); A. O. H. Jarman writes that the final stanzas are irrelevant to the theme of Arthur ("The Delineation of Arthur in Early Welsh Verse", in Kenneth Varty, ed., *An Arthurian Tapestry: Essays in Memory of Lewis Thorpe* (Glasgow: French Department at the University of Glasgow on behalf of the British Branch of the International Arthurian Society, 1981), p. 11); Roger Sherman Loomis gives us an exhaustive exegesis of the mythological allusions in the first four stanzas, but is defeated by the remaining four ("Spoils of Annwn", p. 132); John K. Bollard translates the remainder, but he, too, is loath to comment on its obscurity, except to remark that "the poet seems to be discontented with the lowly men and cowardly monks around him, in contrast to the warriors whom he accompanied on Arthur's expedition to Annwn" ("Arthur in the Early Welsh Tradition", in James J. Wilhelm and Laila Z. Gross, eds., *The Romance of Arthur* (New York: Garland Press, 1984), p. 21).

he is depicted in the manuscript context, i.e., the indigenous man of learning contending with the monks.[9] John T. Koch's translation[10] is more successful at preserving the text's elegance than is Haycock's, which is more interested in getting a *verbum pro verbo* translation — though I direct the interested reader to the linguistic addenda provided by both scholars, which space does not permit me to include.

My aim is to pull the text out from under the exasperation leveled at its ambiguity and make it available to more contemporary theories of textual difficulty: what does a poem such as "Preideu Annwn" reveal about medieval Welsh reception of literacy? privileged knowledge? What did the redactor think he (or she) was copying, and for whom when he put *The Book of Taliesin* together? The title, *preideu annwn*, was added in a different hand and spelling in a space made for it; why this title? Why not "Kaer Sidi" ('Mound Fortress')? These and other questions concern the fundamental mysteries of the entire manuscript and they will never be adequately answered. The choice of title intrigues. Assuming that the redactor understood something of the poem (not a certainty), he may have noticed that it moves in a direction away from describing a raid on the Mound Fortress and towards a criticism of uninformed readers. Deliberate obscurity is an oft-trumpeted feature in medieval Celtic poetry, especially in poems attributed to Taliesin. I submit that "Preideu Annwn" is a kind of meta-text, a poem about the arcane materials of poetry. Its power lies in its studious avoidance of "all connexion with thought" — perhaps the thought connected to reading. Indeed, the text repeatedly points to this asset in its scornful insistence on the ignorance of the monks, the slack shield straps of the "little men of letters", even its refusal to designate the fortress by a single name. It is built on a foundation of shifting words — whether through intention or transmission — which thwarts our efforts to get a "word for word" translation.

Traditionally, *annwfyn* (*annwn*) is the fount of poetic wisdom. Semantically and conceptually, it is ambiguous. Like its Latin cognate *in*, the MW prefix *an* either negates or intensifies, to render *an + dwfyn* 'un-world' or *an + dwfyn* 'very deep', or possibly 'extreme world'; definitely 'other'-world. Its analogy with the Irish *Tír na mBéo* 'Land of the Living', along with its situation underground and later association with hell is well documented.[11] Gweir sings within his equipped prison in *Kaer Sidi*, a name which may be cognate with Irish *síd* 'mound' or 'abode of the gods'.[12] *Kaer Sidi* appears in another poem from *The Book*

9 "'Preideu Annwn' and the Figure of Taliesin", pp. 52–78.
10 "The Spoils of the Unworld", in John T. Koch & John Carey, eds., *The Celtic Heroic Age: Literary Sources for Ancient Celtic Europe and Early Ireland and Wales*, (2nd edn., Malden, Mass.: Celtic Studies Publications, 1995), pp. 290–92.
11 See Loomis, "Spoils of Annwn".
12 Sims-Williams, op. cit., pp. 244–46.

of Taliesin in nearly the same phrase[13] as a place of reward for the poet: filled with music, libation, surrounded at its corners by ocean currents, and above it the "fruitful fountain". "Preideu Annwn" describes these marvels as well, but mixes them, like mingled jet water, with infernal images (l. 20) which bring it closer in character to "Dún Scáith". Having visited such a place and returned with plunder would confer honor on any hero, but it is possible that the text deliberately depicts the poet's seizure of poetic knowledge — from a place containing the cauldron of inspiration — through an adventure which has literally yielded him the Spoils of the Otherworld.

The ancient reification of certain concepts we now think of as abstractions — knowledge, word, mind, "inspiration" — provide us with our old alimentary, respiratory, martial and thesauric metaphors for the production of poetry. Inspiration is not the mere thing of the mind that it is today but is deeply associated with "otherness"; one literally takes in an external and *material* power, and scholars have long noted the relationship between numinous wisdom and eating,[14] a well-established connection in Norse, Welsh, and Irish legend and their cauldrons and salmons of poetry. Knowledge is something material which can be gathered up, as Odin gathered up the runes, as *awen* ('poetic inspiration', from IE *an*, 'breath') is brought up out of the "depths" by the persona of Taliesin in "Angar Kyfyndawt",[15] and in "Messe ocus Pangur bán" the Old Irish poet compares, with artful sophistication, a scholar's reading to his cat's hunting.[16] What the poet consumes or gathers he can expel or strew in the form of "aretalogies" (list of divine virtues) that confound;[17] these decontextualized images acquire magic status as ciphers instead of references where words are no ordinary things "connected to thought"; they are objects hurled. Wordmakers and warriors are an established

---

13 *BT* 34.7: *ys kyweir vyg kadeir yg kaer sidi*, 'equipped is my chair in Caer Sidi'.

14 Walter Ong, "Transformations of the Word and Alienation", in *Interfaces of the Word: Studies in the Evolution of Consciousness and Culture* (Cornell University Press, 1977), pp. 23-24; Paul Zumthor, *Introduction à la poésie oral* (Paris: Seuil, 1983), pp. 14-16; Marcel Jousse, *La manducation de la parole* (Paris: Éditions Gallimard, 1975), p. 7.

15 *BT* 21:20-21: *Awen aganaf. odwfyn ys dygaf,* 'It is Awen I sing. From the deep (or the "world"?) I bring it').

16   Frequently after valorous fights
          a mouse sticks in his net;
          as for me, into my net falls
          a difficult rule hard to understand.

    From *Early Irish Verse*, Ruth P. Lehmann, ed. and trans. (Austin: University of Texas Press, 1982), p. 60.

17 As I have remarked elsewhere regarding the list-like claims made by Taliesin and other figures of esoteric wisdom: "The Mouthful of the Giants: Words and Space in Indo-European Revelation Discourse", in John Miles Foley, et al., eds., *De Gustibus: Essays for Alain Renoir* (New York: Garland, 1992), pp. 266-303.

trope in medieval literature, one which, while it may have strong origins in orality, gains special strength in literacy and the power of the visible letter.[18] This fact also explains why the list is so pleasurable to a medieval audience used to the collectable nature of allusions, and so exasperating to modern editors bent on chasing down references.

"Preideu Annwn" repeatedly juxtaposes the motif of supernatural adventure with the motif of knowledge and song. After the reciter's preface we hear of Gweir's imprisonment in *kaer sidi* and his bitter singing; we are told of his (or the poet's) bardic invocation which will last until Judgment. An uncertain figure, Gweir appears in Triad 53 as one of the Three Exalted Prisoners of Britain, and his full name seems to bestow word-making skills upon him.[19] The stanza closes with Arthur's expedition establishing a pattern that will be followed by the next five stanzas: mention of poetry, reference to esoteric lore, and closure with a refrain which emphasizes a narrow escape from *kaer sidi*. The names given the fortress in the refrain prefigure the contents of the following stanzas, like doors opening into new chambers of meaning. *Kaer sidi* ends stanza one, and stanza two describes objects associated with *annwfyn*. Stanza two closes with *kaer vedwit* 'Fortress of Mead-Drunkenness', and stanza three is full of liquors: bright drink and flowing water. Stanza three ends with *kaer rigor*, a designation that may derive from L. *rigor* 'hardness, rigidity', and stanza four describes daunting fortifications, a 'Fortress of Glass', and an intractable sentinel. *Kaer golud* ('Internal/Intestinal Castle'? 'Castle of Guts'? from MW *coludd*, or 'Castle of Hindrance'? from MW *goludd*) is followed in stanza five by allusions and grammatical structures that are particularly difficult, and which emphasize secrets. The remaining names for the Fortress are uncertain, and the pattern is abandoned in the last two stanzas, which punish monks and their learning. Instead of the tuneful interiors of the Otherworld we have an enclosure of clerics who 'pack together' and/or 'howl'. The poem takes us through ever-expanding spaces (from the prison of Gweir to the imagery of the cosmos) and it closes as it opens,

---

18 The speaker of the first poem of the *Hisperica Famina* likens himself to a warrior, besting other contenders with his word weapons (vol. I, Michael Herren, ed. (Toronto: Pontifical Institute of Medieval Studies, 1974), p. 65); in the first poetical dialogue of "Solomon and Saturn" the individual letters of the Paternoster ambush the devil in the form of warriors (*The Anglo-Saxon Minor Poems*, Elliott Van Kirk Dobbie, ed. (New York: Columbia University Press, 1942), pp. 35–37; 'Buarth Beirdd' of *The Book of Taliesin* may have the meaning of 'Battle Enclosure of Poets' (Ifor Williams and J. E. Caerwyn Williams, *The Poems of Taliesin* (Dublin: Dublin Institute for Advanced Studies, 1975), p. 91), consonant with other martial metaphors used in this text. Scriptural associations of warfare and the word of God are well-attested: see Revelation 1:16, "and out of his mouth came a sharp two-edged sword" (New English Bible).

19 "Gweir ap Geirioed", *Trioedd Ynys Prydein*, Rachel Bromwich, ed. (Cardiff: University of Wales Press, 1961), p. 140.

with a prayer to God and a plea that Christ lift the sadness of the speaker (felt for the deaths of the older sages and vanished heroes?). This poem is hardly the disorderly text of early reputation.

It is dark, though, and evidence of *gair mwys* (punning) is prominent.[20] In my translation of line 49 I try to suggest the ambiguous quality of *cor* (both MW 'assembly' and L. 'chorus') by translating "choir", while putting alternative meanings in parentheses elsewhere. But the most significant play on words unfolds in the opening lines to stanzas four, five, and six. In line 29 the speaker starts his abuse of ignorant men and the vaunting of knowledge for which Taliesin is famous, and we are faced with a number of interpretations. *Llen lywyadur* is problematic, as are *gobrynaf* (from *go* + *prynu*?) and *lawyr*. *Llywyadur* means 'ruler', and can have secular or religious connotations. *Llen* 'learning' may be linked with it in a genitive which leaves the connection between the first and second parts of the line unclear.[21] *Gobrynu* has been glossed as 'deserve, merit', or 'to set value on'.[22] Roger Sherman Loomis translates "I, Lord of Letters, set no value on wretched men."[23] Haycock has "I do not deserve (i.e. I deserve better than) ?readers concerned with the literature of the Lord."[24] Koch translates "I set no value on the director's wretched scribes."[25] But the crux of the matter rests with the repeated word *llawyr* 'little men', which in a martial context means 'cowards' (echoing the sense of *llwfyr* in line 17). The *llawyr* of lines 29, 35, and 43, however, are chastised for their want of knowledge, not their failure in battle, yet the poem erects an important ambiguity here that Haycock collapses in her suggested emendation to *llewyr* 'readers' in all three stanzas.[26] The essential trope is the comparison of men who seek knowledge to the heroes of old who sought booty. False sages produce cacophony, howling in their monasteries; they have tasted neither the poetry nor the champion's portion that Annwn's cauldron boils. True sages produce a blinding poem, full of the ancient treasures of oral wisdom.

In a text where deliberate obscurity is probably compounded by faulty transmission, it is dangerous to make assumptions about intention, irre-

---

20 Haycock (op. cit.) explores the various meanings of *dychnut* and *cunin cor*, concluding that "one cannot help but feel that the poet is deliberately playing on words . . . a characteristic of early Welsh poetry" (p. 75).

21 Haycock uses the caesura to argue that "we are not bound to take *lawyr llen* together", even though *gŵr llên* 'man of letters' "has an exact counterpart in OIr. *fer léiginn*" (p. 72). Encouraged by this analogue, I prefer to translate *llawyr llen* as a compound: 'small men of letters', 'lettered cowards'.

22 Sir Ifor Williams, as cited by Loomis, op. cit., p. 135; Ernest Rhys, introduction to *Le Mort d'Arthur* (London: Dent, Everyman's Library, 1930), p. xvi.

23 Loomis, p. 136.

24 Haycock, p. 72. She also suggests 'deal with, altercate with', taking into consideration the associations of Modern Welsh *prynu* with 'exchange'.

25 "Spoils of the Unworld", p. 291.

26 Haycock, p. 72.

coverable in this case. Regardless of what the poet may have *intended*, though, this poem is compellingly coherent within the context of a prevalent Indo-European metaphor — *wisdom as something material; wisdom as plunder.* Entrance into and egress from a perilous space has further implications for concepts of privileged learning where readers are compared to warriors. Escape and knowledge are beautifully interlaced in the poem, the imagery of interiority allowing the poet to vaunt his wisdom while he hides it. To have knowledge is to have undergone an ordeal inside an enchanted enclosure, and I submit that another central image in this poem is confinement. The author does not identify himself in this text as he does in "Angar Kyfyndawt" (*mitwyf taliessin*), but it is not an impossibility that the reference to Gweir is a name for himself. Gweir is associated with word-making; his prison is "equipped" as is Taliesin's chair in *Kaer Sidi*; his bitter singing is echoed by the sadness expressed at the end of the poem, and in other texts Taliesin boasts of his confinement in marvelous places;[27] singing or making poetry is frequently attached to prisoners, one of the most notable cases to be found in *Canu Aneirin*, where the speaker, who identifies himself as "I not I Aneirin", describes his incarceration in an "underground dwelling".[28] Departing from the more commonplace interpretation of Aneirin's capture in battle,[29] Patrick Ford views it as a form of bardic initiation (the "Dark School" of later tradition) where early Celtic poets submitted to ritual confinement and/or "death" in a shamanic rite.[30] This poem from *Canu Aneirin* presents in microcosm the pattern established by "Preideu Annwn" — a poet and prisoner in a subterranean place, an iron chain around him, who sings of drink and its vessels and who boasts of dissociative powers claimed by Taliesin in other poems: *mi na vi aneirin, ys gwir talyessin* 'I not I Aneirin — Taliesin knows it'. He even seeks to distinguish himself from the *mynawc blin* 'tired, tiresome lord', which in the well-known context of druids and clerics might play on *mynach* 'monk', as if to say, "I am no tiresome lord/monk, making noises in my castle/cloister. I sang *The Gododdin*, like Taliesin in his perilous space."

---

27 In the sixteenth-century text *Hanes Taliesin* by Elis Gruffydd, the speaker boasts that he has been "three times in the prison of Arianrhod", and "in the court of Cynfelyn; / In stocks and fetters a day and a year" (Patrick K. Ford, *The Mabinogi* (Berkeley & Los Angeles: University of California Press, 1977), pp. 172-73).

28 *Canu Aneirin*, Sir Ifor Williams, ed. (Caerdydd: Gwasg Prifysgol Cymru, 1938), pp. 22, 205-6.

29 Kenneth Jackson, *The Gododdin: The Oldest Scottish Poem* (Edinburgh: The University Press, 1969), p. 50. A. O. H. Jarman sees the poem as unequivocally refering to Aneirin's capture in battle: *Y Gododdin: Britain's Oldest Heroic Poem* (Llandysul: Gomer Press, 1990), p. 110.

30 "The Death of Aneirin", *Bulletin of the Board of Celtic Studies* 34 (1987), pp. 41-50.

In both poems, as in "Dún Scáith", something of matter is brought up out of the depths. Below is what I have managed to wrest from my raid on the Spoils of Annwn:

PREIDEU ANNWN — The Spoils or the Cattle of Annwn

I

Golychaf wledic	I praise the Lord,
pendeuic gwlat ri.	prince of the kingly realm.
py ledas ypennaeth	He has extended his sovereignty
dros traeth mundi.	across the world's tract.
bu kyweir karchar gweir	Equipped was the prison of Gweir
ygkaer sidi.	in the Mound Fortress,
trwy ebostol	through the tale
pwyll aphryderi.	of Pwyll and Pryderi.

5
Neb kyn noc ef	No one before him
nyt aeth idi.	went into it,
yr gadwyn trom las	into a heavy gray (blue?) chain;
kywirwas ae ketwi.	a faithful servant it held.
Arac preideu annwfyn	And before (for?) the spoils of Annwfyn
tost yt geni.	bitterly he sang.
Ac yt urawt parahawt	And until Judgment shall last
ynbardwedi.	our (my?) bardic invocation.
Tri lloneit prytwen	Three fullnesses of Prydwen
yd aetham ni idi.	we went into it.

10
| nam seith ny dyrreith | Except seven none rose up |
| ogaer sidi. | from the Fortress of the Mound. |

II

Neut wyf glot geinmyn	I am honored in praise.
cerd ochlywir.	Song is heard
ygkaer pedryuan	in the Four-Peaked Fortress,
pedyr ychwelyt.	four its revolutions.
yg kenneir or peir	My poetry, from the cauldron
pan leferit.	it was uttered.
Oanadyl naw morwyn	From the breath of nine maidens
gochyneuit.	it was kindled.

15
Neu peir pen annwfyn	The cauldron of the chief of Annwfyn:
pwy y vynut.	What is its fashion?
gwrym am yoror	A dark ridge around its border
amererit.	and pearls.

	ny beirw bwyt llwfyr	It does not boil the food of a coward;
	ny rytyghit.	it is not destined.
	cledyf lluch lleawc	The flashing sword of Lleawch
	idaw rydyrchit.	has been lifted to it.
20	Ac yn llaw leminawc	And in the hand of Lleminawc (?)
	yd edewit.	it was left.
	Arac drws porth vffern	And before the door of hellgate
	llugyrn lloscit.	lamps burned.
	Aphan aetham ni gan arthur	And when we went with Arthur,
	trafferth lechrit.	brilliant difficulty,
	namyn seith ny dyrreith	except seven none rose up
	o gaer vedwit.	from the Fortress of Mead-Drunkenness.
III	Neut wyf glot geinmyn	I am honored in praise;
	kerd glywanawr.	song is heard
	ygkaer pedryfan	in the Fortress of Four-Peaks,
	ynys pybyrdor	isle of the flaming door.
25	echwyd amuchyd	Flowing water and jet
	kymyscetor	are mingled.
	gwin gloyw eugwirawt	Sparkling wine their liquor
	rac eu gorgord.	before their retinue.
	Tri lloneit prytwen	Three fullnesses of Prydwen
	yd aetham ni ar vor.	we went on the sea.
	namyn seith ny dyrreith	Except seven none rose up
	ogaer rigor.	from the Fortress of Hardness.
IV	Ny obrynafi lawyr	I do not reward the ruler's
	llen llywyadur	little men of letters.
30	tra chaer wydyr ny welsynt	Beyond the Glass Fortress they did not see
	wrhyt arthur.	the valor of Arthur.
	Tri vgeint canhwr	Six thousand men
	aseui ar y mur.	stood upon the wall.
	oed anhawd ymadrawd	It was difficult to speak
	aegwylyadur.	with their sentinel.
	tri lloneit prytwen	Three fullnesses of Prydwen
	yd aeth gan arthur.	went with Arthur.
	namyn seith ny dyrreith	Except seven none rose up
	ogaer golud.	from the Fortress of Guts (Hindrance?).

V	Ny obrynaf y lawyr llaes eu kylchwy ny wdant wy pydyd peridyd pwy. py awr ymeindyd y ganet cwy. Pwy gwnaeth arnyt aeth doleu defwy. ny wdant wy yrych brych bras y penrwy.	I do not reward little men, slack their shield straps. They do not know which day who was created; (??) (or: created who) what hour of midday (?) Cwy was born. (??) Who made him who did not go (??) (to the) meadows of Defwy? They do not know the brindled ox, thick his headband.
40	Seith vgein kygwng yny aerwy. Aphan aetham ni gan arthur auyrdwl gofwy. namyn seith ny dyrreith o gaer vandwy.	Seven score links on his collar. And when we went with Arthur, dolorous visit, except seven none rose up from the Fortress of God's Peak. (??)
VI	Ny obrynafy lawyr llaes eu gohen. ny wdant pydyd peridyd pen.	I do not reward little men, slack their will. They do not know which day (?) the chief was created,
45	Py awr ymeindyd y ganet perchen. Py vil agatwant aryant ypen. Pan aetham ni gan arthur afyrdwl gynhen. namyn seith ny dyrreith o gaer ochren.	what hour of the midday the owner was born, what animal they keep, silver its head. When we went with Arthur, sorrowful strife, Except seven none rose up from the Fortress of Enclosedness. (?)
VII	Myneich dychnut val cunin cor.	Monks howl (pack together) like a choir of dogs
50	o gyfranc udyd ae gwidanhor. Ae vn hynt gwynt ae vn dwfyr mor. Ae vn vfel tan twrwf diachor.	from an encounter with lords who know it: is there one course of wind? is there one water of the sea? is there one spark of fire of fierce tumult?

VIII Myneych dychnut   Monks howl (pack together)
    val bleidawr.   like young wolves
   o gyfranc udyd   from an encounter with lords
    ae gwidyanhawr   who know it.
55   ny wdant pan yscar   They do not know when midnight
    deweint agwawr.   and dawn divide.
   neu wynt pwy hynt   Nor (the) wind, what its course,
    pwy yrynnawd.   what its onrush,
   py va diua   what place it ravages,
    py tir aplawd.   what region it strikes.
   bet sant yn diuant   The grave of the saint is hidden (lost,
                          vanishing, in the Otherworld)
    abet allawr.   both grave and ground (champion).
   Golychaf y wledic   I praise the Lord,
    pendefic mawr.   great prince;
   na bwyf trist   that I be not sad,
60   crist am gwadawl.   Christ endows me.

IRISH POETRY AND NORSE *DRÓTTKVÆTT*

Gary Holland and John Lindow

UNIVERSITY OF CALIFORNIA AT BERKELEY

The question of Irish influence on Old Norse literature has been discussed for rather more than 100 years. No conclusive or universally accepted results have been reached. General similarities abound —the longer narrative works in both traditions consist of a mixture of prose and verse, and some of the shorter verse forms exhibit comparable metrical structures. Undoubtedly there was contact between Norse speakers and Irish speakers beginning with the Viking Age in Ireland, in Iceland, on the Orkneys, the Shetlands, and the Hebrides; in fact, a number of recent studies assert that the distribution of blood groups and factors among modern Icelanders is more similar to that among the modern Irish than to that among the population of western Norway (for a recent survey of these issues see Gísli Sigurðsson 1988, 35–40). This physical contact has led scholars to argue that the cultural and literary similarities between Norse and Irish came about because of Norse imitation of, or borrowing from, the culturally superior Southerners, who by this period not only preserved in one form or another much of their native traditions, but had also absorbed a strong Latin influence extending even to verse forms, a central interest of Brendan O Hehir. Our negative results do nothing to undermine the broad outlines of the Norse-Irish symbiosis, and we hope that they would appeal to Brendan's sceptical spirit.

The specific issue dealt with in this paper is the influence of Old Irish meters on Norse *dróttkvætt* (research summary in Gísli Sigurðsson 1988, 103–17), a verse form consisting of strophes of eight six-syllable lines with a major syntactic break after the fourth line, and characterized further by a more or less rigid pattern of alliteration, perfect and imperfect internal rhymes (assonance and consonance), and a trochaic cadence. A striking stylistic feature is the use of kennings. Described in this manner, Norse *dróttkvætt* bears a strong resemblance to the classical Old Irish meter *rinnard*, at least in terms of the basic line, and if the Norse eight-line stanza is viewed as consisting of two more elementary four-line units (the helmings), then also in terms of the basic strophic units. Thus, after the Germanist Anton Edzardi's initial exposition of the similarities between the two poetic traditions and his simple assertion that the Norse verse form must have been borrowed from the Irish (1878),[1] scholars have typically been content to cite his paper and accept its basic premise; an early Celticist supporter was Whitley Stokes (1885, 273).

The immediate question arises: why have scholars found it necessary to seek a foreign origin for *dróttkvætt*? The basic assumption seems to have been that *dróttkvætt*, with its rigid metrical structure, its convoluted diction, and its extremely free word order, is somehow isolated within the Germanic poetic tradition and cannot be accounted for as a natural development within this tradition. The typical Germanic verse forms, then, are those represented by *Beowulf*, the Old Saxon *Heliand*, and the Norse Eddic poems — a relatively freely structured, definitely *not* syllable-counting, rhymeless alliterative verse with word order patterns similar to those of prose. Within Norse poetic tradition, *dróttkvætt* has been perceived as atypical *vis-à-vis* the simpler Eddic meters. The Eddic poems are about the gods, about traditional Germanic heroes, or consist in collections of proverbs or bits of practical wisdom, while skaldic verse has as its subject matter contemporary events and characters: praise poems, genealogies, and occasional commemorative verses are the most common types. Furthermore, Eddic poetry was perceived as a popular or folk genre, while skaldic verse is typically court poetry, composed by poets who were ordinarily in the service of a chieftain. According to our late medieval sources, none of which was recorded before the thirteenth century, but which make legitimate claim to far greater antiquity, the early skalds made up a kind of professional class, functioning as quasi-historians within the inner circle of the chieftain's *comitatus*. The similarities with the Irish bards require no comment.

The weight of published scholarly opinion seems to be on the side of those who favor an Irish origin for, or at least a decisive formative influence on, Norse *dróttkvætt*. In addition to Edzardi and Stokes, Andreas Heusler also supported the theory of Irish origin (1956, 285ff.). After these early scholars, the issue lay dormant until 1954, when Gabriel Turville-Petre took it up again, arguing vigorously for the close similarities between the two poetic traditions. In 1957 Jan de Vries published a lengthy restatement and critique of Turville-Petre's ideas in order to bring them to a wider audience (Turville-Petre's article was originally written in Icelandic; an English translation appeared in 1972). In a later work, however, Turville-Petre

---

1 Edzardi thanks the famous Leipzig Celticist Ernst Windisch for *"gütige Mitteilungen"* on Irish metrical matters (1878, 581); presumably, Edzardi had Windisch's support for his thesis.

seems more aware of the differences between Norse and Irish verse forms, and concludes in a more cautious manner:

> Thus it seems that the strict rules governing the syllabic count and the cadence are the only significant features shared in common by Irish and scaldic poetry. These rules are foreign to the traditional Germanic system, and it is hard to believe that they developed among the two northwesterly nations independently (1976, xxvii).

This conclusion is virtually identical to that reached by de Vries. After Turville-Petre, there has been another attempt to argue for a strong form of the Irish influence hypothesis by Bridget Mackenzie (1981), who finds numerous instances of rhymes between lines in Norse court verse, comparing Irish *aicill* rhyme, in which the final syllable of a line rhymes with a word in the next line.

Another recent paper on this subject is by Kristján Árnason (1981), who also supports the hypothesis of Irish influence. He, however, believes that rhythm, not alliteration or assonance, is the central structural feature of the skaldic line. He argues that one basic form of the *dróttkvætt* line contains three heavy stressed syllables and the fact that there are usually six syllables is more or less accidental. Kristján Árnason thinks, following Watkins (1963) and Carney (1971), that strict syllable-counting meters develop from earlier accentual meters, and he further calls attention to the similar stress patterns of Old Irish and Old Norse and maintains that this area of resemblance could well have helped in the importation of the Irish model. Even if all of Kristján Árnason's arguments are correct, however, they could equally well be used to support an inner-Norse development of the *dróttkvætt* line, and in fact such disparate figures as Eduard Sievers (1893, 99) and Aage Kabell (1978, 248ff.) have argued that this meter represents a natural development within the North Germanic tradition.

We drew attention above to the apparent correspondence between the *dróttkvætt* helming and the four-line strophe of classical Irish verse, which scholars from Edzardi (1878, 576, 583) on have used to support the hypothesis of Irish influence on skaldic poetry. Since West Germanic verse is stichic and the earliest Norse poetry of the so-called Eddic type is stanzaic only in a very irregular way, some have seen the Irish strophe as the model for the Norse strophe, transmitted via skaldic poetry to the Eddic poetry. This hypothesis must, however, be rejected, precisely because the Norse strophe consists of two helmings, that is, eight lines. Turville-Petre suggested (1954/1972) that the helming was the basic unit of composition, and this suggestion is not without merit, given the strong caesura between helmings. That so much of the extant skaldic poetry is retained in helmings only, however, has to do with its use as source material (only the helming needed for authority would be cited) and therefore attaches rather to the written transmission and reception of the corpus than to its oral composition. An argument against the idea of a four-line compositional unit may be the

þulur, alliterative list-poems (in *fornyrðislag* meter) of names and synony-
mous nouns which editors have no difficulty in arranging in eight-line
stanzas. Finally, if the skaldic strophe was the model for the Eddic strophe,
the regular use of eight lines in Eddic strophes would suggest that the basic
compositional unit of skaldic poetry was also an eight-line stanza. Thus this
apparent point of correspondence between skaldic and Irish verse must be
abandoned.

The similarities between the Irish and Norse lines have provided the
strongest evidence for the hypothesis of Irish influence on skaldic poetry.
Universally regarded as a development from the Germanic accentual line,
the skaldic syllabic line is virtually unique within Germanic poetry. According to the earlier view, Irish poetry underwent a similar development,
thought by some to be the result of the influence of medieval Latin verse,
and perhaps this development might be regarded as an Irish-Norse parallel.
If, however, Calvert Watkins (1963) is correct in his derivation of the Irish
syllabic meters from what Roman Jacobson termed the "Common
Indo-European Gnomic-Epic line", as seems most likely, then the notion of
influence is unnecessary. (An argument analogous to that advanced by
Watkins for Celtic could, we believe, doubtless be constructed for
Germanic.)

Nevertheless, the possibility of Irish influence on the Norse *dróttkvætt*
line cannot be ruled out at this point (Gísli Sigurðsson 1988, p. 117). Within
the Irish poetic tradition, however, *rinnard* appears to be a fairly uncommon
meter, as can be inferred from its name ('end foot high'), although a number
of sub-variants exists (Murphy 1961, 64). The most common
syllable-counting meters have seven syllables (*deibide* with all its variants,
the seven-syllable *rannaigecht* types, etc.), and the next most common, eight
syllables (Murphy 1961, passim). If an Irish syllabic line provided the model
for the *dróttkvætt* line, why did the skalds avoid the common line of seven
or eight syllables and choose instead the relatively rare line of six syllables?
No explanation has yet been provided.

This is particularly striking since both the Norse and the Irish were
notorious metrical innovators — 102 metrical and dictional (sub)types were
catalogued by Snorri Sturluson, while Murphy (1961), following the earlier
tradition, catalogues more than 80 separate Irish metrical (sub)types. Here
the imprecise nature of the parallels becomes apparent: *rinnard* is formally
equivalent to the *dróttkvætt* line in the number of syllables and form of the
cadence (on which, however, see below), but not in the use of alliteration
and rhyme. The skaldic *hálfhnept*, with its monosyllabic verse ends, recalls
several Irish meters, and sometimes it is found with seven, not six, syllables,
thus recalling *rannaigecht mór*. But the overwhelming majority of the
meters are different in the two traditions, and the parallel is simply that
poets counted syllables and were concerned with the cadence.

Here again the similarity is only incidental. In Irish the cadence may take one of several forms, ranging from stressed monosyllables to tetrasyllables, and the *deibide* meters present a kind of alternating cadence. In contrast, the skaldic meters almost universally demand a trochaic cadence. The only important exception to this rule is a meter in which long monosyllables constitute the cadence. That this cadence is a development of the *dróttkvætt* trochee, however, is proved by the common names of the meter, *hálfhnept* 'half-chopped' or *stýfð* 'cut off'.

Furthermore, the Old Irish lines in *rinnard* (6–2) apparently can end with a trochee defined solely by stress and consequently appear indifferent to the quantity of the penult syllable. Norse trochees, in contrast, are defined both by stress and by syllable weight. Clearly these trochees signal line ends and alert the hearer to start listening for the next alliterations.

Indeed, the alliterations in Norse are structural in that they serve to bind pairs of lines and hence differ from the Irish alliterations, which appear to be optional and which can function to link chains of lines. Classical Bardic poetry uses alliteration in several ingenious ways, but not in the way the skalds use it. Similarly, the morphophonemic system governing the classes of alliterating consonants in Irish is wholly lacking in Norse. Nor is rhyme used identically in the two traditions. *Dróttkvætt* requires an alternation between half and full rhyme in consecutive lines, a prosodic feature found only rarely and ornamentally in Irish.

A further differentiating characteristic of skaldic verse is its dense use of kennings. Although kennings appear occasionally in Irish verse, within Indo-European tradition they are more frequent in Indo-Iranian than in Irish, and in fact kenning-like constructions appear in many of the world's literatures.

Furthermore, kennings fill a different function in Irish verse than in skaldic verse. In Celtic poetry they appear to be primarily decorative, and to be similar to riddles. In skaldic verse, too, they are riddles and clearly ornamental. Yet they are so all-pervasive and omnipresent that it seems more appropriate to understand them as playing a structural role in the verse: that is, the requirements of the verse form with its internal assonance (*aðalhending*) and consonance (*skothending*) are relatively difficult to meet. The possibility of substitution of one lexical item or phrase for another provided by kennings immensely simplifies the poet's task. For example, if one wishes to replace a word like 'battle' with, say, 'the storm of the valkyrie', then what determines the choice among the equivalent alternative storm words and valkyrie names is the alliteration pattern, the particular assonance, and the particular consonance of the lines in which the kenning will appear. Viewed in this way, kennings in skaldic verse are the *semantic* equivalent of oral formulas. Within a *dróttkvætt* stanza each two-line unit has a different alliteration system and a different assonance and consonance. Thus, in a strict sense, the metrical structure of each *dróttkvætt* stanza is different. Although the *þulur* are quite lengthy, during the entire period of composition of skaldic poetry fewer than 100 nouns are replaced by kennings — these are, of course, the most important items from the point of view of the culture: man, prince, woman, battle, ship, gold, silver, horse, etc. (This figure was obtained by simply counting the classificatory headings in Meissner 1921; Holland intends to return to this subject in a separate essay.)

When verse forms are borrowed, they typically are borrowed because of their appropriateness to, or association with, a specific genre. That is, verse forms appear to be linked to certain types of content. One can point to the standard example of the Latin poets' imitation of the Greek meters. Here, the simple fact is that there is no poetry in Irish that is at all similar to *dróttkvætt*.[2] This fact emerges clearly from a reading of the poems contained in Murphy 1956, and from a perusal of the verse samples in Murphy 1961; presumably these sources represent a random sample. The similarities between *dróttkvætt* and *rinnard* are all on an abstract, formal level when the Norse verse is considered in terms of its content and context.

The assumption that a verse form was borrowed from Irish into Norse entails the further assumption of a high degree of bilingualism on the part of at least some Norse skalds. These skalds must also have had some competence in Irish poetics. If this is the case, then one might legitimately expect this bilingualism (and bi-poeticism) to have left some traces in Old Norse in the form of loan words. In fact, there are (according to the data in de Vries 1962, xxi) some two dozen Irish loan words in Norse. None is particularly common, and only five are attested in skaldic verse. These are:

    ingjan 'girl' (< OIr *ingen*).

It is attested only once, in an occasional verse attributed to King Magnus barefoot, describing his love for an Irish girl.

    kapall 'horse' (< *capall* < Latin *caballus*).

Besides a handful of saga and ecclesiastical attestations and continued existence in Modern Icelandic (where it means 'mare'), the term is attested once in skaldic poetry, in the kenning *ýtir brimis kapla* 'man of the horses of the sea', in *Plácitúsdrápa* (49), a twelfth-century life of St. Eustace in verse.

    korki 'oats [?]' (< OIr *corca*).

2 Sophus Bugge argues for a special relationship between *Ynglingatal* and the memorial verses of two Irish poets from the end of the Viking Age (Cinaed hua Artacain, d. 975, and Flann Mainstrech, d. 1056), on the basis of which he concludes that hypothetical earlier Irish memorial poetry provided the model for the composition of *Ynglingatal* (1894, 148–51); Louis Duvau follows him in this (1896, 116–17). However, *Ynglingatal* is isolated in Norse tradition, and, most significantly, it is in *kviðuháttr*, basically a syllable-counting Eddic meter, not in *dróttkvætt*, and therefore it lacks the full range of skaldic features.

Attested only in a *þula* for *sáðs heiti* 'synonyms for grain' found in two minor manuscripts of *Snorra Edda* (*þul.* IV. ddd. 1.; Finnur Jónsson 1912–15, B2, 680), the word is lacking in the extant skaldic corpus.

lung 'longship' (< OIr *long* < Latin [navis] *longa*).

The term is well attested in skaldic poetry (indeed, *Plácitúsdrápa* 49 also appears to use it—an attestation of *lung* not catalogued in Finnur Jónsson (1931, s.v.)—but the manuscript is defective at this point). According to Snorri, it was used by Bragi the Old, regarded by tradition as the first skald. It is not difficult to imagine that longships were a common topic of conversation throughout northern Europe and that the term could have been appropriated from an Irishman by a Norse poet lacking any interest in Irish verse.

tarfr 'steer' (< OIr *tarb*).

The term is attested in a *þula* in the *Snorra Edda* manuscripts for *øxna heiti* 'bovine synonyms' (*þul.* IV. ö. 1; Finnur Jónsson 1912–15, B1, 669) and in a verse in *Eyrbyggja saga* (Einar Ól. Sveinsson and Matthías Þórðarson, eds., pp. 173–74). There it appears as a *heiti* for the bull Glæsir, the killer of the farmer Þoroddr. The verse is spoken by the old blind woman who recognized the bull's supernatural evil and bade the farmer kill him. Although the term has been retained in modern Icelandic and Faroese, its usage in this verse hardly puts Irish loans in a good light.

By way of contrast, Old Norse has 150 secure loans, 90 unsure ones, from Old English, and 75 sure loans, 18 unsure, from Old French (de Vries 1962, xxvii, xxxii). Furthermore, Irish has 140 secure loans and 9 unsure ones from Old Norse, numbers which suggest that Norse was the more prestigious language in the bilingual community and that the burden of bilingualism fell primarily on the Irish. This makes it less likely that Norse poets would borrow Irish verse forms.

Finally, a comparison of Norse poetic terms with the Irish terms listed by Murphy shows no apparent influence and very little in the way of overlap between their basic notions.

In conclusion, there is no clear evidence for the influence of Celtic verse forms on Norse *dróttkvætt*. The development of strict syllable-counting lines from earlier accentual verse must be regarded as independent but parallel developments in these two traditions. After all, they inherited the same Indo-European patrimony.

REFERENCES

Bugge, Sophus. 1894. *Bidrag til den ældste skaldedigtnings historie*. Christiania: H. Aschehoug.

Carney, James. 1971. "Three Old Irish Accentual Poems", *Ériu* 22:23–80.

Duvau, Louis. 1896. "Les poètes de cour irlandais et scandinaves", *Revue Celtique* 17:113–18.

Edzardi, Anton. 1878. "Die skaldischen Versmasse und ihr Verhältnis zur keltischen (irischen) Verskunst", *Beiträge zur Geschichte der deutschen Sprache und Literatur* 5:570–89.

Einar Ól. Sveinsson and Matthías Þórðarson, eds. 1935. *Eyrbyggja saga, Íslenzk fornrit*, 4. Reykjavík: Hið Íslenzka fornritafélag.

Finnur Jónsson. 1912–15. *Den norsk-islandske skjaldedigtning*. 4 vols. Copenhagen: Villadsen & Christensen.

Gísli Sigurðsson. 1988. Gaelic Influence in Iceland: Historical and Literary Contacts: a Survey of Research. *Studia Islandica/Íslenzk fræði*, 46. Reykjavík: Bókaútgáfa Menningasjóðs.

Heusler, Andreas. 1956. *Deutsche Versgeschichte I*. Berlin: W. de Gruyter.

Kabell, Aage. 1978. *Metrische Studien I: Der Alliterationsvers*. München: W. Fink.

Kristján Árnason. 1981. Did *dróttkvætt* Borrow its Rhythm from Irish? *Íslenzkt mál og almenn málfræði* 3:101–11.

Mackenzie, Bridget Gordon. 1981. "On the Relation of Norse Skaldic Verse to Irish Syllabic Poetry", in *Speculum Norroenum: Norse Studies in Memory of Gabriel Turville-Petre*. Ursula Dronke, Guðrún P. Helgadóttir, Gerd Wolfgang Weber, and Hans Bekker-Nielsen, eds. Odense: Odense Univ. Press. Pp. 337–56.

Meissner, Rudolf. 1921. *Die kenningar der Skalden: ein Beitrag zur skaldischen Poetik. Rheinische Beiträge und Hülfsbücher zur germanischen Philologie und Volkskunde*, 1. Bonn: K. Schroeder.

Murphy, Gerard. 1961. *Early Irish Metrics*. Dublin: Royal Irish Academy.

———. 1956. *Early Irish Lyrics, Eighth to Twelfth Century*. Oxford: Clarendon.

Sievers, Eduard. 1893. *Altgermanische Metrik. Sammlung kurzer Grammatiken germanischer Dialekte . . . , Ergänzungsreihe*: 2. Halle: M. Niemeyer.

Stokes, Whitley. 1885. "On the Metre *rinnard* and the Calendar of Oengus as Illustrating the Irish Verbal Accent". *Revue Celtique* 6:273–97.

Thurneysen, Rudolf. 1946. *A Grammar of Old Irish*. Dublin: Dublin Institute for Advanced Studies.

Turville-Petre, Gabriel. 1976. *Scaldic Poetry*. Oxford: Clarendon.

———. 1972. "On the Poetry of the Scalds and the Filid", *Ériu* 22:1–22.

———. 1954. *Um dróttkvæði og írskan kveðskap. Skírnir* 128:31–55.

de Vries, Jan. 1962. *Altnordisches etymologisches Wörterbuch. 2te. verb. Aufl.* Leiden: E. J. Brill.

———. 1957. *Les rapports des poésies scaldique et gaëlique. Ogam* 9:13–26.

Watkins, Calvert. 1963. "Indo-European Metrics and Archaic Irish Verse", *Celtica* 6:194–249.

ALDFRITH OF NORTHUMBRIA AND THE LEARNING OF A *SAPIENS*

Colin Ireland

BEAVER COLLEGE, DUBLIN

The Annals of Ulster at 704 describe Aldfrith son of Oswiu, king of the English, as *sapiens*.[1] The importance of the term *sapiens* has long been emphasized in discussions of early Irish learned culture. Various commentators have confidently asserted that anyone who was called *sapiens* was, of necessity, a cleric or a professor at a monastic school — positions which are not mutually exclusive. The case of Aldfrith *sapiens* is of interest for two reasons. First, the extent of his learning can be confirmed through contemporary non-Irish sources, specifically, through Bede and Aldhelm. Second, by comparing the works and backgrounds of other seventh-century *sapientes*, we can begin to assess the impact of Aldfrith's own learning on Anglo-Saxon learned culture during his reign of Northumbria, c. 685–705.

This paper will examine what is known of those seventh-century *sapientes* who precede Aldfrith in the Annals of Ulster. It will compare these entries with others listed in the Annals of Tigernach,[2] Inisfallen,[3]

1 Seán Mac Airt and Gearóid Mac Niocaill, *The Annals of Ulster (to A.D. 1131)* (Dublin, 1983), pp. 162–63. Abbreviations used in this article are as follows: *AI* = Annals of Inisfallen; *AL* = Ancient Laws of Ireland; *ATig* = Annals of Tigernach; *AU* = Annals of Ulster; *CIH* = Corpus Iuris Hibernici; *FM* = Annals of the Four Masters; *FragA* = Fragmentary Annals; *HE* = Historia Ecclesiastica.
2 Whitley Stokes, "The Annals of Tigernach, third fragment, A.D. 489–766", *Revue Celtique* 17 (1896), pp. 119–263.
3 Seán Mac Airt, *The Annals of Inisfallen (MS. Rawlinson B. 503)* (Dublin, 1944).

the Four Masters[4] and the Fragmentary Annals.[5] These latter sources and *Félire Óengusso*[6] are seldom consistent in assigning the same title or epithet — it is not always clear if *sapiens* should be treated as a noun or an adjective. More importantly, this paper will attempt to identify those texts ascribed to these *sapientes*, if any can be found at all. Even false ascriptions can sometimes tell us something of their reputations in Irish learned circles.

The term *sapiens* is applied in various sources to many persons who are not called *sapiens* in the Annals of Ulster. For the present these other *sapientes* must be ignored. This paper will not attempt to arrive at a definition of *sapiens*. On the contrary, this brief survey will show the desirability of having a thorough study of those Irish and Latin terms applied to the learned classes, including an analysis of how those terms changed through time. Implicit in such an investigation is the need to understand the nature of formal training and education in early Ireland. To appreciate the complexities of the problem we need only ask ourselves, "Could a Northumbrian king have been either a cleric or a professor at a monastic school?"

Laidcenn mac Baíth Bannaig of Clonfert-Mulloe (Cluain Ferta Mo-lua) is the first person called *sapiens* in the Annals of Ulster.[7] Although he is not given a clerical title at his obit in 661, he is listed in the same entry with Tóiméne mac Rónáin, bishop of Armagh (Ard Macha) and Conaing mac Daint, abbot of Emly (Imblech Ibair). No epithet or title is assigned to him in the Annals of Tigernach,[8] Inisfallen[9] or the Four Masters.[10] He composed the *Ecloga de moralibus in Iob*.[11] This work is an abbreviated version of *Moralia in Iob* written by Gregory the Great *c.* 595. Michael Herren has shown that what was formerly known as *Lorica Gildae* is the work of Laidcenn.[12] This *lorica* opens with an invocation to the Trinity and includes a detailed catalogue of body parts

4   John O'Donovan, *Annals of the Kingdom of Ireland by the Four Masters* I (Dublin, 1856).
5   Joan N. Radner, *Fragmentary Annals of Ireland* (Dublin, 1978).
6   Whitley Stokes, *Félire Óengusso Céli Dé: The Martyrology of Oengus the Culdee* (London, 1905; repr. Dublin, 1984).
7   *AU*, pp. 132–33.
8   *ATig*, p. 196.
9   *AI*, pp. 94–95, *anno* 661.
10 *FM*, pp. 270–71, *anno* 660.
11 James F. Kenney, *The Sources for the Early History of Ireland: Ecclesiastical* (New York, 1929; repr. Dublin, 1979), pp. 278–79 §106; Michael Lapidge and Richard Sharpe, *A Bibliography of Celtic-Latin Literature 400–1200* (Dublin, 1985), p. 80 §293.
12 Michael Herren, "The authorship, date of composition and provenance of the so-called *Lorica Gildae*", *Ériu* 24 (1973), pp. 35–51. Kenney, *Sources*, pp. 270–72 §100. Lapidge and Sharpe, *Bibliography*, pp. 80–81 §294.

to be protected.[13] It is evidently the oldest surviving *lorica*. *Félire Óengusso*, at January 12, says of Laidcenn, according to Stokes' translation, "he declared the mysteries of Christ."[14]

The obits for two more *sapientes* are listed at 662. The first of these is Cuimmíne Fota. Both the Annals of Ulster[15] and Tigernach[16] note that he was in his seventy-second year. The Annals of Inisfallen call him *comarbae Brénainn*,[17] and the Four Masters note that he was bishop at Clonfert (Cluain Ferta Brénainn).[18] Dáibhí Ó Cróinín has argued that the descriptive list *De figuris apostolorum* ascribed to him may have been written as early as *c.* 633.[19] This text was also translated into Irish and survives in various versions, some macaronic. A Latin hymn ascribed to him, *Celebra Iuda*, praises the apostles and demonstrates its author's familiarity with the Bible and with Jerome's *De interpretationibus Hebraicorum nominum*.[20] Arguments have been advanced crediting Cuimmíne Fota with the authorship of the letter on the Easter controversy, *c.* 632, addressed to Ségéne, fifth abbot of Iona, and to a certain Béccán.[21] It also seems likely that computistical material was written by Cuimmíne Fota, or a member of his circle.[22] In addition, one of the most comprehensive of the Irish penitentials is associated with his name.[23] Cuimmíne Fota is quoted as an authority in the Old Irish table of commutations[24] and in the Old Irish penitential.[25] The penitential ascribed to him had a wide circulation on the Continent in subsequent centuries. *Félire Óengusso*, at

---

13 Michael Herren, *The Hisperica Famina II. Related Poems* (Toronto, 1987), pp. 76–89.

14 *Críst as rúna rindaid / Laidcenn mac Baíth Bannaig*; Stokes, *Félire*, p. 35.

15 *AU*, pp. 132–33.

16 *ATig*, p. 196 in two consecutive entries.

17 *AI*, pp. 94–95, *anno* 661.

18 *FM*, pp. 270–73, *anno* 661.

19 Dáibhí Ó Cróinín, "Cummianus Longus and the Iconography of Christ and the Apostles in Early Irish Literature", in *Sages, Saints and Storytellers, Celtic Studies in Honour of Professor James Carney*, Donnchadh Ó Corráin, Liam Breatnach and Kim McCone, eds. (Maynooth, 1989), pp. 268–79.

20 J. H. Bernard and R. Atkinson, *The Irish Liber Hymnorum* I (London, 1898), pp. 16–21. Lapidge and Sharpe, *Bibliography*, pp. 148–49 §582.

21 Maura Walsh and Dáibhí Ó Cróinín, *Cummian's Letter* De controversia paschali *and the* De ratione conputandi (Toronto, 1988), pp. 7–15.

22 Dáibhí Ó Cróinín, "A Seventh-century Irish Computus from the Circle of Cummianus", *Proceedings of the Royal Irish Academy* 82 C (1982), pp. 405–30.

23 Ludwig Bieler, *The Irish Penitentials* (Dublin, 1963), pp. 5–7, pp. 108–35; Kenney, *Sources*, p. 241 §73; Lapidge and Sharpe, *Bibliography*, p. 154 §601.

24 Bieler, *Penitentials*, p. 281 §31; Daniel A. Binchy, "The Old-Irish Table of Penitential Commutations", *Ériu* 19 (1962), 47–72, pp. 64–65 §23.

25 Bieler, *Penitentials*, p. 264 §21, p. 266 §2, p. 267 §§12, 15. E. J. Gwynn, "An Irish Penitential", *Ériu* 7 (1914), 121–95, pp. 144–45 §21, pp. 154–55 §2, pp. 156–57 §§12, 15.

November 12, associates Cuimmíne Fota with wisdom (*suíthe*), science (*sous*) and prudence (*tíachrae*).[26]

An extensive body of vernacular literature about Cuimmíne survives. Among the more notable texts is the "Lament for Cuimmíne Fota". This eulogy has been edited twice, first by Gearóid Mac Eoin[27] and then by Francis John Byrne.[28] The former argues that the poem is Middle Irish, the latter that it is Old Irish. They both agree that what is presented as the second stanza is extraneous to the original poem. This stanza appears in the annal entry for Cuimmíne Fota in both the Annals of Ulster[29] and Inisfallen.[30] Versions of the eulogy are included in the Annals of the Four Masters[31] and in the Fragmentary Annals.[32] In the latter two annals the eulogy is attributed to Colmán ua Cluasaig[33] who is described as tutor (*aite*) of Cuimmíne Fota. Several texts associate him with the wise fool Mac Dá Cherda in the time of Guaire Aidni, king of Connacht.[34] Some versions of the tale make Cuimmíne and Mac Dá Cherda half-brothers. The scholia to *Félire Óengusso* repeat the tradition that he was conceived incestuously; in this case, that his father Fiachnae slept with his own daughter. This incestuous birth motif parallels that for other heroic figures, both religious and secular. Among the tales about him are preserved bits of verse which play on his incestuous birth and make him declare that his father is his grandfather, and his sister is his mother.[35]

Sárán ua Crítáin is also listed with Cuimmíne Fota as *sapiens*. But other than his recognition in the Annals of Ulster as a learned person little is known about him.[36] The Annals of Tigernach[37] and the Four Masters[38] list his death but do not give him any epithet or title. He is not listed in the Annals of Inisfallen or the Fragmentary Annals. *Félire*

26   Stokes, *Félire*, p. 234.
27   Gearóid Mac Eoin, "The Lament for Cuimíne Fota", *Ériu* 28 (1977), pp. 17–31.
28   Francis John Byrne, "The Lament for Cummíne Foto", *Ériu* 31 (1980), pp. 111–22.
29   *AU*, pp. 132–33, *anno* 662.
30   *AI*, pp. 94–95, *anno* 661.
31   *FM*, pp. 272–73, *anno* 661.
32   *FragA*, pp. 12–13, *anno* 662.
33   Colmán's *Hymn* is ascribed to this person in its preface; Whitley Stokes and John Strachan, *Thesaurus Palaeohibernicus* II (Cambridge, 1903, repr. Dublin, 1975), pp. 298–306.
34   The *obit* for Guaire Aidni is 663; *AU*, pp. 134–35. For the texts, see Kenney, *Sources*, pp. 420–21 §§209–10. J. G. O'Keeffe, "Mac Dá Cherda and Cummaine Foda", *Ériu* 5 (1911), pp. 18–44; Gearóid Mac Eoin, "A Life of Cuimíne Fota", *Béaloideas* 39–41 (1971–73), pp. 192–205. Seán Ó Coileáin, "The Structure of a Literary Cycle", *Ériu* 25 (1974), pp. 55–125.
35   Mac Eoin, *Béaloideas* 39–41 (1971–73), p. 199, p. 203.
36   *AU*, pp. 132–33, *anno* 662.
37   *ATig*, p. 196.
38   *FM*, pp. 272–73, *anno* 661.

Óengusso at May 15 mentions a certain *Sárán saidbir* 'wealthy Sárán'[39] which the scholia link to various Munster peoples, but the identification is not certain.[40]

The next *sapiens* listed in the annals, at 665, is Ailerán of Clonard (Cluain Iraird).[41] The Annals of Tigernach,[42] Inisfallen,[43] the Four Masters[44] and the Fragmentary Annals[45] all call him *ecnae*. He was one of the many victims of the plague known as *buide chonaill*. Two works are confidently ascribed to him. The first, *Interpretatio mystica progenitorum Domini Iesu Christi*,[46] presents the allegorical interpretation of the names which appear in the genealogy of Christ as found in the Gospel of Matthew. A second text ascribed to Ailerán is the *Carmen in Eusebii canones*, also referred to as *Kanon euangeliorum rhythmica*.[47] This cryptic and dense little poem sets forth the agreements found by the canon to exist among each of the four gospels. There is also a tradition that Ailerán composed a *Life* of St. Brigit.[48] Kim McCone has argued that Brigit's *vita prima*, which reflects an Armagh bias, was composed using original sources from Ultán, Ailerán and Cogitosus. McCone would explain the Armagh bias by arguing that the monasteries of both Ultán and Ailerán are in Southern Uí Néill territory.[49] Ailerán *ecnae* is listed at December 29 in *Félire Óengusso* where the scholia identify him as *fer léigind* at Clonard.[50] Ailerán apparently never achieved the rank of abbot or bishop.[51]

39 Stokes, *Félire*, p. 124.
40 Ibid., pp. 132-33.
41 *AU*, pp. 136-37, *anno* 665. Airerán is a variant of this name.
42 *ATig*, p. 199.
43 *AI*, pp. 96-97, *anno* 666.
44 *FM*, pp. 276-77, *anno* 664.
45 *FragA*, pp. 14-15, *anno* 665.
46 See the new edition by Aidan Breen, *Ailerani Interpretatio Mystica et Moralis Progenitorvm Domini Iesv Christi* (Blackrock, 1995).
47 Kenney, *Sources*, pp. 280-81 §107(ii); Lapidge and Sharpe, *Bibliography*, p. 83 §300. Mario Esposito, "Hiberno-Latin Manuscripts in the Libraries of Switzerland", *Proceedings of the Royal Irish Academy* 30 C (1912-13) pp. 1-14, pp. 3-5.
48 Mario Esposito, "Notes on Latin Learning and Literature in Mediaeval Ireland. — IV", *Hermethena* 24 (1935), 120-66, pp. 125-30.
49 Kim McCone, "Brigit in the Seventh Century: a Saint with Three Lives?", *Peritia* 1 (1982), 107-45, pp. 134-41; Seán Connolly, "Vita Prima Sanctae Brigitae", *Journal of the Royal Society of Antiquaries of Ireland* 119 (1989), 5-49, pp. 6-7.
50 Stokes, *Félire*, p. 255, pp. 262-63.
51 Paul Byrne, "The Community of Clonard, Sixth to Twelfth Centuries", *Peritia* 4 (1985), 157-73, p. 171.

Cenn Fáelad mac Ailello (*ob.* 679) is the next *sapiens* listed.[52] The Annals of Tigernach[53] and Inisfallen[54] also describe him as *sapiens*. The Four Masters called him *suí i n-ecnu* 'professor in [Latin] learning'.[55] The etiological legend about his head wound received at the Battle of Mag Roth in 637, and his cure involving the loss of his *inchinn dermait* 'brain of forgetting' at the house of Briccíne in Túaim Drecain, has been the subject of much discussion.[56] The outlines of the legend are repeated in texts as disparate as *Suidigud Tellaig Temra*,[57] the saga *Cath Maige Roth*,[58] the law tract *Bretha Étgid*,[59] and the grammar *Auraicept na nÉces*.[60] The entry in the Annals of Ulster describe him as Cenn Fáelad mac Ailello mac Báetáin which agrees with the genealogies and confirms his relationship to the Cenél nÉogain branch of the Northern Uí Néill.[61]

None of the surviving writings ascribed to Cenn Fáelad can be attributed to him with the same confidence with which works are ascribed to Laidcenn, Cuimmíne Fota or Ailerán. All surviving works are in Irish, none are Latin texts. In the case of Cenn Fáelad we are relying on his reputation based on ascriptions to understand what was meant by *sapiens*.

From the evidence of the annals he would appear to have been trained as a professional poet. Several poems in various annals are ascribed to him which deal with sixth-century victories by the Northern Uí Néill. Only stanzas in the Annals of Ulster will be discussed here. The corpus of poems ascribed to Cenn Fáelad throughout the annals deserves a separate study. None of the annals ever gives a patronymic when they cite

52   *AU*, pp. 144–45, *anno* 679.
53   *ATig*, p. 205.
54   *AI*, pp. 98–99, *anno* 678.
55   *FM*, pp. 286–87, *anno* 677 (*sai in eccna*).
56   See, for example, Eoin Mac Néill, "A Pioneer of Nations", *Studies* 11 (1922), pp. 13–28, pp. 435–46; Proinsias Mac Cana, "The Three Languages and the Three Laws", *Studia Celtica* 5 (1970), 62–78, pp. 62–66; P. L. Henry, *Saoithiúlacht na Sean-Ghaeilge* (Baile Átha Cliath, 1978), pp. 215–17. J. E. Caerwyn Williams agus Máirín Ní Mhuiríosa, *Traidisiún Liteartha na nGael* (Baile Átha Cliath, 1979), pp. 80–82; Pádraig Ó Riain, "Conservation in the Vocabulary of the Early Irish Church", in *Sages, Saints and Storytellers, Celtic Studies in Honour of Professor James Carney*, Donnchadh Ó Corráin, Liam Breatnach and Kim McCone, eds. (Maynooth, 1989), 358–66, p. 363 and notes; Kim McCone, *Pagan Past and Christian Present in Early Irish Literature* (Maynooth, 1990), pp. 23–24; J. E. Caerwyn Williams and Patrick K. Ford, *The Irish Literary Tradition* (Cardiff and Belmont, Mass., 1992), pp. 87–88.
57   R. I. Best, "The Settling of the Manor of Tara", *Ériu* 4 (1910), pp. 121–72.
58   John O'Donovan, *The Banquet of Dun na n-Gedh and the Battle of Rath* (Dublin, 1842).
59   *The Ancient Laws of Ireland* III (Dublin and London, 1873), where it is given the title "Book of Aicill". See Fergus Kelly, *A Guide to Early Irish Law* (Dublin, 1988), p. 272 §33.
60   George Calder, *Auraicept na nÉces / The Scholars' Primer* (Edinburgh, 1917).
61   Michael A. O'Brien, *Corpus Genealogiarum Hibernae* (Dublin, 1962), p. 135.

stanzas ascribed to him, but simply say something like "*Cenn Fáelad cecinit*".

The Annals of Ulster have stanzas ascribed to Cenn Fáelad for the Battle of Dergaige. This battle is entered twice, first at 516 and again at 517.[62] It is described as a victory by Fiachu mac Néill over the Failge in which Mag Mide was taken from the Laigin. In the entry at 516 two stanzas are included about Fiachu's victory, but no attribution is made. In the entry at 517, in a later hand, the second stanza of the previous entry is repeated, this time ascribed to Cenn Fáelad. This same stanza is also found attributed to Cenn Fáelad in the Annals of Tigernach[63] and in the Four Masters[64] at the entry for this battle.

A stanza ascribed to Cenn Fáelad is found at the obit for Máel Fothartaig mac Suibne, king of Uí Tuirtri, who died in 669.[65] The Four Masters[66] contain the same stanza ascribed to Cenn Fáelad at this entry. This verse differs from the others ascribed to Cenn Fáelad in the annals by dealing with contemporary events. Cenn Fáelad himself was to die only ten years later. Furthermore, the Uí Tuirtri are not Uí Néill, they are Airgialla. According to writings about St. Patrick,[67] the Uí Tuirtri were to be found on the western shore of Lough Neagh.[68] Daire Luráin, the cite at which Cenn Fáelad is supposed to have done so much of his work, is located within this territory, near the present Cookstown, Co. Tyrone.[69] This stanza appears to eulogize a royal patron.

Another text, *Dúil Roscad(ach)*, is ascribed to Cenn Fáelad in the Trinity MS. H 3.18 version of *Bretha Étgid*.[70] *Dúil Roscad* is known only through citations in other works. For example, it is cited in the law

---

62 *AU*, pp. 62–65.
63 *ATig*, p. 127.
64 *FM*, pp. 164–67, *anno* 507.
65 *AU*, pp. 138–39.
66 *FM*, pp. 280–81, *anno* 668.
67 *FM*, p. 280 note k. Ludwig Bieler, *The Patrician Texts in the Book of Armagh* (Dublin, 1979), p. 266.
68 Cf. Gearóid Mac Niocaill, *Ireland before the Vikings* (Dublin, 1972), p. 39, where he says they were situated at the north end of Lough Neagh before 600.
69 Edmund Hogan, *Onomasticon Goedelicum* (Dublin and London, 1910), p. 328.
70 *AL* iii 550.10–11 = Daniel A. Binchy, *Corpus Iuris Hibernici* (Dublin, 1978), iii 925.39–40.

text *Cóic Conara Fuigill*,[71] in *Sanas Cormaic*,[72] and in O'Davoren's Glossary.[73]

Bretha Étgid, at least in part, is also ascribed to Cenn Fáelad. The introduction states that Cormac mac Airt composed those parts of the text which contain the word *blaí* 'exemption, immunity from liability', and those parts that contain the phrase *a mheic, ara fesser* 'my son, that you may know'.[74] Cenn Fáelad allegedly composed the remainder in Daire Luráin in the time of Domnall mac Áedo mac Ainmirech of the Cenél Conaill, that is, between *c.* 628–642.

Cenn Fáelad is cited in *Míadslechta* on a point concerning the *suí canóine* 'professor of the scriptures or canon law'.[75] *Bretha Nemed Toísech* also contains a quotation by Cenn Fáelad concerning the place of the church in judgements. In the recent edition by Liam Breatnach the quotation reads as follows: "The truth of nature is a noble truth — it is not an oath (alone) which a judge adjudicates on — 'twin of judgment' is referred to analogy, it is declared to be the basis; scriptural text judges it as the third."[76] The citation stresses three important features: (1) *fír aicnid* 'truth of nature'; (2) reliance on similar cases for precedents; (3) reliance on scripture (*teistemain*).

The prologue (*brollach*) to *Auraicept na nÉces* is also sometimes referred to as *Lebor Cinn Fáelad*. As with *Bretha Étgid*, it is said to have been composed in Daire Luráin in the time of Domnall mac Áedo.[77] In some manuscript versions this is embellished to say that Cenn Fáelad revised the work in Daire Luráin together with the greater part of the scriptures.[78] Anders Ahlqvist, who re-edited the canonical portion of the *Auraicept*, counsels caution with regard to the ascription of any part of this work to Cenn Fáelad, but he does not dismiss the possibility.[79]

71　Rudolf Thurneysen, "*Cóic Conara Fuigill*: Die fünf Wege zum Urteil", *Abhandlungen der preussischen Akademie der Wissenschaften*. Jahrgang 1928. Phil.-Hist. Klasse. Nr. 2 (Berlin, 1928), p. 60 §142.

72　Kuno Meyer, "*Sanas Cormaic*, an Old-Irish Glossary", *Anecdota from Irish cripts* IV (ed. O. J. Bergin, R. I. Best, Kuno Meyer, J. G. O'Keeffe, Halle and Dublin, 1912), p. 70 §827.

73　Whitley Stokes, "O'Davoren's Glossary", *Archiv für celtische Lexikographie* II (eds. Whitley Stokes and Kuno Meyer, Halle, 1904), 197–504, p. 269 §458, p. 303 §664, p. 347 §896.

74　*AL* iii 84.12–13 = *CIH* i 250.17, iii 925.35.

75　Eoin MacNeill, "Ancient Irish Law. The Law of Status and Franchise", *Proceedings of the Royal Irish Academy* 36 C (1921–24), 265–316, p. 313. *AL* iv 356.8–10 = *CIH* ii 586.14–16.

76　Liam Breatnach, "The First Third of *Bretha Nemed Toísech*", *Ériu* 40 (1989), 1–40, pp. 5, 12–13 §8.

77　Calder, *Auraicept na n-Éces*, pp. 6–9, 174, 182, 224.

78　Ibid., p. 182.

79　Anders Ahlqvist, "The Early Irish Linguist, an Edition of the Canonical Part of the *Auraicept na nÉces*", *Commentationes Humanarum Litterarum* 73, 1982 (Helsinki, 1983), p. 18.

Cenn Fáelad's prominence is stressed in later writings. The Middle Irish saga *Cath Maige Roth* includes the story of his head wound received in that battle, making Congal Cláen, king of Dál nAraidi, his attacker. The tale relates that Briccíne took care of him for a year at Túaim Drecain and repeats that Cenn Fáelad 'renewed' *Auraicept na nÉces* at Daire Luráin.[80] In another Middle Irish tale, *Suidigud Tellaig Temra*, Cenn Fáelad is anachronistically presented in the time of Diarmait mac Cerbaill, *c.* 545–65, as a wise man called upon to arbitrate in the settling of the Manor of Tara.[81] Elsewhere there is a prophecy of future calamity ascribed to him[82] which is reminiscent of the one by Ferchertne in *Immacallam in dá Thúarad*[83] and the one by the Morrígan in *Cath Maige Tuired*.[84]

Cenn Fáelad is not mentioned in *Félire Óengusso*, not even in the scholia as published by Stokes. However, the scholia identify a certain Breccbúaid listed at September 5 as Briccíne of Túaim Drecain in Breifne.[85] Given the prominent role played by Cenn Fáelad in later Irish tradition it is surprising that the person responsible for his cure and early instruction is recognized in the *Félire* but Cenn Fáelad is not.

The next *sapiens* mentioned, at 686, is Banbán "a wise man surpassing all others".[86] The Annals of Tigernach provide the additional information that he was *fer léigind* at Kildare[87] and the Fragmentary Annals describe him as a *scriba* there.[88] As we will see in the discussion of our next *sapiens*, there seems to have been a tradition of scribes at Kildare. In addition, the Annals of Ulster at 725, in an entry that also lists two other scribes, enters the obit of Colmán Banbáin *scriba* at Kildare.[89] It is tempting to think of this Colmán as being named after the Banbán under discussion. Banbán is probably the same person who is credited with writing the law tract *Cáin Fhuithirbe*, *c.* 680.[90] Due to the history and nature of *Cáin Fhuithirbe* one might expect a person with

80 O'Donovan, *Battle of Magh Rath*, pp. 278–85.
81 Best, *Ériu* 4 (1910), pp. 121–72.
82 Roland Smith, "A Prophecy Ascribed to Cendfaelad", *Revue Celtique* 46 (1929), pp. 120–25.
83 Whitley Stokes, "The Colloquy of the Two Sages" (Paris, 1905), pp. 36–49 §§175–266; = *Revue Celtique* 26 (1905), 4–64, pp. 36–49 §§175–266.
84 Elizabeth A. Gray, *Cath Maige Tuired: The Second Battle of Mag Tuired* (Irish Texts Society LII, London, 1982), pp. 72–73 §167; John Carey, "Myth and Mythography in *Cath Maige Tuired*," *Studia Celtica* 24–25 (1989–90), 53–69, pp. 66–69.
85 Stokes, *Félire*, p. 192, pp. 202–3.
86 *AU*, pp. 148–49, (*Mors Banbāin ōs cāch sapientis*).
87 *ATig*, p. 209.
88 *FragA*, pp. 36–37 §92.
89 *AU*, pp. 178–79.
90 Liam Breatnach, "The ecclesiastical element in the Old-Irish legal tract *Cáin Fhuithirbe*", *Peritia* 5 (1986), 36–52, pp. 46–47.

associations in the south of Ireland. In this regard one should note that at November 26 *Félire Óengusso* lists a *Banbán, bruth óir oíblech* 'Banbán, a sparkling mass of gold'.[91] The single scholium identifies this Banbán as bishop of Leighlin (Lethglenn), Co. Carlow.[92]

Cáin Fhuithirbe is said to have been compiled by three persons working in cooperation. Díblíne instituted it, Banbán wrote it — which reinforces his identification as a scribe —, and Amairgen arranged it.[93] Compare their cases with Cenn Fáelad who was said to have "renewed" certain texts, and to have put a thread of poetry on them.

The next *sapiens* listed is Lóchéne Menn, obit 696, who was also abbot of Kildare.[94] The Fragmentary Annals also call him *sapiens*.[95] The Four Masters call him *eagnaidh*,[96] and the Annals of Tigernach, *duine ecnaid*.[97] All of these annal entries note his rank as abbot. He is the one case among the *sapientes* under discussion to be consistently given the same ecclesiastical title by all sources. He is also the only *sapiens* of concern to us who met a violent death (*iugulatus est*). Little else is known of Lóchéne Menn but he is mentioned in the genealogies as *optimus scriba Scottorum*.[98] This latter information supports the description of Kildare as a foundation with a rich scribal tradition.

An entry in the Annals of Ulster at 702 is ambiguous as to how many people listed are intended as *sapientes*.[99] Of the four other chronicles consulted, none has a similar entry. Four names could be intended as *sapientes*. It seems unlikely that the first, Garbán Mide, is intended by the term. He was king of Meath and also guarantor of the *Cáin Adomnáin*.[100] The second person in the entry, Colcu mac Moenaig, is a more likely candidate. He was abbot of Lusca and also a guarantor for *Cáin Adomnáin*.[101] The Annals of Inisfallen call Colcu bishop and king of Lusca, but the editor feels that "king" is a scribal error.[102] Judging by the syntax of the entry, it seems most likely that only the last two names are intended to be covered by *sapientes*. However, the problem is compounded by the fact that these two names are unusual. They may have been epithets, if they refer to real persons at all. One is called

---

91   Stokes, *Félire*, p. 237.
92   Ibid., p. 248.
93   Breatnach, *Peritia* 5 (1986), pp. 43–44.
94   *AU*, pp. 156–57.
95   *FragA*, pp. 44–45 §133.
96   *FM*, pp. 296–97, *anno* 694.
97   *ATig*, p. 215.
98   O'Brien, *Corpus*, p. 152 [142^{b}31].
99   *AU*, pp. 160–61.
100 Máirín Ní Dhonnchadha, "The guarantor list of *Cáin Adomnáin*, 697", *Peritia* 1 (1982), 178–215, pp. 181, 211 §83.
101 Ibid., p. 180, pp. 190–91 §20.
102 *AI*, pp. 100–101, *anno* 700.

'Lūath Foigde' and the other 'Crach Erpais'. *Lúath* is apparently the adjective 'swift'. *Foigde* may be the feminine noun 'begging, mendicancy; entertainment, hospitality'. *Crach* may be the rarely attested adjective 'harsh, rough'. *Erpais* looks like the genitive singular of an unattested *o*-stem noun. On the other hand, it could be a preterite singular of the verb *erbaid* 'entrusts, commits, grants'.

Aldfrith mac Ossu is called *sapiens* at his obit in 704 (*recte* 705).[103] Many sources use his Irish name, Flann Fína. The Annals of Tigernach describe him as an *ecnaid*,[104] and the Fragmentary Annals call him *ecnaid amrae* 'splendid scholar' and *dalta* 'pupil' of Adomnán.[105] Irish genealogies are consistent in making his mother a member of Cenél nÉogain, and they agree that Cenn Fáelad mac Ailello *sapiens* was his second cousin.[106]

English sources concur in acknowledging Aldfrith's learning. Bede, on more then one occasion, calls him "a very learned man in the scriptures" (*vir in scripturis doctissimus*)[107] and elsewhere he describes him as "a very learned man in all respects" (*vir undecumque doctissimus*).[108] This latter phrase Bede also applied to the noted English churchman and intellectual, Aldhelm. Stephan, who wrote the *Life* of St. Wilfrid sometime between 709 and 731, called Aldfrith a *rex sapientissimus*.[109] Roughly a century after Aldfrith's death, Alcuin of York, who gained fame as a scholar at the courts of Charlemagne, referred to Aldfrith as being *rex simul atque magister*.[110]

English sources confirm Aldfrith's education among the Irish. The anonymous *Life* of St. Cuthbert states that he spent time at Iona.[111] Bede's prose *Life* of St. Cuthbert states variously that Aldfrith was "among the Irish isles" (*in insulis Scottorum*)[112] or "in the regions of the Irish" (*in regionibus Scottorum*) for the love of learning.[113] These phrases could mean that Aldfrith was in Ireland itself and not merely in the Irish territories in Britain.

---

103 *AU*, pp. 162-63. See my article, "Aldfrith of Northumbria and the Irish Genealogies", *Celtica* 22 (1991) pp. 64-78.
104 *ATig*, p. 219.
105 *FragA*, pp. 54-55 §165.
106 O'Brien, *Corpus*, 135 [140ª30]. Ireland, *Celtica* 22 (1991) pp. 69, 73, and note 50.
107 Bertram Colgrave and R. A. B. Mynors, *Bede's Ecclesiastical History of the English People* (Oxford, 1969) = *HE* iv 26.
108 *HE* v 18.
109 Bertram Colgrave, *The Life of Bishop Wilfrid by Eddius Stephanus*, (Cambridge 1927) p. 90.
110 Peter Hunter Blair, *The World of Bede* (Cambridge, 1970), p. 180.
111 Bertram Colgrave, *Two Lives of Saint Cuthbert* (Cambridge, 1940), p. 104.
112 Ibid., p. 236.
113 Ibid., p. 238.

A number of texts in Irish have been ascribed to Aldfrith under his Irish name Flann Fína. No Old English or Latin texts are attributed to him. A large collection of Old Irish maxims ascribed to Flann Fína survives. The maxims are secular in tone and stress an ethical outlook which agrees with the teachings of the Church, but they contain no theological message.[114] Although their contents agree with Aldfrith's reputation, the maxims lack linguistic features which might suggest a seventh-century date of origin. Another text ascribed to Flann Fína is a poem in praise of Ireland which describes the special features of various parts of Ireland. Prominence is given to Ailech, thus stressing the connection with Cenél nÉogain.[115] A Middle Irish religious text is also ascribed to Flann Fína. It begins "Woe to the man who loves mankind, and who does not love God who loves him."[116]

We derive our clearest impressions of Aldfrith's learning by examining Latin texts which we know he received from other writers. Bede tells us that Adomnán presented him with a copy of *De locis sanctis* which Aldfrith had copied and distributed.[117] This is almost certainly how Bede came to know that work which he later embellished and cited extensively in his own *Historia ecclesiastica*.[118]

De locis sanctis has been accessible in an edition since 1958, but it has not received the critical study it deserves. Many commentators accept the view that Adomnán took this work down in dictation from Arculf. But Adomnán contributed more to the work than to serve as a mere amanuensis. Its editor, Denis Meehan, stated, "The finished product reveals its compiler as a man of relatively high critical standards, good scriptural scholarship, and painstaking accuracy in the manipulation of his material".[119] Thomas O'Loughlin has argued that Adomnán was intent on using Arculf's testimony to portray the accuracy of scripture in its depiction of the Holy Places.[120] In this context it makes sense that Aldfrith, whom Bede described as a *vir in scripturis doctissimus*, should have ensured that copies of the work were disseminated throughout his kingdom.

De locis sanctis must have also appealed to the curiosity of peoples on the northwest fringe of Europe since it describes places which would

---

114 I am currently preparing an edition of these Old Irish maxims.
115 Paul Walsh, "A poem on Ireland", *Ériu* 8/1 (1915), pp. 64–74.
116 *Maircc don duine carus duíne ocus ná car Día nod·car*; Vernam Hull, "Wise sayings of Flann Fína (Aldfrith, King of Northumbria)", *Speculum* 4 (1929) pp. 95–102.
117 *HE* v 15.
118 *HE* v 16, 17.
119 Denis Meehan and Ludwig Bieler, *Adamnan's De Locis Sanctis* (Dublin 1958), p. 6.
120 Thomas O'Loughlin, "The Exegetical Purpose of Adomnán's *De Locis Sanctis*", *Cambridge Medieval Celtic Studies* 24 (1992), pp. 37–53.

have seemed exotic to them. As Marina Smyth says in discussing the seventh-century Irish text *De mirabilibus sacrae scripturae* "this same independence from purely religious motivations in favour of simple intellectual curiosity surfaces also in *De locis sanctis* of Adomnán of Iona".[121] A work of this nature would have satisfied the demands of both scriptural scholarship and intellectual curiosity.[122]

Aldfrith received from Aldhelm the long five-part *epistola ad Acircium*. Although Aldhelm never specifically names Aldfrith, this letter is addressed to the one "who governs the kingdom of the northern empire and dispenses rule over a famous royal realm".[123] It can only refer to Aldfrith. The *exordium* speaks obliquely of a close spiritual relationship between the two which dated back at least twenty years. The work includes a typological essay on the number 7 and a treatise on Latin metrics, concentrating on hexameters, which displays a wide familiarity with various Latin authors. Aldhelm boasted of being the first author of a Germanic race to have written so on metre. It also includes a collection of one hundred *enigmata* 'mysteries',[124] ostensibly to serve as metrical examples for the treatise on metrics. These treat a wide range of subjects, some very exotic, like elephants and unicorns. Others show Aldhelm to have been a keen observer of his own immediate surroundings.[125] In the final section Aldhelm exhorts Aldfrith to heed the work presented to him and not to neglect his own studies, particularly of the Holy Scriptures, despite the weight of his secular responsibilities. Because of the personal nature of the *exordium* and conclusion we must assume that Aldfrith fully understood Aldhelm's florid Latin style.

Aldhelm's encouragement of Aldfrith to maintain his studies, particularly of the scriptures, confirms Bede's description of him as *vir in scripturis doctissimus*. The wide range of subjects in Aldhelm's *epistola*,

---

121   Marina Smyth, "The Physical World in Seventh–Century Hiberno-Latin Texts", *Peritia* 5 (1986), 201-34, p. 211.

122   Aidan Breen suggests to me that it would be worth comparing other *itineraria* of the early Middle Ages to Adomnán's work which is longer than any of them, a remarkable feat in itself for a man who never travelled beyond Ireland and Britain.

123   [*illvstri acircio*] *aqvilonalis imperii sceptra gvbernanti, illvstris regalis regni regimina dispensanti*; R. Ehwald, *Aldhelmi Opera*, Monumenta Germaniae Historica, Auctores Antiquissimi XV (Berlin, 1919), 61.3–5. For a translation, see Michael Lapidge and Michael Herren, *Aldhelm, the Prose Works* (Ipswich and Totowa, 1979), pp. 34-47.

124   James H. Pitman, *The Riddles of Aldhelm* (New Haven, Conn., 1925); Michael Lapidge and James L. Rosier, *Aldhelm, the Poetic Works* (Cambridge, 1985), pp. 70-94.

125   M. L. Cameron, "Aldhelm as a naturalist: a re-examination of some of his *enigmata*", *Peritia* 4 (1985), pp. 117-33.

especially in the *enigmata*, must have appealed to a *vir undecumque doctissimus*.

Of the *sapientes* we have discussed there are six persons to whom we can attribute works. For three of these, Laidcenn, Cuimmíne Fota, and Ailerán, their works are in Latin and of a specifically religious nature. For the remaining three, Cenn Fáelad, Banbán and Aldfrith (Flann Fína), only texts in Irish are ascribed to them. These Irish texts are not primarily religious in their purposes despite associations with the Church in subject matter and evidence of ecclesiastical training for their authors. For example, Cenn Fáelad is cited as an authority on points of law which concern the Church in *Míadslechta* and *Bretha Nemed Toísech*. If we can believe the tradition about *Auraicept na nÉces*, we must assume that Cenn Fáelad had acquired his grammatical knowledge through Latin authors. Banbán is described as *scriba* and *fer léigind* of Kildare. More importantly, the ecclesiastical associations of *Cáin Fhuithirbe* have been clearly demonstrated.[126] As for Aldfrith, Bede reported on his piety and described him as *vir in scripturis doctissimus*, Adomnán presented *De locis sanctis* to him, and Aldhelm encouraged him to pursue his studies of the Holy Scriptures.

We know that some *sapientes* held ecclesiastical office. From the nature of the works ascribed to others we can feel secure that they were clerics. But in the cases of Cenn Fáelad and Aldfrith there simply isn't enough evidence to argue convincingly that they were clerics. Texts ascribed to Cenn Fáelad deal primarily with secular topics. The quotations ascribed to him involving the Church in *Míadslechta* and *Bretha Nemed Toísech* only show that he worked in conjunction with clerics, not that he was one. If Aldfrith were, or had been, a cleric, it seems likely that clerics like Bede, Aldhelm or Adomnán, would have intimated as much.

The mythopoeic tendencies of later Irish literary tradition are already evident in this brief survey. Cenn Fáelad is portrayed as a contributor to this tendency in the ascriptions to him in the annals of stanzas about the sixth-century military victories by the Uí Néill against their southern neighbors. These verses helped form the basis of an Uí Néill dynastic myth. We do not need to accept the ascriptions of these stanzas to Cenn Fáelad himself in order to appreciate how he was being portrayed by the annalists.[127] These mythopoeic tendencies are even more tangible in the poems and tales that evolved around the historical figures of Cenn Fáelad and Cuimmíne Fota. This development is particularly interesting because these *sapientes* have been transformed and elevated to the status of

---

126 Breatnach, *Peritia* 5 (1986), pp. 36–52.
127 Compare the discussion of the "synthetic historians" by Eoin Mac Neill, *Celtic Ireland* (Dublin, 1921, rev. ed. 1981), pp. 25–42.

cultural heroes. They contradict the expectation that "heroic age" heroes will be warriors or kings.

This brief historical survey shows that the seventh-century Irish *sapientes*, like scholars in monastic schools throughout Early Medieval Europe, turned their attention to such topics as scriptural and patristic exegesis, penitentials and computistics. But unlike their colleagues elsewhere in Europe, they frequently composed tracts on non-theological topics. Furthermore, they could eschew Latin as the only legitimate learned language and convey their works to posterity through their own vernacular.

READING THE UNREADABLE: "GWARCHAN MAELDERW" FROM *THE BOOK OF ANEIRIN*

Kathryn A. Klar and Eve E. Sweetser

CELTIC STUDIES PROGRAM
UNIVERSITY OF CALIFORNIA AT BERKELEY

INTRODUCTION[1]

"Gwarchan Maelderw" is traditionally thought of as the most opaque part of the Gododdin corpus, and one of the most difficult texts in Welsh. There is no agreed-upon translation or interpretation of its contents. Its obscurity, moreover, has been suggested by some critics to be deliberate.[2] Without denying that the text presents obscure and complex contents, it is however possible to tackle some of the problems of this "problem text" by relatively standard means. In this paper, we will argue that careful metrical analysis reveals previously

1 The work contained in this paper was the last collaborative project we were able to work on with Brendan O Hehir during his final illness. Preceding joint work sessions had laid the foundations for the one long, intense afternoon of excited discussion with Brendan which laid out many of the central ideas in the paper. We wrote an initial draft for presentation at the 1991 UC Celtic Conference, which we were able to read to Brendan the week before the conference. He was unable to attend the conference session on *Llyfr Aneirin* as he had hoped to do, but his intellectual presence was surely tangible throughout the session — and nowhere more than in this work, here printed in a more final form. This piece is his, as much as ours. We present it here in his honor — with much gratitude for our years of delight and enlightenment in working with Brendan, for the sharing of friendship and humor, and for the continuing benefits of those collegial years, as we go on with the scholarly endeavor.
2 An illuminating discussion of deliberate obscurity in Early Welsh poetry is to be found in chapter 7 of Higley 1993; see also her paper in this volume.

unsuspected internal divisions: "Gwarchan Maelderw"'s celebrated lack of coherence is naturally less surprising if there is no one poem to be coherent. (The other *gwarchanau* also seem to be non-unitary in contents, as Klar (1988) has argued.) The remaining group of texts is still a difficult one, and we will not presume to offer a full interpretation here. What we hope to contribute is an improved understanding of what texts are present, as a prolegomenon to future textual interpretation.

1. LLYFR ANEIRIN: THE BACKGROUND

Llyfr Aneirin or *The Book of Aneirin* (South Glamorgan County Library MS 2.81) holds pride of place among Welsh medieval manuscripts for several reasons, not the least of which is that its contents comprise some of the oldest vernacular verse in Western Europe. The manuscript itself was compiled into its present form during the thirteenth century, probably during the third quarter of that century,[3] early on in what became a great flowering of manuscript production in Wales. But internal reconstruction allows us fairly surely to recognize ninth–tenth century prototypes for much of the poetry; themes and specific events allow us to postulate much earlier composition dates — sixth to eighth centuries — for the original versions of some of the poems.[4]

Although the manuscript production is of fairly good quality,[5] this volume was not put together in its final form only to be carefully stored in a private collection and brought out on special occasions. Rubbed and soiled outer pages and the marginal comments of later, well-known poets make it clear that this little book had a long history of practical use. At least one of the sources which we can postulate (cf. O Hehir 1988, pp. 71ff.) from internal evidence was a small collection — some 51 poems —

3　Huws 1989 (pp. 4ff./34ff.) places Scribe A in the third quarter of the thirteenth century, and Scribe B later than A in the second half of that century.

4　Sir Ifor Williams' arguments for seeing an earlier text behind the extant one can be found in the preface and notes to his edition of *Canu Aneirin* (1938 [1970]) and in the essays in *The Beginnings of Welsh Poetry* (1972); Jackson (1969) also argues for a very early composed text, represented in the manuscript in a form much altered by transmission. More recent philological treatment of these issues has come from numerous scholars: particularly relevant here are D. Simon Evans (1978) and John Koch (1985/6, 1988). For general issues of language dating in Welsh, there is a prolific literature: we refer readers of course to Jackson 1953, and for the early poetry, to Roberts 1988 as a whole.

5　The authors are grateful to the South Glamorgan County Library and the National Library of Wales for hospitable assistance in examining the manuscript of *Llyfr Aneirin*. The manuscript is a small one (approximately 163–170 mm in height by 127–120 mm in width (Huws 1989, p.2/32)), but the vellum is of fairly high quality, and most of the ink is very good and dark. Parts of it have carefully done blue and red capitals, and there are a number of rubrics — comments and titles inserted into the body of the text in red ink.

put together specially as a funerary offering to a warrior, Owain, Marro's only son, killed under unknown circumstances at a very young age.

That initial collection may have been a treasured and guarded privately-held manuscript, subsequently copied and added to by the first of the scribes of the *Book of Aneirin*. The *Book of Aneirin* itself was not. It is not likely to have been strictly a public document either; the practice of poetic composition and performance was a professional matter conducted in a guild-like manner, and the different bardic schools contended with one another over the proper way of doing their business. To some extent, the finer points of poetic composition were closely guarded secrets, and a book like this likely had a wide circulation among poets, but not outside those circles. It was compiled, we believe, by monastic poet-scribes out of earlier manuscripts or individual pieces; it was owned and used by poets in the bardic schools to aid in teaching the techniques of older (i.e., not contemporary) verse. It may have been commissioned by a noble patron well-versed in *cerdd dafod*. But nothing of certainty survives about a patron of this type with regard to the *Book of Aneirin*.

High Medieval Welsh poets were nothing if not antiquarians; the very fact that this little book was preserved virtually intact when so little else was, and when so much was wantonly or inadvertently destroyed in succeeding centuries by those bent on destroying the power of Welsh princes or the social glue of native Welsh language and culture, attests to its poet-possessors' sense of its worth even in their own time. From a poetic point of view the book shares with only a few other manuscripts the distinction of containing verse which looks both backward in time to the rhymed, stress-metered origins of British verse, and forward to the strict syllabic conventions of later Welsh verse (Klar, O Hehir and Sweetser 1983/4; Klar and Sweetser 1988). It was archaic in form in 1275, but not yet completely outdated, and held in great esteem by practicing bards. We can infer that respectable poets knew much of this old verse and revered the tradition it represented — but nonetheless didn't understand it very well at times. In 1932, Saunders Lewis proposed — correctly, we think — that the *Book of Aneirin* among others contained (partly at least) didactic and pedagogical material, some the work of student poets.[6] The book's use in bardic schools is consonant not only with its physically worn condition, but also with the varied repertory of poetic forms represented in the contents — and the Gwarchan Maelderw section of the text is a good example of this variety.

---

6 Lewis' view is presented, provocatively, in the first chapter of his (unfinished) history of Welsh literature (1932), p. 5.

Most of the text (pp. 1–24 and 30–38 of the manuscript)[7] is comprised of some 130 individual, short heroic elegies to warriors slain in battle. A number of these warriors are said to have fought (and presumably died) at the disastrous battle of Catraeth, which both medieval poets and modern scholars have seen as a sixth-century border skirmish near the present Yorkshire town of Catterick. Many of the elegies are not specific as to where the praised hero fought or died; but the gist of the collection as a whole seems to be recounting the battle of Catraeth, and an early "core" of genuine "Catraeth" verse no doubt attracted to it many poems of similar thematic type. The usual (sometimes severe) problems of interpretation aside, these elegies are generally quite readable and understandable: in no sense are they deliberately obscure.[8] There is another collection of a different type of verse, on pp. 25–30 of the manuscript, this group consisting of five textual units, each of which is specifically referred to as a *gwarchan* or *gorchan*.[9] Whereas the individual short elegies of the rest of the manuscript are never given either titles or specific descriptions, these five units have specific titles: *gorchan tutvwlch, gwarchan* (or *gorchan*) *adebon, gorchan kynvelyn, gwarchan kynvelyn ar ododin*, and *gwarchan maelderw*.[10] Elsewhere we have dealt extensively with what a *gwarchan* is (cf. Klar 1988) — only a brief summary is possible here. The word means, variously (and interconnectedly) "teaching, lesson, or (lit.) incantation." The *gwarchanau* as a genre were most likely poems composed and used in order to convey bardic knowledge about themes, stories, events, heroes, styles, and not least of all, metrical technique. A salient characteristic of the *gwarchanau* texts we have is that, with one exception ("Gwarchan Kynvelyn ar Ododin"), they are made up out of a number of smaller units: "Gwarchan Tutvwlch" is three poems unified by formulaic opening and closing devices; "Gwarchan Adebon" is a collection of thirteen proverbs unified by rhyme scheme; *Gwarchan Kynvelyn* is several poems linked by various metrical devices. ("Gwarchan Maelderw" follows this pattern as

7 We shall use the following system for referring to locations in the "Gwarchan Maelderw" text: for location in the Gododdin manuscript, page number x and line number y on that page, we shall write *G* x.y; for location in Williams' 1938 edition, we shall write *CA* followed by the relevant line numbers in his lineation system for the entire Gododdin text. "Gwarchan Maelderw" is thus *G* 28.18–30.11; or alternatively, *CA* 1412–1480.

8 This is not, of course, the whole story. Besides interpolations (such as the celebrated Dinogad cradle–song), there are also poems in the text such as the so-called "reciter's preface" and *Nyt wyf vynawg blin*, which seem to be about the act of traditional poetic composition. But more of this later.

9 The standard view is that there are only four *gwarchanau*. But internal analysis clearly reveals the collation, through scribal error, of two originally separate corpora into one. See Klar (1988) for specific discussion of this.

10 We will throughout use the (archaizing) spelling *gwarchan* to indicate this poetic genre. We have chosen this spelling partly to avoid confusion with modern Welsh use of the term *gorchan*.

well, as we shall demonstrate below.) "Gwarchan Kynvelyn ar Ododin",
and the third of the three Tutvwlch poems, are strictly poetic narrative
recountings of the specifics of the Battle of Catraeth, and deal not with
individual warriors — these poems are not elegiac — but with the battle
as a whole. All of these pieces are among the most metrically skilful
verses in the manuscript. But still — we are working in the realm of the
readable.

2. "GWARCHAN MAELDERW": THE UNREADABLE

All of the verse so far described has been customarily ascribed to one of
Wales' legendary proto-bards, Aneirin. Whatever its ultimate origin, this
attribution comes to us from the rubric at the top of page 1 of the manuscript — "This is the Gododdin — Aneirin sang it." Whether this was
meant to apply as well to the *gwarchanau* is a separate critical problem,
and one which we certainly can't resolve here (see O Hehir 1988). But
when we move on to the last of the *gwarchanau* — "Gwarchan
Maelderw" — we are faced with several new problems in situating the
text for interpretation.

First of all, in a rubric (the so-called "long rubric") preceding the
"Gwarchan Maelderw", this *gwarchan* is attributed not to Aneirin, but to
another proto-bard, Taliesin. It is said, in fact, that this one composition
is worth more in a bardic competition than all the verse of the Gododdin
and its attached *gwarchanau* combined; i.e., more than all the short
elegies and the other teaching poems which make up most of the manuscript contents.[11] So here we are, poised for a composition of unparal-
leled skill and execution. We have read the rest of the *Book of Aneirin,*
we know the themes, the heroes, the vocabulary, the formulas. But what
do we find? At first glance — and at second and third — we simply can't
make sense of these obviously rhymed, alliterated and very Welsh-
sounding words. We think of the scene in the prose tale of Taliesin,
where the poet sits inconspicuously in a corner of King Maelgwn

---

11 The rubric reads: "[Here ends "Gwarchan Kynfelyn".] The singing of a single
song is worth every *awdl* of the *Gododdin* as regards prestige/honor in a poetry
competition. Each one of the *gwarchanau* is worth three hundred and sixty-three.
This is because of the memorials in the *gorchaneu* enumerating the men who went
to Catraeth. No more should a bard go to a competition without this poetry than
should a warrior go to battle without arms. [Here immediately begins "Gwarchan
Maeldderw": Taliesin sang it and gave prestige/honor to it. As much as the *odleu*
of the entire *Gododdin* and its three *gwarchan(eu*) in a poetry competition.]"
(The above is our translation, with preservation of the manuscript's variation in
spelling between *gorchan* and *gwarchan*. The rubric is on p. 11 of *G*, and on p. 55
of *CA*, following 1411.)

Gwynedd's court and puts a spell on each of the poets who go to pay homage to the King, making sure that they can produce no sound but *blerwm blerwm* as they attempt to tell King Maelgwn how good and wise and generous and powerful he is. We think of glossalalia — inspired non-sensical utterance. And we suddenly and at last find ourselves in the realm of the unreadable.

While difficulties abound in the rest of the *Book of Aneirin*, they are generally of types with which we are all familiar: scribal miscopyings of various sorts, marginalia inserted as text, hapaxlegomena, etc. Not so in "Maelderw". The words, many of which we can read individually, do not go easily together. Some of the words are simply non-sensical. Ifor Williams, the most respected commentator on the contents of the *Book of Aneirin*, the scholar whose work and teaching opened up the study of early Welsh verse to several generations of students, had this to say about it:

> It corresponds exactly to *Gwarchan Adebon*, since it is a collection of proverbs, except that its proverbs are worthy of the inspiration of Hell...it is a dark piece, but to the man of the red ink its utter obscurity was its glory, at least for the purpose of poetic competition, and no doubt there is bitter experience behind the words of some bard which were preserved for us in the *Book of Taliesin: An maglas blaen derw / o warchan maelderw.* If the meaning of that is that this *gwarchan* ensnared him and others, I can sympathize entirely: it ensnared me.[12]

At the risk of anticipating ourselves, let us say immediately that the "Gwarchan Maelderw" is not simply a collection of proverbs, though there is indeed some gnomic material in it. Ifor Williams' stature and ability being what they were, subsequent scholars seemed content to accept his interpretation and evaluation of the text, and leave the unreadable, ensnaring "Gwarchan Maelderw" alone. And their judgment was not entirely misplaced. There was no theoretical framework for the metrics of early Welsh verse which could even propose a scansion into certain lines, much less discern what might be meaningful groupings of

---

12 Our translation; the original Welsh follows:

> Cyfetyb i'r dim i Warchan Adebon, canys casgliad o ddiarhebion yw, eithr bod ei ddiarhebion ef yn deilwng o awen Afagddu. ... Darn tywyll yw, eithr i ddyn yr inc coch ei dywyllwch caddugol oedd ei ogoniant, o leiaf i amcan cerdd ymryson, a diau fod profiad chwerw y tu ôl i eiriau rhyw fardd a gadwyd inni yn Llyfr Taliesin,
>
>> An maglas blaen derw
>> o warchan maelderw.
>
> Os ystyr hynny yw i'r gwarchan hwn ei faglu ef ac eraill, medraf gydymdeimlo i'r byw. Maglodd finnau.
>
>   (Williams 1938, pp. lix–lx.)

The Taliesin text cited by Williams occurs in the *Cat Godeu* (ll. 19–20 on p. 25 of Evans' (1910) facsimile edition).

words. Most scholars examining the early Welsh poetic texts have seen metrical structures which do not conform to later Welsh metrical canons: in general, the tendency has been to see the earlier texts as representing defective transmissions, or incomplete and primitive versions, of metrical structures rather like the high medieval and later ones.[13] We disagree with this interpretation, and prefer to treat the early poetic corpora on their own terms; we have argued elsewhere that a short-lined, stress-metrical analysis best fits the data (Klar, O Hehir and Sweetser 1993/4, Sweetser 1988). A scenario for the development from this earlier metrical canon to later ones is presented in Klar and Sweetser (1988).

Before moving on to our analysis of "Gwarchan Maelderw", we would like to recount one more event in the history of its redaction. In 1801 a group of Welsh antiquarians led by Owain Myfyr (Owen Jones) began publishing a collection known as the *Myvyrian Archaiology of Wales*, in which were to be included the first printed versions of much early Welsh prose and verse. When the contents of the *Book of Aneirin* were printed, the Myvyrian editors did not know where the "Gwarchan Maelderw" ended; they simply printed it and all the poetry on the remaining pages of the manuscript (i.e., a number of the short heroic elegies) as if they were one continuous composition — one huge poem — of epic length, in fact, relative to the length of the other pieces. It was not until several generations later that a respected but iconoclastic Welsh antiquarian and literary critic, Thomas Stephens, realized that, in fact, the "Gwarchan Maelderw" ended on page 30 of the manuscript, and the sequence of short elegies resumed. It was not a complete understanding of the text; Stephens merely states that "*Gorchan Maeldderw* contains a number of verses evidently belonging to the Gododdin, which find no place in any of the ordinary copies of that [verse]" (1888, p. 339). Stephens was no more able to "read" with understanding the "Gwarchan Maelderw" than his predecessors or successors; he was, however, brilliantly and intuitively sensitive to the text; given the materials he had to work with, his insight is remarkable.

3. THE "GWARCHAN MAELDERW" POEMS:
METRICAL AND TEXTUAL EXAMINATION

We have completed a metrical analysis of the "Gwarchan Maelderw" portion of the *Book of Aneirin* (i.e., *G* 28.18 -30.11; *CA* 1412-1480). On metrical grounds, we shall argue that the text appears to consist of four

---

13 We have discussed this issue elsewhere: see Klar, O Hehir and Sweetser 1983/4, Sweetser 1988. Haycock 1988 examines the Book of Taliesin for metrical regularity, and proposes a systematic inventory of metrical structures to be found in that text; her analysis involves both syllable count and accentual patterns.

distinct poems, which will be presented below in metrically analyzed form. Our hypothesis is that the final section is the true "Gwarchan Maelderw". Two shorter poems of similar thematic content begin the text, followed by a short heroic elegy of the kind found throughout the A and B texts, followed finally by the section of the text to which the title applies. We will explain the conjunction of thematic and metrical structures which have led us to this conclusion. The accompanying translation is our own very tentative one, and should in no way be taken as a final reading of the contents of these poems, but simply as an aid to following our present argument. For this reason, we have tried to keep it as literal and uninterpreted as possible, even though a smoother and more coherent English text would certainly be possible with a little interpretation.

The rest of the paper is, then, in three main sections. First, the remaining part of the body of the paper is a discussion of the "Gwarchan Maelderw" text, with our arguments for dividing it into four (or possibly more) poems, followed by a brief section summarizing our conclusions. Two further sections follow the text of the paper: a presentation of the text itself, with our suggested metrical lineation and division; and finally our translation of the text. But first, four paragraphs to set out the basics of our metrical system.

3.1. METRICS

We refer readers to our own past work with Brendan O Hehir, for full discussion of the metrical patterns of the Gododdin corpus. We should mention here that in general we find short lines of either two or three accentual feet (i.e, including two or three beats or poetic accents). A given poem is normally consistent in line-length. These lines may occur singly, or in groups of two or more; these stanzaic groupings we have called *rhannau*, in a loan-translation of the cognate Irish *rann* ("stanza, quatrain"). The *prifodl* (or main rhyme) links the ends of *rhan*-final lines throughout a poem (single lines, which may be seen as the final and only line of a minimal *rhan*, also conform to the *prifodl*).

Within a *rhan*, it is usual to find alliteration or rhyme linking lines to each other; the most regular pattern is for the end of one line to be linked to the beginning of the next. When these *rhan*-internal links are rhyme, the rhyme need not be final, but may involve stressed non-final syllables of the words in question. Thus, a common stanzaic pattern might be:

$$\begin{array}{l} \text{————a} \\ a\text{————b} \\ b\text{————p} \end{array}$$

This stanza could then be part of a longer poem which involved other lines or stanzas all ending with a rhyme in "p", the *prifodl* or main rhyme. In some poems, all the *rhannau* are two-line (cf. *Kaeawc kynhorawc/ aruawc eg gawr*, *G* 2.5–12, *CA* 46–56), in others they may all be one-line, or they may vary in length. Three-stress lines tend towards appearance as single lines, rather than groupings of lines; the norm in a three-stress-lined poem is thus simply end-rhyme between the single lines. However, it is possible in the *Gododdin* text to find *rhannau* of quite varied length (e.g., mixtures of one-line, two-line and three-line *rhannau*) within a single poem of two-stress lines: in such cases, the *prifodl* will not occur at even intervals, but at the ends of *rhannau*, wherever they take place.

These short, accentually regular lines are thus intended to replace Williams' and others' longer syllabic (but very irregularly syllabic) lines[14]. First and last lines of poems, and also names, sometimes involve metrical irregularity (see Sweetser 1988). In this text, as elsewhere in the *Gododdin* manuscript, scribal use of periods frequently coincides with the end of a *rhan*; that is, periods occur immediately following a *prifodl*. However, this is not invariably the case, as we shall see below: a whole group of *prifodlau* may pass without a period, and, though rarely, periods do occur in non-*rhan*-final position (our suggestion is that these periods are not metrical in function).

Obviously one can only judge a shift in metrical pattern, or an irregularity in a metrical pattern, against some standard of a contrasting regular metrical pattern. Our claim is that, given a metrical analysis of this text, it becomes clear that breaks or shifts in the metrical pattern coincide with thematic and other suggestions of discontinuity. These are our arguments for a non-unitary "Gwarchan Maelderw" text.

3.2. THE POEMS OF THE "GWARCHAN MAELDERW" TEXT: HOW MANY, AND WHY?[15]

POEM ONE.
The first poem is lines 1–14 of our text (*G* 28.18–29.3; *CA* 1412–1425). This portion of text can be given a satisfactory regular analysis as consisting of three-stress lines with end-rhyme *(prifodl)* which changes several times in the course of the poem. There is at least one flaw in the rhyme-scheme of this poem as we have it (see note 20). Periods mark the ends of all but one of the three-stress lines (or single-line *rhannau*).

The content is often fairly simple locally, but globally opaque. One coherent interpretation might be that the poem describes a trance-voyage

---

14 Loth 1900–2[1969], vol.2, part 2., chap. 5 is an interesting early inventory of the kind of syllables which tended to be "superfluous" in trying to reach a regular syllable count; see our discussion of this in Klar, O Hehir and Sweetser 1983/4.

15 In reading this analysis, our readers will need to refer regularly to the following text and translation.

on the part of a bard. The text starts with a liminal setting: a castle which is supernaturally white and shining, set on a coast. This is a *topos* or theme recognized by scholars as being connected with supernatural journeys in both Germanic and Celtic traditional literature.[16] The poem continues with images of a cold wandering (*gwibde adoer*), and a "famous seeker of sleep" (a bard in a trance?). The protagonist may be an enchanter (if *hutei* is to be read as "he would enchant"), and is present at graves and at a "crooked hill." It is unclear whether the poetic quest is successful, as the poet ends by composing "neither a composition of great sadness nor a curse with a very fearsome result." Whether this means he failed to compose, or that he composed something more auspicious (e.g., the work we are reading) is unclear. At any rate this poem seems added to the start of the *gwarchan*, perhaps in the role of a reciter's preface, like the poem concerning the underground Aneirin in his trance.[17]

POEM TWO (*G* 29.3-9; *CA* 1426-1435; 15-32 of our text).
The following portion of text begins with a new capital in the manuscript: *Tervyn torret*. Poem One likewise began with a capital D (in *Doleu*), but within the poem no capitals were used. Metrically, it is two-line *rhannau* of predominantly two-stress lines, with a good deal of Irish rhyme in the *prifodlau*. Periods mark the ends of all the *rhannau* except the first and the eighth.

Poem Two does seem to be thematically related to the preceding lines, although the capital and the metrics argue for a new section of text. It appears to be praise for a successful "warrior" who may well be a metaphorical poetic warrior, a bard:[18] initially a "boundary" is "broken" (liminality could again be metaphorical here), and elsewhere the subject is described as an "illuminator and seeker" (*disgleiriawr ac archawr*) and said to have no companions in the *awel* "wind" — or "spirit/inspiration". Both light and vision, and breath or wind, are metaphorically connected to prophecy and spiritual vision/inspiration, in the Indo-European tradition. Ford (1987) has discussed this theme with respect to other parts of the *Gododdin* text. Reference to a red dragon (line 25) can be seen as a

---

16 The supernatural light, or bright object, on a coast or a boundary at the beginning of a journey, is part of the "Hero on the Beach" theme first recognized by David Crowne (1960) as being a pervasive one in early Germanic literature. Renoir (1988, pp. 96ff. and 201) resumes and cites some of the subsequent literature on this theme and related ones. In an orally presented paper at the University of California Celtic Conference in April 1989, Mary Niepokuj argued that the same theme is manifested in Welsh medieval tales such as the Mabinogi and *Owain*.

17 See Patrick Ford's (1987) discussion of the *Nyt wyf vynawg blin* poem in the Gododdin manuscript (*G* 12.9-13; *CA* 538-552).

18 See Haycock (1983/4) and Higley (this volume) for treatments of *Preiddeu Annwn* as a metaphorical poetic foray, rather than a literal military one.

heroic theme for warriors, or as an inspirational vision for a bard. A maxim such as "the praise of virtue is a binding bond" (ll.19–20) could certainly be a maxim for poets, but could also be a description of reputation as a motivation to warriors. As in most traditional Indo–European societies, the early Welsh relationship between hero and elegiac poet was a bond which bound in both directions, ideally obligating poets to praise and heroes to be glorious and earn praise. Finally he is said to know the death-dwelling (*Trengsyd a gwydei*), and to go on a grave-journey (*[g]orthur teith*), which suggest either a magical being or a bard who has lived through ritual "death" in initiation and in composition. And the mysterious *neb ae eneu* 'no one begot/bore him' (or perhaps, 'the one who begot/bore him') suggests a supernatural or mantic being.

The metrics of this poem are regular: two-line *rhannau* of two-stress lines seem a defensible analysis throughout this portion of text. The rhyme scheme, however, poses some problems for any analyst, whatever line-lengths are being considered. As will be seen in our notes, the off-rhymes of *adawavn* with the previous verses in *-on*, and of *-awl* with *-awt* at the start of the poem, are not full rhymes in either Welsh or Irish tradition. One particular wrinkle in this poem's structure is that the final *rhan* seems quite unconnected with the immediately preceding text by either *prifodl* or alliteration; however, it is linked by both rhyme and alliteration to the **first** *rhan* of the poem, in a pattern as complex as later regular *cynghanedd*. Besides alliterative effects, the stressed syllable of *teithyawl* (line 16) rhymes with *teith* (line 31), while *torret* (line 15) and *thedyt* (line 32) also rhyme.

The linking of the beginning and end of Poem Two is of course one argument in favor of identifying that poem as a distinct unit. Although more complex than Irish *dúnad(h)*, there is a related flavor to this poetic tactic, and of course both recall the acknowledged Indo-European poetic tendency to compose in "rings", whether in short or long poems. Further evidence for dividing the text up at these points is found in the metrical shift from 3-stress to 2-stress lines, in the switch from no capitals to starting small sections of text with capitals, and (we maintain) in the thematic structure of the contents. Besides the minor and ambiguous issue of capitalization, *tervyn torret* seems at least appropriate thematic material for starting a poem. In the earlier part of the Gododdin manuscript, poems can be found beginning with lines concerning broken ranks (*G* 7.6; *CA* 250), attacks on the border (*G* 31.18; *CA* 258) and related topics.

POEM THREE (*G* 29.9–12; *CA* 1436–1442; lines 33–39 of our text).
The third poem is a short heroic elegy, one which would not be out of
place in the A or B text of the Gododdin corpus. It begins, following
traditional patterns, with a description of the hero's host setting out for
battle ("his retinue is set, a great wall, ash-trees on the sea"), and ends
by praising the hero and finally giving his name in a traditional closure,
"fair Kenan, a wall in the vanguard". Its metrics and rhyme are unprob-
lematic: the lines are three-stress throughout (except perhaps the final
naming of the hero; we elsewhere address the issue of metrical oddities in
first and last lines; cf. Sweetser 1988), and there is line-final rhyme in *-or*
throughout. It is only seven lines long, seems patently heroic rather than
meta-poetic in nature, and refers to *esgor eidin* "the fort of Eiddin"
(Edinburgh), which may partially explain how it got into the general
vicinity of the A and B texts.

The perceptive reader may already have noted that our lineation of
this short poem still differs from Williams', which breaks after *osgord*
rather than after *mavr,* and contains a long line (1438) *ny dheli. na
chywyd gil na chyngor.* It is unclear to us what suggested a line-break
after *osgord* to Williams; we suggest that *mawr* is at least a more plausible rhyme for the following six *-or* rhymes (especially given the possible
rhyming of *-awn* with *-on,* above, in line 36 of the *Maelderw* text).
Further, our break after *mawr* gives a *rhan* or stanza whose lines are
linked by alliteration of *mavr* and *mur.* This kind of alliterative linking of
the end of one line to the beginning of the next, within a *rhan,* is a
normal pattern in the poetics of the Gododdin corpus.

But a more serious issue is Williams' line 1438, *ny dheli. na
chyngwyd gil na chyngor.* This is clearly too long, in fact twice as long as
the *Menit e osgord* line just two lines higher. Further, the scribe's period
after *ny dheli* strongly suggests that there is a line-break hiding around
here, and that we should start a new line with *na chyngwyd.* Yet Williams
is correct in observing that this line is the distance between two *-or*
rhymes, and hence should be a unit in a poem rhyming in *-or.*

We think this problem of aberrant line length is not only solvable, but
in a way that further confirms our metrical and thematic divisions
between sections of the *Maelderw* text. If *ny dheli i*s assumed to be a
textual gloss (translation "it doesn't continue" rather than "he does not
hold"), then not only do line-lengths suddenly regularize and rhyme-
scheme become simple, but the gloss itself appears to refer to the break
between Poems Two and Three. A scribe remarked the discontinuity in
an earlier copy of this text (metrical or thematic discontinuity? we wish
we could know what was evident to him). In some subsequent recopying,
his comment was shifted from the margin to the end of line two of the
new poem; perhaps this was the end of a manuscript line in the glossed
text, and hence the physical location of the gloss.

It may also be noted that the scribe once again stopped beginning short sections with capitals at this point: Poem Three has only its initial capital, and henceforth the text is nearly capital-less. The use of periods in this text is irregular: the last three of the seven lines have final periods, and the others do not. The period following *ny dheli* seems irrelevant to the structure of the poem; if this phrase is an interpolated gloss, then it may have brought its period with it from the margin, but at any rate we need not explain the period metrically — a relief, since *dheli* rhymes with nothing else in the poem, and all the other periods mark a *prifodl*.

POEM FOUR (*G* 29.13–30.11; *CA* 1443–1480; lines 40–80 of our text). The rest of the *Maelderw* text, beginning *gossodes ef gledyf*, is the genuinely difficult and confusing portion. It may in itself consist of more than one poem: there is one capital (*Ystofflit*) within it, and there may be some thematic and/or metrical discontinuities. Periods occur frequently but irregularly after rhyme-words; and one period (after *collwyd*, line 54), like the one following *ny dheli*, seems unlikely to be demarcating any multi-foot metrical unit.

This is the part of the text which presumably should properly be called the *Gwarchan Maeldderw*, since Maeldderw is mentioned in it rather than elsewhere in the text. There are also thematic links with the mantic Poems One and Two, whether we read *hu tei enwlyd elwit* "thus he was called Tei the very-pleasant" in Poem One, or *hutei* giving "he enchanted, he was called very-pleasant." For in this text we once again find *hu tei*, and once again it could have either translation. Further, this textual chunk (whether it should be "Poem Four" or several poems) is evidently mantic in its contents. References to hazel-trees as well as to Maeldderw (the "oak-lord") immediately make us think of *Cat Godeu*. Lines 59–61 (*CA* 1463–4) have explicit textual parallels in *Cat Godeu*, some in the same passage which refers to a "Gwarchan Maelderw",[19] suggesting that the author of *Cat Godeu* had access to some text related to the one we are examining here. There is also much here which could simply be traditional heroic elegy; however, as mentioned above, it

19 Cf. *Cat Godeu* 18–20, Evans 1910 p. 25:

> andeilas blaen bedw.
> andatrith datedw.
> an maglas blaenderw
> o warchan maelderw.

Other phrases which parallel this "Gwarchan Maelderw" passage occur on Evans p. 24: *blaen llin blaen bun* (line 11); *gwern blaen llin* (line 15).

appears to have been conventional to write about prophetic and poetic "forays" as if they were military forays.[20]

One particular portion of this text deserves comment thematically. Lines 68–76 (Williams 1470–76) could be read as a description of a ritual sequence of events.

> kentaf digonir can welw
>
> kynnwythic lleithic llwyrdelw
>
> kyn y olo gouudelw
>
> taf gwr mawr y wael
> maelderw.
>
> delwat dieirydaf
> y erry par ar delw
>
> rwysc rwyf bre
> [rymun] gwlat rymun rymdyre.[21]

This translates something like: "First the pale-white (one? horse?) is made (suffices?), a wild throne (couch) whole-shaped, before the covering of the afflicted shape[22] — a great man grows ill: Maeldderw. The most terrible form awaits: a spear in the form of the authority of the lord of the hill: he joined the land, he ran to me." The text continues to say that someone (the lord of the hill? Maeldderw?) victoriously descended on the hill-country. To us the sequential structure here, and the possible mention of a white horse (*canwelw* is the color of supernatural animals such as Rhiannon's horse in *Pwyll*), together with a throne and a spear, suggest a ceremonial description. If so, the origins of the content here are archaic indeed.

This "Poem Four" section is metrically more difficult than Poems 1–3. The first portion is in regular couplets of two-stress lines, while later we see things which can only be three-stress (like the potentially ceremonial excerpt just quoted). There may be more than one poem here as well, or there may be separate portions of a single poem which are metrically different from each other. It does mention Maeldderw at a crucial point (the height of the ritual, if that is what the text is really about). Our hypothesis is that its mantic material brought it into the same text as the two preceding mantic Poems One and Two, which became prefaces to it.

---

20 Cf. above, footnote 17.
21 Is one of the *rymun*s a copy of the other, and superfluous?
22 Or read *gofiddelw*, 'pillar, upholder' rather than *gofud-delw* 'afflicted form'.

4. CONCLUSIONS

Our reconstructed history of this text is thus, in brief, that the first two poems were prefaced to the thematically related "Gwarchan Maelderw", while the short elegy (Poem Three) may have been incorporated as part of a general project of gathering older poetry. A similar incorporation of a Llywarch poem into the Gododdin text is discussed in Gruffydd (this volume); the Dinogad cradle-song (*CA* 1101–1117, *G* 22.12–20) presumably found its way into the corpus in the same general manner, but with less justification in that (although part of the same older poetic tradition) it is not "high" heroic matter like the A and B texts. A later copyist took the whole four-poem sequence as a single unit and labelled the whole as "Gwarchan Maelderw"; while the Myfyrian Archaiology editors were unable to identify the end of "Gwarchan Maelderw", this prior redactor failed to identify its beginning. Some early reader noted the oddity of Poem Three's presence in this larger unit with a gloss *(ny dheli)* that was subsequently incorporated by another copyist, to the confusion of later editors.

In order to make it credible that this text contains first a textual intrusion (Poem Three), and then a gloss on that intrusion which itself becomes an intrusion, one must posit several stages of manuscript transmission. This is not surprising or troubling. Our corpus is clearly a good deal older than this manuscript, as we have elsewhere said (our guess is not six or seven centuries older, but perhaps three). Moreover, the *gwarchanau* are generally a more archaic and corrupt text than the A and B texts, arguing potentially that they have an older source and more intervening manuscript transmission. As mentioned above, the "Gwarchan Maelderw" text has poetic anomalies not typical of the rest of the *Gododdin* corpus, although it shares general rules of metrics with the A and B poems. Perhaps some of these deviations are archaisms.

We hope that the framework used in this paper has provided insight into the structure of this portion of the *Book of Aneirin*. If we are correct in subdividing the text as we have, the divisions should provide a useful basis for future work on the content, and help us make the unreadable readable.

TEXT OF "GWARCHAN MAELDERW"[23]

POEM ONE

Doleu deu ebyr am gaer.
ym duhun am galch am glaer.
gwibde adoer a dwyaer.

clodryd keissidyd kysgut.   [*CA* 1415]
brithwe arwe arwrut.   5

ruthyr anorthwe a uebir.[24]

adwy a dodet ny debit.

odef ynyas dof y wryt.[25]

dygwgei en aryf en esgut.   [*CA* 1420]

hu tei enwlyd elwit.   10
gwr a ret pan dychelwit.

Kywely krym dy krymdwyn.
kyueiliw nac eiliw etvrwyn
nac emmel dy dywal a therwyn.   [*CA* 1425]

23 Our lineation is numbered continuously throughout the Maelderw text. We have at intervals incorporated line numbers from Williams' edition, labelled *CA*, for the reader's convenience in comparing the two lineations of the text.

24 *uebir*. This word does not rhyme with anything. It does not rhyme with *debit*, two lines below; although we have mentioned elsewhere the use of "Irish rhyme" in the *Book of Aneirin*, by Irish rules r and t cannot belong to the same class. Despite the work of Williams, and of later researchers such as Donovan (1975) and Rowland (1990), a global analysis of early Welsh rhyme may yet reveal more complexity to early Welsh rhyming patterns.

25 *wryt* and the following rhyme-word *esgut* present problems: although they share final consonants with adjacent lines, they are not obviously full rhyme. Note that they do take up full rhymes observed elsewhere in the poem, however.

POEM TWO

Tervyn torret   15
tec teithyawl[26]

nyt aruedauc e uolawt.
diffryderas y vrascawt.

Molawt rin
rymidhin rymenon.   20

dyssyllei trech   [CA 1430]
tra manon.

Disgleiryawr ac archawr
tal achon

ar rud dhreic   25
fud pharaon.

Kyueillyaur en awel
adawavn.[27]

Trengsyd a gwydei
neb ae eneu   30

y ar orthur teith   [CA 1435]
teth a thedyt.

POEM THREE

Menit e osgord mavr
mur onwyd ar vor[28]

[ny dheli.][29]

26 *teithyawl* This does not rhyme with -awt. Irish rhyme class L consonants (strongly
   pronounced [voiced] liquids) rhyme with /m/, /nn/, /ng/, /ll/ and /rr/.
27 *adawavn*. Is this proposed to rhyme with -on?
28 *vor*. Does this rhyme with the preceding *mavr*? It certainly need not, as it
   alliterates with the following *mur*, making a good two-line *rhan*. But it is unusual,
   in this corpus, to find non-end-rhymed material in a three-stress-line passage.
29 As discussed above, we see these two words as a gloss, incorporated into the text
   by a copyist.

na chyngwyd gil na chyngor   35
gordibleu eneit talachor
nyt mwy ry uudyt y esgor.
esgor eidin rac dor.
kenan kein mur e ragor.

"POEM FOUR"

gossodes ef gledyf   40
ar glawd meiwyr.

budic e ren
eny annavd wledic.

y gynnwithic kynlas
kynweis dwuyn dyvyneis.   45

kychuech ny chwyd   [CA 1450]
kychwerw kychvenyches

kychwenychwy enlli weles.
a lenwis miran mir edles.
ar ystre gan vore godemles.   50

hu tei idware yngorvynt   [CA 1455]

gwyr goruynnaf ry annet.
en llwrw rwydheu ry gollet.

collwyd[30]. medwyd[31] menwyt.

gogled run ren ry dynnit.   55
gorthew am dychuel dychuelit.   [CA 1460]
gorwyd mwy galwant no melwit.
am rwyd am ry ystoflit.

---

30 *collwyd*. The period here is a difficulty. Is this additional text ? — a restatement of
   ry gollet? and if so, by whom — poet or glossator?
31 *medwyd*. Williams prints this as two words, *med wyd*, although the manuscript has
   med at the end of a line, and *wyd* at the beginning of the next line. Evans prints a
   hyphen at the end of the line: *med-/ wyd*.

Ystofflit llib llain
blin blaen   60
blen blenwyd.

trybedavt y wledic   [*CA* 1465]

e rwng drem
dremrud dremryt

ny welet y odeu dhogyn ryd.   65
ny welet y odeu dhogyn fyd
mor eredic dar digeryd.

kentaf digonir can welw
kynnwythic lleithic llwyrdelw
kyn y olo gouudelw   70

taf gwr mawr y wael
maelderw.[32]

delwat dieirydaf
y erry par ar delw

rwysc [*CA* 1475] rwyf bre   75
[rymun] gwlat rymun rymdyre.
ysgavl dhisgynnyawd wlawd gymre
nac ysgawt y redec ry gre.
godiweud godiwes gwlat vre.
ny odiweud o vevyl veint gwre. [*CA* 1480] 80

---

32 Note the presence of the name *maelderw* in a line alone, presumably not a full two-stress line; the metrically irregular use of names in rhan-final and poem-final lines is common in the Gododdin corpus (cf. Sweetser 1988).

KLAR AND SWEETSER TRANSLATION

POEM ONE

Meadows of two estuaries about a fortress[33]
awaken me because of whiteness and brilliance
a wandering very cold and very bloody

praise-generous seeker of sleep[34]
dappled web bloody rough-red   5

invincible rushing was faced

a hurdle was set, there was no retreat

suffering in battle, tamed his valor

he would frown intensely in arms actively

he would enchant — very pleasant he was called[35] 10

a man who runs when he is called

bedmate of a crooked (round) house on a crooked hill[36]
composing neither a composition of great sadness
nor a curse very fearsome its result[37]

(end Poem One)

---

33 This initial sequence — a shoreline, a fort, and white light — is what suggests that this is a "hero on the beach" (see above) about to have an encounter with the supernatural.

34 Both "praise-generous" and "seeker of sleep" could be kennings for "poet," since poets are elegiac praisers by profession, and may go into trance states (see above discussion) in search of inspiration.

35 Or: "Thus he was called Tei the very pleasant."

36 I.e. a grave on a mound?

37 Perhaps, therefore, composing something more auspicious — praise of someone alive? Or mantic and prophetic poetry?

POEM TWO

A boundary (was) broken   15
fair travelling

his praise was unstinted[38]
he was anxious about his greatness

the praise of virtue
is a binding bond[39]   20

he would gaze intently
over trifles[40]

illuminator and requester
of the payment of pedigrees[41]

about a red dragon[42]   25
for the benefit of a pharaoh

companions in the wind/spirit[43]
they would allow

death-dwelling he knew
no one bore him   30

upon a grave journey
teat and fathering[44]

(end Poem Two)

---

38 Cf. "Praise-generous" in the preceding poem, line 4.

39 This is gnomic, and a very Indo-European piece of wisdom; Pindar and other early praise poets would have agreed. One is "bound" to praise virtue, in that it is a part of the social fabric to give glory to courage and generosity (society demands it, and is maintained by it, in this world-view); and the act of praise is a bond (social, financial, and artistic) between patron and poet.

40 Or: 'over maidens'.

41 "Illuminator" could mean either prophet or poet — "one who sheds light on the unknown" or "one who confers glory"? "Requester of the payment of pedigrees" sounds exactly like a poet who requires due compensation for praising a lineage.

42 A good Welsh symbol, of course.

43 I.e. companions in poetic or prophetic inspiration? The connection between Indo-European words for 'wind' or 'breath' and words for 'inspiration' is well-known.

44 Lines 29–32 can be read as being about a ritual or spiritual death and rebirth; the poet encounters death, abandons his previous self ("no one bore him"), and is reborn — his "grave journey" is his new "teat and fathering" as he is reborn in poetry or prophecy.

POEM THREE (plausible title: "Kenan the Fair")

His great retinue was set
a wall of ash-trees before the sea[45]

[it does not continue]

neither a retreat nor a deliberation   35
an overlively soul is the payment of tumult[46]
no more he moved his enclosure
the fort of Eiddin before the door[47]
Fair Kenan, a wall in the vanguard[48].

(end Poem Three)

POEM FOUR (or possibly Four and Five)

(the "Gwarchan Maeldderw" section of the text)

He placed a sword   40
on the puny men's dike

for the benefit of a prince
in the protection of a lord

to fierce Kynlas
first wading of the ford's depths   45

he did not fall sweetly
bitterly he arose

mutual-desiring he saw a flood
which filled the mournful seas
on the border in the morning heaped   50

45 The ash-trees here are a kenning for spears, but may have helped the poem get into
the vicinity of the very tree-oriented poetic passages in Poem Four?
46 A gnomic piece of advice: cf. *Proverbs* 11:29, "He that troubleth his own house
shall inherit the wind"?
47 I.e., His troop stood as steadfast as the fort?
48 A very standard kenning for a hero, in the rest of the Gododdin corpus: and it is
also normal to end an elegy with the hero's name and a particularly appropriate
kenning or description: e.g. 'glorious Eithinyn, battle-wall, combat-bull' (*G* 10.18–
19, *CA* 427) or 'Tutvwlch harsh in battle, a barred fortress' (*G* 32,6–7, *CA* 761).

[Break here?][49]

He would enchant, he would compete ardently

the most ambitious of men he was born
on the path of riches he was lost

it was lost, it was drunken, delight[50]

the north of Lord Rhun was taken   55
Gorthew would return — he returned
wooded-slope they called it more than honeysuckle
a very easy way he tamed anger

he tamed wrath of blade-slander
grievous vanguard   60
? was ?ed

tripod [51]of the troop

between dream red dream
a dream-ford

(if) the purpose of a liberal ration is not seen   65
(then) the purpose of a beneficial ration is not seen[52]
a plowed sea — a blameless lord

First the pale-white[53] (one) is made
fierce couch, whole shape
before the covering of afflicted shape   70

a great man grows ill
Maeldderw

---

49 Ll. 40–50 could be an elegy, although they could also be a part of a metaphorical
   poetic-foray poem, including reference to fords and beaches, liminal zones.
50 This line could also read 'hazel trees, drunken trees'.
51 Tripod — i.e., support. Another standard formula for a hero.
52 I.e., "Giving ungenerously is pointless"?
53 *canwelw* seems to be a gleaming white shade which is (among other things) the
   color of Rhiannon's magical steed in the *Pwyll*. It may have supernatural
   connotations here as well.

the most terrible form
awaits, a spear in form

authority of the lord of the hill   75
he joined the land, he joined, he ran to me
Ysgawl attacked
not as a shadow that runs did he do it
he overtook overtaking the highland
he did not overtake so much as a mite of shame.   80

ABBREVIATIONS

G = South Glamorgan County Library MS. 2.81; reproduced in Daniel Huws (ed.) 1989, *Llyfr Aneirin: a Facsimile* (pub. The South Glamorgan County Council and the National Library of Wales).

CA = Sir Ifor WIlliams (ed.) 1938, *Canu Aneirin* (Caerdydd: University of Wales Press).

REFERENCES

Crowne, David K. 1960. "The Hero on the Beach: An Example of Composition by Theme in Anglo-Saxon Poetry." *Neuphilologische Mitteilungen* *61*:362–72.

Donovan, Patrick J. 1975. Mydryddiaeth Canu Aneirin a Chanu Taliesin. M.A. thesis, University of Wales at Aberystwyth.

Evans, D. Simon. 1978. "Iaith Y Gododdin." In Rachel Bromwich and R. Brinley Jones, eds., *Astudiaethau ar yr Hengerdd*. Caerdydd: University of Wales Press. Pp. 89–122.

Evans, J. Gwynogvryn. 1910. *Facsimile and Text of the Book of Taliesin*. Lanbedrog.

Ford, Patrick K. 1974. *The Poetry of Llywarch Hen*. Berkeley, CA: University of California Press.

———. 1977. *The Mabinogi and other medieval Welsh tales*. Berkeley, CA: University of California Press.

———. 1987. "The Death of Aneirin." *BBCS* 34: 41–50.

Gruffydd, Geraint. (this volume) "The *englynion* in *Llyfr Aneirin*."

Haycock, Marged. 1983/4. "'Preiddeu Annwn' and the Figure of Taliesin." *Studia Celtica* 18–19: 52–78.

———. 1988. "Metrical models for the poems in the Book of Taliesin." In Roberts (1988), pp. 155–178.

Higley, Sarah Lynn. *Between Languages: the Uncooperative Text in Early Welsh and Old English Nature Poetry*. University Park, PA: Pennsylvania State University Press. 1993.

———. (this volume) "The Spoils of Annwn: Taliesin and Material Poetry."

Huws, Daniel. 1989. Introduction to *Llyfr Aneirin: a Facsimile*. Cardiff and Aberystwyth: South Glamorgan County Library and The National Library of Wales.

Jackson, Kenneth. 1953. *Language and History in Early Britain.* Edinburgh: Edinburgh University Press.

———. 1969. *The Gododdin, The Earliest Scottish Poem.* Edinburgh: Edinburgh University Press.

Klar, Kathryn A. 1988. "What are the *Gwarchanau?*" In Roberts (1988), pp. 97–137.

Klar, Kathryn, Brendan O Hehir and Eve E. Sweetser. 1983/4. "Welsh Poetics in the Indo-European Tradition." *Studia Celtica* 18–19: 30–51.

Klar, Kathryn A. and Eve E. Sweetser. 1988. "Remarks on the development of medieval Welsh metrics." In Gordon W. MacLennan (ed.), *Proceedings of the First North American Congress of Celtic Studies.* Ottawa.

Koch, John T. 1985/6. "When was Welsh Literature First Written Down?" *Studia Celtica* 20–21: 43–66.

———. 1988. "The Cynfeirdd Poetry and the Language of the Sixth Century." In Roberts (1988), pp. 17–41.

Lewis, Saunders. 1932. *Braslun o Hanes Llenyddiaeth Gymraeg.* Caerdydd: University of Wales Press.

Loth, Joseph. 1900–1902. *La métrique galloise depuis les plus anciens textes jusqu'à nos jours.* (3 volumes: vol. 1, and vol. 2 parts 1 and 2; originally printed as vols. 9–11 of *Cours de littérature celtique,* ed. by H. d'Arbois de Jubainville and J. Loth) [reprinted 1969, Osnabrück: Otto Zeller].

Morland (Morland O Hehir), Laura. 1992. "Caedmon and the Germanic Tradition." In John Miles Foley, ed., *De Gustibus: Essays for Alain Renoir.* New York: Garland Publishing, Inc. Pp. 324–358.

O Hehir, Brendan P. 1988. "What is the Gododdin?" In Roberts (1988), pp. 57–96.

Renoir, Alain. 1988. *A Key to Old Poems: The Oral-Formulaic Approach to the Interpretation of West Germanic Verse.* University Park PA: Pennsylvania State University Press.

Roberts, Brynley F. (ed.) 1988. *Early Welsh Poetry: Studies in the Book of Aneirin.* Aberystwyth: National Library of Wales.

Rowland, Jenny. 1990. *Early Welsh Saga Poetry.* Woodbridge: D. S. Brewer.

Stephens, Thomas. 1888. *The Gododin of Aneurin Gwawdrydd.* (Printed for the Honourable Society of Cymmrodorion) London: Whiting and Co.

Sweetser, Eve E. 1988. "Line-structure and rhan-structure: the metrical units of the Gododdin corpus." In Roberts (1988), pp. 139–154.

Williams, Sir Ifor. 1938. *Canu Aneirin.* Caerdydd: University of Wales Press.

———. 1972. *The Beginnings of Welsh Poetry,* ed. by Rachel Bromwich. Cardiff: University of Wales Press.

NARRATIVE OPENERS AND PROGRESS MARKERS IN IRISH

Proinsias Mac Cana

DUBLIN INSTITUTE FOR ADVANCED STUDIES

In an earlier article (1973, 107–9; cf. 1991, 70–72) I referred to the familiar practice of medieval Irish storytellers and redactors of opening their narrative with a sentence deviating from the normal VSO prose order; thus **Rí amra** [subj.] *ro boí for Laignib .i. Rónán mac Aeda* 'There was a wondrous king over the Leinstermen, Rónán son of Aed' Fing. R. 1, **Ardrí** *ro gab for Hérind .i. Túathal Techtmar mac Fiachach Findolaid meic Fheradaig Fhindfhechtnaig* 'A high-king ruled over Ireland . . . ' *LL*37639 (*Bórama Laigen*), **Rí maith** *ro gab Mumain .i. Mairid mac Cáiredo* 'A good king ruled over Munster, Mairid son of Cairid' *LU* 2926 (*Aided Echach meic Maireda*), **Mórrí mórbrethach** *ro gab os Herind* 'A great king of weighty judgements ruled over Ireland, Cormac son of Art' *LU* 4041 (*Senchas na Relec*), **Óenach** *dogníthe la Ultu cecha blíadna . . .* 'An assembly was held by the Ulstermen every year' Serg. CC 1. Whereas normally in Irish, V-second statements are used to identify the initial constituent as distinct from other possible referents, these narrative openers constitute one of several sub-categories in which the effect of the inverted order is to mark or contextually to "load" the whole statement and not merely the fronted element.

Most often, as in the examples cited, the fronted constituent at the beginning of a tale serves to introduce a famous personage, reflecting the preoccupation of the learned literature with kings and heroes. But occasions or events could be similarly pre-posed, and in this regard the opening of *Serglige Con Culainn* corresponds to the characteristic *Sealg/ Fleadh mhór-adhbhal . . . do comóradh le . . .* 'A great hunt/feast was held by . . . ' of the later romantic tales. Dr. Alan Bruford suggested that the V-second opening of these tales is one of the declamatory devices that typify this later phase of medieval Irish storytelling (Bruford 1969, 37), which of course immediately raises the question whether it is an inherited or an innovational feature.[1] The fact that it occurs in earlier tales would seem to rule out the second alternative, and this is perhaps borne out by the use of subject-initial openings in a number of Middle Welsh tales, as in the initial sentence of the first of the Four Branches of the *Mabinogi*: **Pwyll, Pendeuic Dyuet**, *a oed yn arglwyd ar seith cantref Dyuet* 'Pwyll prince of Dyfed was lord over the seven cantrefs of Dyfed' *PKM* 1.1.[2]

It may also be significant that V-second order still occurs quite frequently in modern popular tales not confined to the romantic genres of Early Modern Irish (though my impression is that it is much less common in Ulster tales than in those from Munster and Connacht); thus the following examples from a Connacht collection: **Bean** *do bhí ann agus bhí triúr mac aici* 'There was a woman who had three sons', **Inghean áird-righ Ghréige** *[do] chuir cuntas chuig Fionn* . . . 'The daughter of the high-king of Greece sent a message to Fionn', **Ceathrar dearbhráthar** *do bhí ionnta* 'There were four brothers of them', **Duine-uasal** *do bhí ann, agus bhí sípéaraidh (maor caorach) aige* 'There was a gentleman who had a shepherd' (de h-Íde 1933, 116, 156, 168, 258), or these from a Kerry storyteller: **Gabha** *a bhí ann* . . . 'There was a smith . . . ', **Beirt driothár** *a bhí ann fadó* . . . 'There were two brothers long ago . . . ', **Sagart óg** *a bhí ann* . . . 'There was a young priest . . . ', **Leas-mháthair** *a bhí ar a' nGárlach Coileánach* . . . 'The G.C. had a stepmother . . . ', **An tiarna talún** *a tháinig isteach i dtig athar a' Ghárlaig a' lorg cíosa* 'The landlord came into the Gárlach's father's house for the rent', **Sagart óg** *a tháinig as a' gcóláiste* 'A young priest had come from college', **Spailpín ó Bhaile 'n Sgeilig** *a chuaig thar cnoc suir a' buin phrátaí* 'A spalpeen from B. went east over the hills to pick potatoes' (Ó Duilearga 1948, 127, 141, 157, 159, 288; the translations are those in Ó Duilearga

---

1   The high frequency of V-second incipits in the Early ModIr romantic tales is well illustrated by the collection entitled *Gadaidhe Géar na Geamh-oidhche*, edited by "Triúr cómhdhalta do Chuallacht Chuilm Cille" (Baile Átha Cliath, 1915): of the seven tales included, six begin with a V-second sentence. In fact one of them flaunts the conventional structure by stretching it beyond the point of syntactic dislocation (*Áirdrí uasal, onórach* . . . *do ghaibh ceannas* . . . *darbh' chomhainm Feidlime mac Criomhthainn* 'A noble, honourable . . . high-king held sway . . . whose name was F. mac C.' (93)): here we have the familiar sequence of fronted noun + attributive adjective + verb + naming formula, but whereas normally there is only one or at most two attributive adjectives, here the noun is separated from its verb by a series of forty-four adjectives and adjectival phrases.

2   One notable disparity between the Irish and Welsh instances is that the latter have a proper name as the fronted constituent, but this may be due simply to stylistic divergence and to the more limited nature of the Welsh corpus.

and MacNeill 1981). It is interesting that the anecdote beginning **An tiarna talún . . .** (p. 157) is followed by another which has virtually the same opening sentence, but with normal V-first order: *Do tháinig tiarna 'n talún isteach lá eile i dtig athar a' Ghárlaig ad iarraig ciosa.* Presumably the reason for this is that the second anecdote was sequential to the first and it was therefore unnecessary to repeat the marked opener.

The combination of the medieval and modern Irish evidence and that of medieval Welsh suggests, though obviously it does not prove, that the use of V-second order to begin a narrative was traditional in Irish and perhaps also in Insular Celtic as a whole. At the same time the indications are that its use was optional and that it was but one of several modes of marking the opening of a discrete narrative.

Another closely related opener to which I have already adverted (1973, 108) is the *nominativus pendens* (or left dislocation) construction, e.g. **Fróech mac Idaith do Chonnachtaib**, *mac side do Bé Find as sídib* 'Fróech mac Idaith of Connacht, he was son of Bé Find from the fairy mounds' TBF 1, **Diarmait mac Aeda Sláne**, *Sinech Cró rod n-alt* 'Diarmait mac A.S., it was Sinech Cró who reared him' *LU* 9568, **Conaire mac Mese Buachalla**, *is é ortae i mbruidhin ui Dergae . . .* 'Conaire son of Mess Buachalla, he it was who was slain in the hostel of Ua Dergae' Zu ir. Hdschr. i, 27, **Temair na ríg** *is sí bá dodgnás díles do cech ríg no gebed Herind* 'Tara of the kings was the proper residence of every king who acceded to the sovereignty of Ireland' *LU* 4206. It is still a familiar feature of Modern Irish story-telling; the following instances are from *Peadar Chois Fhairrge*, a group of tales collected from a County Galway storyteller: **Micil Mhág Cing** *ba éard a bhí ann figheadóir* 'Micil Mhág C. was a weaver' p. 29, **Seán Ó Lopáin as Béal an Daingin** *bhí sé foghlumtha agus ina sgoláire* 'Seán Ó Lopáin from B. was learned and a scholar' 53, **Seán Ó Bia i mBaile na Páirce, Spidéal,** *tá sé ina chomhnuidhe san teach a bhfuil sé le seacht mbliana fichead* 'Seán Ó Bia in B. has been living in the house where he is now for twenty-seven years' 75, **Máirtín Ó Loideáin** *bhí sé ina bháille uisge agus ina bháille coille ag Coirnéal Ó Dálaigh* 'Máirtín Ó L. was a water bailiff and a wood bailiff for Colonel Ó D.' 104, **Ochtar ban as Indreabhán, thíos le fairrge,** *chuadar ar buaile amach ar an gCloich Bhric ins an áit ar a dtugtar Formaol* 'Eight women from Indreabhán down by the sea went booleying [on transhumance] on C. B. at the place that is called F.' 105.[3] It is in a

---

3 In one instance where the editor has an opening V-second sentence, it is also possible to read it as a *nominativus pendens*. The text has **Lochlannach** *a bhí ina chomairleach ar oibreacha i 'Meireacá. Bhí m'oncal Colm ag obair faoi* 'A Scandinavian was works officer in America. My uncle Colm was working under him' (op. cit., 52), but syntactically the two sentences could just as easily be understood as one, with the first a complex *nom. pendens* consisting of antecedent

way remarkable that in regard to this dual feature of narrative technique the popular storyteller of Modern Irish should remain in such substantial harmony with the usage of the earlier literature, given that this has been mediated to us by many generations of active redactors, more or less exclusively monastic in the pre-Norman period and of more varied provenance in subsequent centuries.

For our immediate purpose one of the most relevant productions of the medieval redactors is the capacious frame-tale *Acallam na Senórach* which dates from about the end of the twelfth century, for here, whatever its precise motivation, we have a skillful and sensitive *literatus* "com-posing" within the compass of a single text a numerous collection of tales and anecdotes about Fionn and the Fiana drawn from a variety of sources, probably both written and oral. However, for reasons which we need not go into here, the traditions of the Fionn cycle had received relatively little recognition in the manuscripts of the monastic scribes and redactors of the Old and early Middle Irish period (cf. Mac Cana 1987, 92–97, McCone 1986, 2 *et passim*), and many of the stories told or alluded to in the *Acallam* are not found in earlier texts; even if we suppose that some are fabrications of the author, there can be little doubt that most derive from oral storytelling, whether learned or popular. The title, "The Converse of the Old Men", indicates the device which is used to justify the size and structure of the anthology and to authenticate its account of characters and events that long preceded the coming of Christianity and of writing: Caoilte mac Rónáin, one of the leading members of the Fian, survives the extinction of the heroic brotherhood and lives long enough to meet St. Patrick in the midst of his Christianizing mission. As he accompanies Patrick around the Irish countryside he responds to the saint's queries about the places they pass — hills, rivers, plains and other notable features of the terrain — by recounting the ancient events from which they took their names. The result is thus a thesaurus of placename lore complementary to the great collection of prose and verse *dindshenchas* which was compiled in the late MIr period. For our present purpose the essential thing is that all these topographical explanations take the form of individual stories, some extremely short, others relatively long, and it may therefore be useful to survey briefly how exactly these narratives are presented to the reader/auditor.

The normal pattern comprises the question posed by Patrick or another onlooker followed by Caoilte's explanatory response. The response is frequently preceded by an introductory 'Caoilte answered . . . ' (*frecrais Caoilte*) or may include the *inquit* form (*ar Caoilte*); in some

---

noun + relative clause, though there might be a slight discrepancy in sentence stress in the spoken language.

cases both are found, in other cases neither. It may also alternatively be preceded by a variety of introductory phrases such as *Adér frit a fhírinne* 'I shall tell you how that came about', *Do geba-su a fhis sin uaimsi* 'You will get the explanation of it from me' (this in reply to the interrogative statement *nil a fis acaind cid dia fuilet na hanmanna ata orro* 'we do not know the origin of their names'). In the great majority of instances the beginning of the etiological story is marked by its constituent order, which is normally V-second, e.g.

> *Do fhiafraig Muiredach do Cháilti: 'cidh fa tucadh Almha uirre?'* *Freagrais Cailte*: '**óclach do Thuaith dé Danann** *do bhí isin Brugh braenach breacsholus . . .* ' M. asked C.: 'Why was it called Almha?' C. answered: 'There was a warrior of the TDD in the dewy bright-speckled *síd*-dwelling . . . '
>
> (Stokes 1900, 1252–54)

> *'Adhbur a haidheda?' ar Conall. 'Ata limsa duit,' ar Cailti '.i.* **mathair ⁊ athair Guill meic Morna** *ro ailestar hí . . .* ' '[What was] the cause of her death?' asked Conall. 'I have it for you,' said C.: 'Goll mac Moran's mother and father reared her . . . '
>
> (2111–13)

> *Is ann sin do fhiarfaig rig Eirenn: 'cá lín do rígaib Eirenn leis a tucad ferann don Fheind?' Fregrais Cailti sin . . . .i.* '**Rí** *ro gabusdur Eirinn .i. Feradach Fechtnach* ⁊ *. . .* ' Then the king of Ireland asked: 'How many kings of Ireland were there by whom land was given to the Fiann?' C. answered: 'A king ruled over Ireland, namely F.F., and . . . '
>
> (2468–71)

> *'rob ail liumsa a fhis d'fhagbail uaitsiu cia ic á raibe in dúnad út ann.'* '**Dá óclach gráda d'Fhind mac Cumaill** *ro bói ann .i. Cellach Braenbili* ⁊ *Moling Luath . . .* ' 'I would like to find out from you who had that fort there.' 'There were two trusted warriors of Fionn mac Cumaill's, C.B. and M.L. . . . '
>
> (2631–35)

> ⁊ *crét ima tucad Tulach in trir ar in tulaig seo?' . . .* '**Rí** *ro bí ar Albain .i. Iruath mac Ailpin, rí Alban,* ⁊ *ro badur tri hingena aici . . .* ' 'Why was this hill called the hill of the three?' 'There was a king over Alba, I. mac A., king of Alba, and he had three daughters . . . '
>
> (3384–89)

'cid fá tucadh Carn Manannáin ar an carn so?' '**Óclach do Thuaith dé Danann**', *ar Cáilte, '.i. Aillén mac Eogabail, tuc grádh do mhnái Mhanannáin meic lir . . .* ' 'Why was this cairn called C.M.?' 'There was a warrior of the T.D.D. who fell in love with the wife of M. mac L.'

(3648-50)

'Ocus crét fa tucad Raith in bantrachta ar in raith sea?' ar rí Muman re Cailti. . . . '**coeca ban [n]gressa is ferr bói a nEirinn** *do thinoil in flaith Find . . .* ' 'And why was this rath called the Rath of the Women?' the king of Munster asked C. . . . 'The leader Find assembled the fifty women best at needlework in Ireland . . . ' [In this instance the fronted noun is object.]

(5535-38)

'cid imma tucad in Garbthanach ar in n-inad sa?' Fregrais Cailte in ceist sin .i. '**Airdrí** *ro gabustar Eirinn .i. Tuathal Techtmar . . .* ' 'Why was this place called the G.?' C. answered that question: 'A high-king ruled over Ireland, namely T.T. . . . '

(4125-27)

A rough and rapid survey of the *Acallam* that does not lay claim to complete statistical accuracy gives a count of forty-one segments of narrative which vary considerably in extent but which are individually sufficiently autonomous to be regarded as stories or at least as anecdotes (one might perhaps expand this figure somewhat by adopting a more liberal view of what constitutes a separate narrative). Of these, thirty begin with a V-second sentence as in the examples just cited, and it is clear that for the author of the *Acallam* this was the normal and most appropriate way of denoting the incipit of a story. On the other hand, his use of the *nom. pendens* construction as a narrative opener — as distinct from its frequent occurrence in the general body of his prose — is relatively sparing, more sparing than the general run of Old and Middle Irish narrative would lead us to expect. I have noted only three instances, and of these two might be contested as not conforming to the *nom. pendens* usage *stricto sensu*:

'In fetrais, a naemchleirig, soithfir dom riachtain-sea i cath buidnech Beindi hEtair thair?' 'Cá soithfir sin alé?' ar Pátraic. '**Mane mac rig Lochlann** *ro bói sleg neimnech aici,* ⁊ *ní therna duine di riam gan éc nó gan beith ainbech acht co ngontái di hé . . .* ' 'Do you know, holy cleric, how I found myself in difficulty in the great battle of Howth in the east?' 'What difficulty was that?' asked Patrick. 'Maine, son of the king of Lochlainn, had a virulent spear, and no one wounded by it ever escaped without death or blemish.'

(6789-93)

'ca ferr duind ní da fiarfochamais na senchus na ratha so .i. Raith Áine?' 'Atá acumsa inní dia tá sin,' ar Cailte, '.i. **Áine ingen Mugh[d]uirnn, ingen rig Alban anall,** ⏋ *ro badur fir Alban íc a rada ria: "Cid taíssiu, a rigan, gan feis re fer maith ind Albain nó a nEirinn?"'* 'What could we more fittingly ask you than the history of this rath, that is, Ráith Áine?' 'I know its origin,' said Caílte, 'that is, Áine the daughter of M. king of Alba yonder, the men of Alba were saying to her, "Why have you not married a worthy man in Alba or in Ireland?"'

(3055–60)

'Cred 'ma tucad Cnoc in eolaire ar in cnoc-sa, a Caílti?' ar Patraic. **'In t-aenduine is ferr delb don Ádhamcloind** ⏋ **do droing delbda duineta .i. Eolair mac righ in domain móir anoir,** ⏋ *dorinde a curu* ⏋ *a muinnterus re Find . . .* ' 'Why was this hill called Cnoc in Eolaire, Caílte?' said Patrick. 'The man most favored in form of the family of Adam and comely humankind, namely Eolair son of the king of the great world in the east, made covenants and alliance with Find.'

(7560–64)

The first of these instances of *nom. pendens* is straightforward, but the other two are complicated by the fact that the constituent in question, that printed here in bold, is followed by the conjunction *ocus* (⏋). The effect of this is syntactically to attach to the following text the constituent word or phrase which, as *nom. pendens*, would be detached from it. It might conceivably be argued that in the second example *Áine ingen M.* etc. simply stands in apposition to the preceding *inní dia tá sin* and that it is so indicated by the sign *.i.*. This is improbable. It will be seen from several of the instances of V-second openers quoted above from *Acallam na Senórach* that *.i.* is sometimes used as a scribal sign introducing the explanatory narrative, and in some sequences such as that at ll. 2468–71 the constituent following *.i.* cannot possibly be in apposition to a preceding referent. Another such mark of the scholastic authorship of the text is the very occasional use of the formulaic response *Ní annsa* to introduce the explanatory in-tale (as in 1065 and 2203). As regards the third instance (7560–64), the fact that the scribe/author inserts *.i.* between the two nominal constituents of the passage in bold shows that he understood them as appositional phrases, not as a copula sentence, which would be the only other conceivable interpretation.

My third category of narrative openers in *Acallam na Senórach* consists of those episodes—nine of them by my reckoning—which begin with the initial adverbial *Fecht n-aen / Aen do ló / Laithe n-aen* 'One time' / 'One day'. It is of course true that there are scores upon scores of connecting sentences within the narrative which begin with adverbial phrases, but normally these do not serve specifically to mark the opening of a discrete segment of narrative, which seems to be precisely what the three adverbs in question are intended to do:

'Crét tuc dóibhsium in maithius mór sin?' ar Pátraic. **'Fecht n-aen** *dá táncatar d'agallaim a n-athar co Fert na nDruadh fria Temhraig aníartúaid, "Cán-asa táncubair, a óca?" ar sé'* . . . 'What brought them that great wealth?' said Patrick. 'Once when they came to speak to their father at F. na nD. to the north-west of Tara, he asked them: "Whence have you come, men?"' . . .

(359–63)

'crét fa tucad Glenn na caillige ar an nglenn-so thís?' . . . **'Aen do ló** *do bhí Find ⁊ in Fhiann annso, ⁊ atchonncamar amuit chailligi . . . cucainn, . . .* ' 'Why was this valley called G. na C.?' . . . 'One day Find and the Fiann were here, and we saw an old witch coming towards us, . . . '

(3960–63)

'Cred ima tucad Raithin na n-ingnad ar in raithin seo? . . . ' **'Laithe** **n-aen,'** *ar Cailte, 'da tangamarne tri catha na Féine conici in tulaig sea ⁊ atchonncamar in triur óclach sin ar ar cind . . .* ' 'Why was this little rath called R. na nI.?' . . . 'One day that we came with three troops of the Fiann to this hill,' said C., 'we saw three warriors before us . . . '

(5448–53)

'Crét fa tucad Benn bán in retha ar in n-inad so?' . . . **'Feacht n-aen** *da raibi Find mac Cumaill ar in tulaig-sea atchonncadur in mnái ara cind . . .* ' 'Why was this place called B.B. in R.?' . . . 'Once when Find mac C. were upon this hill they saw a woman before them . . . '

(5635–39)

'⁊ créd 'má tucad Callann ⁊ Cuillenn ar in inad so' . . . **'Laithe** **n-aen,'** . . . *da raibe Find mac Cumaill ac Raith chuiri . . . ⁊ ní cían ro bamar ann . . . co faccamar in tricha cairptech . . .* ' 'And why was this place called C. and C.?' . . . 'One day that F. mac C. was at R. Ch. . . . and we were not there long until we saw thirty charioteers . . . '

(5733–42)

'Ocus cred 'ma tucad Daire in coccair ar in inad-so?' . . . **'Feacht n-aen** *da tainic Find mac Cumaill . . .* ⁊ *ni cían ro bamar ann co faccamur in t-aenduine dar n-indsaigid . . .* ' 'And why was this place called D. in C.?' . . . 'Once when F. mac C. came . . . and it was not long until we saw a single person coming towards us . . . '

(5911–19)

'cret 'ma tucad Raithin na Sénaighechta ar in raithin seo?' . . . **'Laithe n-aen** *da raibe Find annso ina tshuidhe . . .* ⁊ *atconncamar triar scoloc maelruad dar n-indsaighid . . .* ' 'Why was this little rath called R. na S.?' . . . 'One day that Find was sitting here . . . and we saw three cropped and red-haired farmers coming towards us . . . '

(6144–48)

'Cid imma tucad Lia in imracail ar in lia so?' ar se. **'Fecht n-aen** *da tangadur meic Morna co Cuaill Chepain . . . ac fogail* ⁊ *ac díbeirg ar Fhind* ⁊ *ar in Féin,* ⁊ *doriachtamar-ne tri catha na Féine co mullach tshléibe Cairnd . . .* ' 'Why was this stone called L. in I.?' said he. 'Once when the sons of Morna came to C.C. . . . raiding and plundering Find and the Fian, and we came, three battalions of the Fian, to the top of Sliab Cairn . . . '

(7844–51)

What is significant about these adverbial usages is precisely that they are found in conjunction with the question and answer formula which typically introduces individual stories and anecdotes in the *Acallam*; in other words, they constitute one of the syntactic options acceptable or appropriate in this position, one that is already attested in the incipits of several OIr stories. For example, *Compert Con Culaind* opens with **Láa n-áen** *ro bátar mathi Ulad im Chonchobur i nEmain Macha* 'One day the nobles of Ulster were with C. in E.M.' (*LU* 10558), the third of the trilogy of tales in *Tochmarc Étaíne* has **Fecht** (*LU, Fechtas* YBL) **n-aili** *asraracht Eochaid Airem rí Teamrach la n-alaind a n-aimsir tsamrata . . .* 'Another time on a lovely summer day E.A. king of Tara arose . . . ' (Bergin and Best 1938, 174–75), and *Cennach ind Ruanada* 'The Champion's Bargain', the heady final episode of *Fled Bricrenn*, has **Fecht n-and** *do Ultaib i nEmain Macha iar scís óenaig* ⁊ *cluchi, dolluid Conchobar* ⁊ *Fergus mac Róig* ⁊ *mathi Ulad olchena . . .* 'Once (upon a time) when the Ulstermen were in E.M. weary from the gathering and the games, C. and F. and the other nobles of Ulster came . . . ' (Henderson 1899, 116). This last piece is found as an independent text (beginning *Fecht n-aen . . .*) in Edinburgh, Advocates' Lib. Ms. XL — fortunately so, since it is seriously defective in the other mss. of *Fled Bricrenn* — but Thurneysen, perhaps correctly, dismisses the possibility that it may have once existed as a separate story (1921, 447–48). Nonetheless, its opening phrase does set it apart somewhat from the body of the tale, which may of course be part of the conscious artistry that is so evident through this text: to the best of my recollection this is the only instance of initial *fecht n-and* in the whole tale. It may be noted incidentally that, as in the case of the *nom. pendens*, there seems to be some tendency to treat the phrase introduced by the conjunctional adverb as an absolute clause and to insert a coordinating ⁊ (*ocus*) before the main clause. This is true of five of the eight instances cited above from the *Acallam*. Of the remaining three, the first (359–63) has the conjunctional clause followed by a direct question, as if it constituted a complete statement, 5635–39 is syntactically regular since it has no ⁊, and 3960–63 is regular because *Aen do ló* is not followed by conjunctive *dá* and therefore functions as a simple non-conjunctional adverb.

The choice of these three particular adverbs as narrative openers is, of course, semantically controlled. Unlike *(Is) annsin, iarum*, etc., which are used as discourse connectors or progress markers punctuating the internal sequence of the narrative, these three adverbs indicate a historic past, a *passé défini*, which isolates what follows from the preceding narrative rather than relating it to it temporally and sequentially. That being so, we need not be surprised to find a similar functional discrimination in the use of adverbs reflected in some ModIr tales. Perhaps the nearest equivalent to *Laithe n-aen* and *Aen do ló* in ModIr is *Aon lá amháin*, and we might therefore expect to find this also occurring as a narrative opener. In fact a cursory examination of de h-Íde (1933) reveals eleven such instances of *Aon lá amháin* and one each of *Aon oidhche amháin* and *Aon am amháin* (cf. MIr *Fecht n-aen*) marking the beginning of discrete tales or episodes (pp. 26, 37, 39, 42, 51, 138, 151, 197, 211, 227, 240, 243, 246). In only one case does it stand at the very outset of the story text (p. 197), but in several texts where the opening paragraph or paragraphs serve to set the scene and introduce the principal character(s) and the succeeding paragraph sets the action of the story in motion, it is the latter which opens with *Aon lá amháin* (pp. 26, 42, 51, 227). One might appropriately compare the medieval tale *Serglige Con Culainn* which has the V-second sentence already cited (*Óenach dogníthe la Ultu cech blíadna* 'An assembly was (lit. 'used to be') held . . . ') as its incipit and then, after a brief explanatory or scene-setting passage, switches from the general to the specific and signals the change with the adverb *fechtas and*, an occasional variant of *fecht n-and*: *Fechtas and trá fertha óenach la hUltu i mMaig Murthemni* 'Once (lit. 'one time') an assembly was held by the Ulstermen in M.M.'; and having adverted to the *Serglige* one might go on to note the use of *laithe n-and* 'one day' — its only occurrence in the text — to introduce the second phase of the story that opens with the invitation or summons to the Otherworld: *Lathi n-and resint shamfhuin aile cind blíadna, a mbátar Ulaid imbi isin taig . . . tánic fer chucu isa tech . . .* 'One day before the next Samain at the end of the year when the Ulstermen were with him in the house . . . a man came towards them into the house' (Dillon 1953, lines 1, 7, 87–91).

The significant thing is that the ModIr adverbial *aon lá amháin* (with its variants)[4] functions within the narrative in a different way from the various other adverbs scattered throughout the text as indicators of the relative location of events in the chronological sequence: *Ann sin* 'then', *Lá ar na mhárach* 'the next day', *Ar maidin lá ar na mhárach* 'next morning', *Leis sin* 'with that', *Seal gearr 'na dhiaidh sin* 'a short while after that', and so on. In other words, where the adverb *aon lá amháin* is used in ModIr storytelling it has virtually the same function as its semantic correspondents had in MIr and, like the V-second sentence and the *nom. pendens*, it indicates a continuity in storytelling technique from medieval to modern times, at least in regard to the use of specific narrative openers.

At the same time it is well to keep in mind that our three types of marked openings do not appear, on the evidence of the extant texts, to have ever been used consistently to highlight either the absolute incipit of a narrative or the incipit of an in-tale or episode. On the contrary, many medieval tales and the great majority of modern ones do quite well without them, and it seems reasonable to suppose that, while these devices were characteristic of traditional storytelling, they were not essential to it. One example will illustrate this flexibility. It has been noted by others that the saints' Lives employ many of the same structural and stylistic features as secular narrative, and this correspondence is already evident in the earliest of the vernacular Lives, that of St. Brigit (which has been assigned to the ninth century and is roughly three-quarters in Irish and one-quarter in Latin and is likely to have been based on a Latin original).

---

4   Cf. for example the rhythmical opening used by the Donegal storyteller Micí Sheáin Néill: **Lá de na laethanta agus uair de na huaireanta** *a raibh Fionn Mac Cumhaill agus a chuid fear ag seilg trí chuid sléibhte Thír Chonaill, lean siad eilit aon lá amháin go domhain amach ins an tsliabh agus d'imigh sí orthu ina n-ainneoin agus d'fhág sí folach sléibhe orthu* 'One of the days and one of the times that Fionn M.C. and his men were hunting in the mountains of Donegal, they followed a hind this day (lit. 'one day') deep into the mountain, but despite their efforts she got away from them and disappeared' (Maguidhir 1973, 1). It is particularly interesting that Micí should have followed his introductory adverbial phrase with the semantically redundant *aon lá amháin*: the probable reason, I would suggest, is that he declaimed the initial adverbial as an opening flourish, marked as much for function as for sense, and was not therefore conscious of the tautology involved.

Incidentally, Professor Séamus Ó Catháin of University College, Dublin, reminds me that in spoken narrative, at least in northern Irish, the numeral *aon* of *aon lá amháin* is unstressed.

Its laconic prose has no instance of V-second sentence or *nom. pendens* as narrative opener, but in the sole manuscript which preserves the Life, Rawl. B.512, it is followed by a short MIr text divided into seven thematic segments or paragraphs dealing with some of the saint's miraculous deeds, and of the incipits of the seven segments five are V-second, one is *nom. pendens*, and only the last is V-initial (Ó hAodha 1978, xxix–xxx, 1–16, 17–19). Obviously the purpose in using the marked order here is to individuate the several episodes in the series by syntactically highlighting the beginning of each. Whatever his precise hagiographical or artistic motivation, it is evident that the author of this text saw his composition as a series of distinct events or *historiettes*, whereas the OIr *Bethu Brigte* aims at a somewhat more unified and continuous treatment of the saint's life, however imperfect its realization. Nevertheless, since its staple ingredient is miraculous incident or miraculous action, the narrative of the text inevitably consists for the most part of a succession of separate happenings within the continuum of the saint's life-span. This combination of disjunction and continuity affects the relationship between successive episodes and the manner in which each of them is introduced. Most of them are temporally qualified by an adverb or adverbial phrase, and when an episode is thought of as clearly sequential in time to the preceding one, this is indicated in the Irish text by the use of *iarum* 'thereafter', *gair iarum* 'shortly afterwards', *arabarach* 'on the next day', *Isin Domnach cetnu na Casc* 'On the same Easter Sunday', *dia Luain arabarach* 'on the following day, Monday', *Dia Mairt arabarach* 'On the following day, Tuesday', or by a temporal adverbial clause. There is also one small cluster of passages where the author switches to a different syntax for his temporal marker: each one of the series §§35, 36, 37, 39 begins with the emphasizing syntagm *Ba and-sin* 'It was then' followed by a preterite sentence, essentially the same linking device as the ubiquitous progress marker *Is and-sin* + preterite sentence of the *Acallam*, and finally §42 has the slightly variant *Ba iar sin* 'It was after that'. On the other hand, some sections of the narrative are not set in any specific time sequence, and these are introduced by the temporally isolating *Fecht n-and* 'Once (upon a time)' and *Laa n-and* 'One day'. Others again combine isolating *fecht* with the linking adjective *aile*: *Fecht n-aile* 'Another time, on another occasion', but *aile* is devoid of temporal reference and its only function here is to provide some little anchorage for the individual episode within its immediate context.

The functional disparity between adverbial progress markers and narrative openers is simply a reflex of their semantic disparity: 'Once upon a time' normally comes at the beginning of a story and 'then' or 'the next day' somewhere in the middle, and given that most traditional Irish tales follow a linear development and a straight time sequence, it is natural that progress markers will vastly outnumber narrative openers, except in texts such as *Bethu Brigte* which by their nature tend to be thematically and structurally episodic. The reason I chose to examine *Acallam na Senórach* for the purpose of the present essay was precisely that it was a frame-story encompassing within its overall unity a large number of discrete tales devoid of chronological sequence, each one of which was explicitly demarcated from the others and from its continuous narrative setting. On the other hand a text like *Táin Bó Cuailnge*, though comparable in its length and episodic structure, is quite different in the way its constituent parts are conjoined. However loose and linear their composition, they all, with the exception of the retrospective account of Cú Chulainn's "boyhood deeds", belong to the same thematic sequence, each linked causally and chronologically to what has gone before and what follows after. Consequently, in contrast to the *Acallam*, the *Táin* offers little occasion for the use of narrative openers but abounds in adverbs and adverbial phrases functioning as progress markers.

The signal exception is the "Boyhood Deeds of Cú Chulainn", which constitutes a distinct complex tale within the compass of the main narrative but outside its time-frame, and in view of the way in which the intales of the *Acallam* are regularly introduced, it is perhaps worth noting that the section of the *Táin* recounting Cú Chulainn's youth begins with the question and answer formula: '*Cinnas fir,*' or Ailill, '*in Cú rochúalammár la hUltu?*' . . . '*Ní handsa ém,*' ol Fergus. . . . 'What kind of man,' asked Ailill, 'is this Hound whom we have heard of among the Ulstermen?' . . . 'I can tell you that' [lit. 'That is not difficult'], said Fergus. . . . (O'Rahilly 1976, 12.374–76). In the mss. the title of the *Macgnímrada* is inserted a little later at the point where Fergus begins his continuous account of Cú Chulainn's career, but the section actually opens with the question and answer which marks it out from the preceding narrative.5

One thing that emerges clearly, and hardly surprisingly, from our brief survey of the evidence of the written literature is that its authors and

---

5 Cf. *Acallam na Senórach* 3114–17: *Is annsin ro fhiarfaig rí Ulad do Chailti: 'Atait da fhert ar Tráig Rudraigi annseo, ⁊ cid dia fuilet?' 'Issim meabrach inní dia fuilet,' ar Cailte '.i. da mac d'Aed mac Fhidaig, meic Fhintain, do rí[g] Connacht aniar, do hadhlaiced ann'* Then the king of Ulster asked Caílte: 'There are two mounds here on T.R.; how did they come to be there?' 'I know how they come to be there,' said Caílte: 'Two sons of Aed m. Fidaig m. Fhintain, the king of Connacht in the west, were buried there. . . . ' Here the story is introduced by the usual question and answer, and the explanatory narrative begins with a V-second sentence. However, the actual battle in which the two sons of the king of Connacht were killed does not commence until l. 3146, and this is where Ms. Laud 610 furnishes the marginal title *Cath Traga Rudraigi inso* 'This is the [story of the] Battle of Tráig Rudraigi'.

redactors did not work to any rigid set of rules or conventions with regard to how a story should be introduced; otherwise there would be a much greater degree of uniformity than exists in the extant corpus of texts. The presumption is that this stylistic freedom obtained also in the oral tradition both before and within the era of writing, though it must always be kept in mind that texts of the medieval, and especially the OIr period, while they doubtless retain many of the features of oral narrative, need not and probably should not be thought of as closely reflecting the overall structure, proportions, and style of their oral counterparts where such existed; even the tales of modern storytellers, though in general they have been recorded more or less verbatim from the oral telling, have undoubtedly in some instances been influenced by earlier written versions. But even if we assume, as seems most likely, that Irish storytellers throughout history, and before it, could exercise a measure of eclecticism in framing the incipits of their tales, the evidence shows that certain options of matter and form were felt to be particularly appropriate for this purpose. As regards the matter, it was common to begin by introducing a character of primary importance, though not necessarily the main protagonist of the tale, as in the medieval *Rí amra ro boí for Laignib .i. Rónán mac Aeda* 'There was a wondrous king over the Leinstermen, Rónán son of Aed' in *Fingal Rónáin, Buí rí amra airegda for Érinn, Eochaid Feidleach a ainm* 'There was a wondrous and noble king over Ireland called E.F.' in *Togail Bruidne Da Derga* (Knott 1936, line 1), and the modern *Do bhí beirt i nUíb Ráthach fadó gurbh ainm dóibh Cluasach Ó Fáilbhe agus an Ceannaidhe Fionn* 'There were two men in Uíbh R. long ago called C. Ó F. and the C.F.' (Seabhac 1932, 64), *Bhí seanlánú ann sa tseanaimsir. 'Sé an ainm a bhí ortha Siobhán agus Domhnall* 'There was an old couple long ago. They were called S. and D.' (162). As for the form, the storyteller frequently underscored the opening of his narrative by using V-second word order or the *nom. pendens* construction, and sometimes he began with a historical adverb such as *fecht n-and* or *lá n-and* to set the ensuing narrative clearly in the context of *senchas* or traditions about the past. The role of the historical adverb is self-evident, since it is semantically controlled, but the syntactic marking by word order in this position perhaps requires a little further comment.

I have sought to show elsewhere (1991, 62–72) that non-contrastive fronting was, and is, used in spoken and written Welsh and Irish to convey a range of nuanced emphasis relative to both the implicit and the explicit context. It frequently serves to supply information relating to a preceding question, statement, or situational prompt, so that in essence its functional range may be summarized fairly accurately as responsive/explicative, and it seemed to me that this might be part of the reason why the V-second sentence was regarded as a particularly appropriate narrative opener, in view of the fact that the medieval tale was typically told to an audience and that it was the function of the storyteller to respond to his audience's expectation by recounting to them the lives and exploits of certain legendary characters of the distant past. Now the evidence which I have surveyed (though far from exhaustively) in the present essay brings that conjecture into much clearer focus. Throughout *Acallam na Senórach* a tale is told as a direct answer to a specific question, and thus the initial V-second sentence is justified in purely syntactic terms as a simple responsive. It is a combination which is also extremely common in texts which present in catalogue form thematically related items of traditional knowledge, as for example the *Dindshenchas* and *Cóir Anmann*, those solid repositories of etymological and heroic/mythological lore concerning the names of famous places and persons respectively. Given the preoccupation with the "backward look" and with ultimate origins which colors so much of Irish literature, one can safely assume that the telling of a tale in response to a request for information must have been a constant of oral tradition (as well as being in some sense implicit in the normal reciprocity of audience and storyteller): in Séamus Ó Duilearga's edition of the repertoire of the Kerry storyteller Seán Ó Conaill the very first anecdote begins with a V-second sentence, **Blonag Naomh Mhártain** *a dhin iad sin* 'They were made from St. Martin's fat', and provides the answer to the printed heading *Conus a tháinig luchaig agus franncaig agus cait agus muca sa dúthaig* 'How mice, rats, cats, and pigs came into the world' — which, even if not punctuated as a question, is certainly an invitation to an answer (Ó Duilearga 1948, 1). Though the editor does not say whether the precise wording of the heading derives from the storyteller, it is clear that its substance did, since it is presupposed by the opening sentence of the narrative that follows.

The question then is whether my former suggestion that the V-second opener is related to the broad category of responsive/explicative statements suffices by way of explanation, or whether one should make this more specific by assuming an integral pattern comprising a question and a following narrative by way of response, but with the question component implicit or underlying in the majority of instances. It may be recalled that one of the most banal features of medieval Irish literature is the combination of a question with the phrase *ní (h)anse*, lit. 'it is not difficult', as preface to an item of traditional lore or learning (cf. the instances in *Acallam na Senórach* referred to above). This has its reflex in the Latin *non difficile*, which also prefaces answers to questions and which is considered to be a Latinization of the Irish and is included among those characteristic features which are used to identify certain

Latin texts as being of Irish origin (McNamara 1972, 340–41). But even if this were not so, it is safe to presume that the question and answer form was the staple of pedagogy in the learned schools of Ireland before the invention and spread of writing in the vernacular. When Plato, speaking in the name of Socrates, associates the acquisition of true and enduring knowledge in the Greek context with the dialectic of oral question and answer (*Phaedrus* 276), he is assuming a praxis which is not confined to Greece but which may be regarded as inherent in oral learning in general. The question and answer formula that turns up so frequently in written Irish literature may thus be a remnant of the system of learning and instruction which was current in the native schools before the adoption of writing, and it does not seem unreasonable to envisage the question and answer mode of introducing narratives as a continuity from that earlier environment. This is not a direct answer to the question posed at the beginning of this paragraph; on the other hand this may be one of those instances where to ask a question is at least as important as to answer it.

REFERENCES

Bergin, Osborn, and R. I. Best, eds. 1938. *Tochmarc Étaíne. Ériu* 12:137–96.

Bruford, Alan. 1969. *Gaelic Folk-tales and Medieval Romances*. Dublin.

de h-Íde, Dubhglas. 1933. *An Sgeuluidhe Gaedhealach*. Dublin.

Dillon, Myles. 1953. *Serglige Con Culainn*. Dublin.

Henderson, George, ed. 1899. *Fled Bricrenn: The Feast of Bricriu*. London.

Knott, Eleanor, ed. 1936. *Togail Bruidne Da Derga*. Dublin.

Mac Cana, Proinsias. 1973. On Celtic Word-order and the Welsh 'Abnormal' Sentence. *Ériu* 24:90–120.

———. 1987. *Fianaigheacht* in the Pre-Norman Period. In *The Heroic Process: Form, Function and Fantasy in Folk Epic*, Bo Almqvist, Séamus Ó Catháin, and Pádraig Ó hÉalaí, eds., 75–99. Dún Laoghairi, Co. Dublin.

———. 1991. Further Notes on Constituent Order in Welsh. In *Studies in Brythonic Word Order*, James Fife and Erich Poppe, eds., 45–80. Amsterdam/Philadelphia.

McCone, Kim R. 1986. Werewolves, Cyclopes, *Díberga*, and *Fíanna*: Juvenile Delinquency in Early Ireland. *Cambridge Medieval Celtic Studies* 12:1–22.

Mac Giollarnáth, Seán. 1939. *Peadar Chois Fhairrge*. Dublin.

McNamara, Martin. 1972. A plea for Hiberno-Latin Biblical studies. *The Irish Theological Quarterly* 39:337–53.

Maguidhir, An tAth. Seosamh. 1973. *Maith thú, a Mhicí* (eagrán leasaithe). Muineachán/Dún Geanainn.

Ó Duilearga, Séamus, 1948. *Leabhar Sheáin Í Chonaill*. Dublin.

Ó Duilearga, Séamus, and Máire MacNeill. 1981. *Seán Ó Conaill's Book*. Dublin.

Ó hAodha, Donnchadh, ed. 1978. *Bethu Brigte*. Dublin.

O'Rahilly, Cecile, ed. 1976. *Táin Bó Cuailnge: Recension I*. Dublin.

Seabhac, An [Pádraig Ó Siochfhradha]. 1932. *An Seanchaidhe Muimhneach*. Dublin.

Stokes, Whitley, ed. 1900. *Acallam na Senórach*. In *Irische Texte* IV.i, W. Stokes and E. Windisch, eds. Leipzig. (Numbers in present article refer to lines. I leave my quotations as in this edition, except, for convenience, to print his italicized expansions in roman.)

Thurneysen, Rudolf. 1921. *Die irische Helden- und Königsage*. Halle (Saale).

THE HAGIOGRAPHIC POETICS OF *CANU CADFAN*

Catherine McKenna

CITY UNIVERSITY OF NEW YORK GRADUATE SCHOOL
MEDIEVAL STUDIES PROGRAM

For some time now, Welsh scholarship has generally assigned the three *Gogynfeirdd* poems in honor of saints — Cynddelw's *Canu Tysilio Sant*, Llywelyn Fardd's *Canu Cadfan*, and Gwynfardd Brycheiniog's *Canu i Ddewi*[1] — to the genre of bardic eulogy or courtly panegyric. In his 1948 Rhŷs Lecture on "The Court Poets of the Welsh Princes", for example, John Lloyd-Jones claimed that *Canu Tysilio* and *Canu Cadfan* "are primarily eulogies on Meifod, the holy sanctuary of the realm of Powys, and St. Cadfan's foundation at Tywyn, Meirionydd".[2] J. E. Caerwyn Williams presented essentially the same view in his 1970 survey of *Gogynfeirdd* poetry, according to which

Nid yw'r awdl i Dysilio nemor amgen na mawl i Meifod, 'gwydua brenhined' (Madog ap Maredudd a fu f. 1160 a Gruffydd Maelor a fu f. 1191) a

---

1   *Canu Tysilio Sant* of Cynddelw is preserved in MS. NLW 6680 B (the Hendre-gadredd manuscript), f. 32r-v and in Jesus College MS. III (the *Red Book of Hergest*), cols. 1165-69. It has been edited, with a Modern Welsh paraphrase, in Nerys Ann Jones and Ann Parry Owen, eds., *Gwaith Cynddelw Brydydd Mawr I*, Cyfres Beirdd y Tywysogion III (Caerdydd: Gwasg Prifysgol Cymru, 1991), pp. 15-50. The *Canu i Ddewi* of Gwynfardd Brycheiniog is also preserved in NLW MS. 6680 B, ff. 79r-82v, and in Jesus College MS. III, cols. 1186-92. It has been edited, with a Modern Welsh paraphrase, by Morfydd E. Owen, in *Gwaith Llywelyn Fardd I ac Eraill o Feirdd y Ddeuddegfed Ganrif*, Cyfres Beirdd y Tywysogion II (Caerddyd: Gwasg Prifysgol Cymru, 1994), pp. 435-92. *Canu Cadfan* of Llywelyn Fardd, preserved in NLW MS. 6680 B, ff. 19r-21r, is edited, with a Modern Welsh paraphrase, by Catherine McKenna, in *Gwaith Llywelyn Fardd I ac Eraill o Feirdd y Ddeuddegfed Ganrif*, Cyfres Beirdd y Tywysogion II (Caerddyd: Gwasg Prifysgol Cymru, 1994), pp. 3-32. This essay had its origins in a paper read to the Eighth International Congress of Celtic Studies in Swansea.

2   John Lloyd-Jones, "The Court Poets of the Welsh Princes", Sir John Rhŷs Memorial Lecture for 1948, *Proceedings of the British Academy* 34 (1948), pp. 167-97, and separately (London, 1948), at pp. 16-17 of the latter publication.

'brenhinawl loc' Powys. . . . Mae'r 'Canu i Gadfan' yn debyg i'r 'Canu i Dysilio' oblegid fel yr oedd yr olaf yn folawd i Meifod, y mae'r cyntaf yn folawd i eglwys Tywyn.[3]

The *awdl* to Tysilio is hardly more than praise of Meifod, 'tomb of kings' (Madog ap Maredudd who died in 1160 and Gruffydd Maelor who died in 1191) and 'the royal fold' of Powys. . . . The *Canu i Gadfan* is like the *Canu i Dysilio*, since as the latter was a eulogy of Meifod, the former is a eulogy of the church of Tywyn.

His views were echoed by D. Myrddin Lloyd, who wrote in 1977 of *Canu Cadfan* that it is

a long poem nominally in praise of St. Cadfan but in fact to the church of Tywyn, Merioneth, and its *clas* of resident clergy whose hospitality the poet had enjoyed. It is a eulogy of civilized life as seen at Tywyn under the abbot Morfran.[4]

And the most recent editors of *Canu Tyssilyaw* call praise of place "the key to *Gogynfeirdd* poetry to the saints and one of the principal purposes of this poem":[5]

[Y]n ogystal â chanmol ei dysg a'i hamddiffyn, molir Meifod am ei chroeso a'i lletygarwch i feirdd, ac yn arbennig i Gynddelw ei hun. . . . Y mae'r pwyslais cryf ar y Feifod gyfoes yn awgrymu mai cerdd i'r fynachlog ydyw hi'n bennaf ac mai Abad y fynachlog fyddai'r noddwr mwyaf tebygol iddi.[6]

In addition to the praise of its learning and its protection, Meifod is praised for its welcome and its hospitality to poets, and especially to Cynddelw himself. . . .

These observations are perfectly valid as far as they go, but in their strong emphasis on the praise of place and their preoccupation with questions of bardic patronage, they implicitly dissociate the saint poems from the hagiographical traditions represented in prose lives of the saints.[7] Recent years have seen considerable interest in hagiography among scholars in various disciplines, interest that has generated new ways of thinking about saints' traditions, and it seems to me appropriate

3　J. E. Caerwyn Williams, "Beirdd y Tywysogion: Arolwg", *Llên Cymru* 11 (1970), 3–94, at pp. 89–90.
4　D. Myrddin Lloyd, "The Poets of the Princes", in A. O. H. Jarman and Gwilym Rees Hughes, eds., *A Guide to Welsh Literature*, vol. 1 (Swansea, 1977), 157–88, at p. 180.
5　"*Wrth droi at yr elfen gyfoes o foli sefydliad(au) a gysylltir ag enw'r sant, credir ein bod yn dod at allwedd canu'r Gogynfeirdd i'r saint ac un o brif ddibenion y gerdd hon*", Jones and Owen, op. cit., p. 16.
6　Jones and Owen, op. cit., n.1, pp. 16–17.
7　Morfydd Owen's edition of Gwynfardd Brycheiniog's *Canu i Ddewi*, however, discusses common elements in the poem and the Latin life of Dewi. Op. cit., n.1, pp. 435–36.

to re-examine the saints' poems of the *beirdd y tywysogion* in the light of
such new ideas. This kind of open re-reading, I think, is a particularly
appropriate way to commemorate Brendan O Hehir, who asked stark
questions like "What is the *Gododdin*?"[8] We need to re-evaluate our
scholarly assumptions from time to time, and even when we do not as a
result alter our judgments significantly, we may develop new and useful
perspectives, or at least begin to ask new and potentially productive
questions. This essay will confine itself to consideration of just one of the
three "saint poems" in the *Gogynfeirdd* corpus, *Canu Cadfan* attributed
to Llywelyn Fardd, in the hope that re-examination of that text will open
a discussion of the relationship of all three to the rich and varied tradition
of medieval hagiography.

Canu Cadfan is preserved in the Hendregadredd manuscript (NLW
6680B), where it is attributed to Llywelyn Fardd.[9] There were, apparently, two poets known as Llywelyn Fardd, one of whom flourished in
the latter half of the twelfth century, the other *ca.* 1215–80. The poem to
St. Cadfan may be confidently attributed to the first Llywelyn Fardd on
the basis of its reference, in line 60, to Abbot Morfran of Tywyn, who
was alive in 1147.[10]

Previous scholarship has focused on the ways in which the poem
belongs to the tradition of bardic eulogy in Wales, a tradition that goes
back to the sixth-century bards Aneirin and Taliesin.[11] There can be no
doubt that *Canu Cadfan* participates fully in that tradition as it was practiced by the twelfth- and thirteenth-century Welsh court poets known as
Gogynfeirdd or *beirdd y tywysogion* 'poets of the princes'. This is evident
in its opening invocation of God, in its self-consciousness about itself as
an act of celebration, in its gratitude for past blessings and its prayers for
continued well-being within the precincts of Cadfan's foundation at
Tywyn, and in its use of traditional *awdl* measures ornamented with
internal rhyme and alliteration. Emphasis on the poem's traditional
structure has led scholars to attempt to identify for it a patron, that is, an

8   Brendan O Hehir, "What is the *Gododdin*?" in Brynley F. Roberts, ed., *Early
    Welsh Poetry: Studies in the Book of Aneirin* (Aberystwyth: National Library of
    Wales, 1988), pp. 57–95.

9   John Morris-Jones and T. H. Parry-Williams, *Llawysgrif Hendregadredd* (Caer-
    dydd, 1933), pp. 42–48. The text appears in folios 19r–21r, written in the hand
    that has been labelled "llaw α" *ca.* 1300. See Daniel Huws, "Llawysgrif Hendre-
    gadredd", *National Library of Wales Journal* 22 (1981–82), pp. 1–26.

10 According to the Red Book of Hergest version of the *Brut y Tywysogion*, Abbot
    Morfran served as steward of the Castle of Cynfael, holding that stronghold for
    Cadwaladr ap Gruffudd ap Cynan against his nephews, Hywel ab Owain Gwynedd
    and Cynan ab Owain Gwynedd. See Thomas Jones, ed., *Brut y Tywysogion* (Red
    Book of Hergest version) (Cardiff, 1940), *s.a.* 1147; see also J.E. Lloyd, *A
    History of Wales* (3rd ed.; London, 1939), pp. 206, 490.

11 In addition to the works cited above, see Catrin S. B. Davies, "Cerddi'r Tai
    Crefydd", M.A. Thesis, University College of Wales, Bangor (1972).

object of its praise and a potentially responsive audience for its artistry. The great bulk of *Gogynfeirdd* poetry, after all, consists of songs in honor of living or recently deceased princes, composed in the self-evident anticipation of direct and fairly immediate reward; it is a literature driven by patronage, and the question of how a particular poem functioned in the cultural milieu that produced it quite rightly leads to the questions "for whom was it made? By whom did the poet expect to be rewarded?" In this case it is very probable that the correct answer to these questions is indeed Abbot Morfran and the *clas* of Tywyn, the patrons that have generally been associated with *Canu Cadfan*. It is even possible, perhaps likely, that a poem in honor of Cadfan was actually commissioned by Morfran, as a means of magnifying the fame of his monastery, its political and cultic significance.

This does not mean, however, that the poem can be defined as a eulogy of Abbot Morfran, nor that it is simply a praise of place aimed at pleasing those in whose power it lay to extend the hospitality of that place. Rather, the probable involvement of Morfran and his community in its genesis encourages a reading of the poem that is sensitive to the ways in which it fosters the cult of Cadfan, since the development of that cult may be assumed to have been one of Morfran's principal interests, both devotional and practical.

Writing of the practice of hagiography in the later Middle Ages and the Counter Reformation in their important book *Saints and Society*, Donald Weinstein and Rudolph Bell state that

> The hagiographer's main contribution was to shape . . . received material according to the current, partly implicit, pressures of the saint-making process, including the tastes of his bishop, the interests of his house or order, political interests, and, not least, the expectations of local devotees, both clerical and lay. In short, as Delehaye pointed out, the hagiographer was not a biographer, at least in the modern sense. He was an agent of a mythmaking mechanism that served a variety of publics, and he took his cues where he found them, often from very modest, nonclerical sources.[12]

Even though Weinstein and Bell are primarily concerned with the kind of text that we would define as a *vita* proper, this observation is pertinent to our understanding of *Canu Cadfan*. As far as we know, Llywelyn Fardd was working with a rather amorphous body of "received material" in composing his *awdl*; as Elissa Henken's studies of Welsh hagiographic traditions have shown, this poem is itself the earliest and principal textual

---

12 Donald Weinstein and Rudolph M. Bell, *Saints and Society: The Two Worlds of Western Christendom, 1000–1700* (Chicago and London, 1982), p. 13.

source that we have for traditions connected with Cadfan.[13] And the suggestion that the hagiographer had to satisfy "the expectations of local devotees" prompts us to remember that in twelfth-century Wales, where the prose *vita* was a new form, the panegyric *awdl* was traditional, familiar, expected. It should not be surprising to discover that it was the form into which material pertaining to Cadfan was cast when the abbot of his monastery and a poet fiercely loyal to the regional interests of Meirionydd, where Tywyn is located, sought both to celebrate the saint and to extend the influence of his foundation. To a considerable extent, *Canu Cadfan* really is a poem about the saint, which is what it quite explicitly claims to be in line 8, where Llywelyn Fardd announces his intention *y uoli Kaduan, kedwyr noted* 'to praise Cadfan, the refuge of warriors'. Although its overt organization is that of conventional bardic eulogy, there are in the poem implicit structures that share with many medieval *vitae* the twin functions of spiritual edification and assertion of ecclesiastical privilege.

To understand fully this hagiographical, as opposed to the celebratory, dimension of *Canu Cadfan*, two considerations must be borne in mind. One is that the importance of the "saint" in the medieval Church had to do less with his suitability as a model to be imitated than with his power to protect his devotees and to intercede for them with God. This preoccupation with power in saints' cults is evident in a range of practices including miracle stories, use of relics, and invocation of the saints. A corollary of this fact is that the saint's cult did not only commemorate its object as someone who had lived a holy and supernaturally powerful life *in the past*, but also, as the practice of invocation and, in some cases, testimony to ongoing miracles, demonstrates, as a still powerful *living presence* in the life of the devotee. This being the case, there is no reason why a celebration of the saint himself should confine itself to rehearsal of details from his life on earth; the works that he undertook from his honored position in heaven, his present intervention in the lives of his adherents, would be of equal or greater relevance to them. If the fact that the *vita* itself was a form that typically encompassed only the temporal biography obscures the importance to saints' cults of the activity of their ongoing spiritual lives, it should be remembered that the *vita* proper was only one of a variety of hagiographic forms, others of which, such as the *miracula* and the *translatio*, did indeed concern themselves with events that followed the physical death of the saint.

The second of the two considerations relevant to a hagiographical reading of *Canu Cadfan* is that while a saint's *vita* is a narrative form, and as such essentially linear in its chronology, the bardic *molawd*, or

---

13 Elissa R. Henken, *Traditions of the Welsh Saints* (Cambridge, 1987), esp. pp. 174–77, and idem, *The Welsh Saints: A Study in Patterned Lives* (Cambridge, 1991).

praise poem, is neither narrative nor linear. While it alludes to specific achievements of its patron's career, it does so briefly, with no particular regard for chronology, and intersperses these biographical references with celebratory epithets, metaphors, and comparisons to prominent figures of the Welsh tradition, as well as with assertions about the value of praise poetry and requests for reward.

The *Arwyrain Owain Gwynedd*,[14] a poem in praise of Owain Gwynedd attributed to the same Llywelyn Fardd who is said to have composed *Canu Cadfan*, will serve as an example of the structure of secular eulogy. Its ten opening lines praise Owain with such locutions as *ardemyl gwir* 'temple of truth' and *eryr gwŷr* 'eagle of heroes', and with a comparison to a legendary magnanimous king, Mordaf. In the same passage, the poet makes reference to the act of praise in which he is engaged and its worthiness. In the next forty lines or so we find oblique allusions to the history of the poet's relationship with the prince — Llywelyn Fardd has some grounds for reproaching Owain, to whom he has returned after spending time in Powys in the service of the recently deceased Madog ap Maredudd. Only in the final twenty-six lines is there any mention of particular places over which Owain has dominion — the rivers Taf and Tren, Eryri, and Porthwygyr in Anglesey — and of a battle to which the poet was witness,

> Pan uu gyfaruot y modrydaf
> A llwoed Lloegrwys, pwys diffwyssaf. (lines 65–66)

> When there was a meeting between the chief
> and the hosts of England, mass most grim.

These are no more than passing references, however, scattered among further eulogistic metaphors and reminders of the rewards due to poetry. Not even meaningful fragments of a biography of Owain Gwynedd could be extracted from the *Arwyrain Owain*.

Bearing in mind the typical structure of the medieval Welsh *molawd*, along with the saint's role as a mediator, both before and after death, of divine power to his devotees, it is possible to read *Canu Cadfan* and its celebration of the foundation at Tywyn in new light, to see the poem as fully participatory in the purposes and techniques that shaped other forms of hagiography in the Middle Ages.

14 NLW MS 6680B (MS Hendregadredd) folios 88r–v, written in hands N and E, *ca.* 1300–25; edited, with a Modern Welsh paraphrase, by Catherine McKenna, in *Gwaith Llywelyn Fardd I ac Eraill o Feirdd y Ddeuddegfed Ganrif,* Cyfres Beirdd y Tywysogion II (Caerdydd: Gwasg Prifysgol Cymru, 1994), pp. 33–44.

Tywyn, in *Canu Cadfan*, is far more than a place of material hospitality, although it is certainly that, especially near the end of the poem.[15] At the outset, what is most important about Tywyn is that it is an enduring manifestation of God's favor to Cadfan, favor apparent in the power that the saint was able to exercise and that has remained immanent in his foundation.

That Cadfan had special powers derived from God is quite explicit in lines 109–110, where there is a reference to one of his miracles:

> Ef goreu gwyrtheu wrth y gennad,
> Dillwg tan yman y mywn dillad.

> He performed miracles with [God's] permission
> by unleashing fire here in clothing.

It is equally clear that by virtue of his God-given supernatural powers Cadfan was able to maintain the honor and integrity of the territory at Tywyn that God himself had granted him:

> Llunywys y Dews dewis edryd — itaw
> Pan doeth o Lydaw ar lydu bedyt. (lines 37–38)

---

15 Especially in lines 150–162:

> Ac nyd oes eissyoes eisseu yndi,
> Namyn heirt a beirt a bartoni,
> Namyn het a met y mewn llestri,
> Namyn hawt amrawt yn ymroti — a bart
> A gwyr hart heb gart, heb galedi,
> Ac eurgrawn a dawn a daeoni,
> Ac eurgreir kyweir kywiw a hi,
> Ac angert a chert a cheinyedi—llawen,
> Ac amgen yw yn llenn na Llanddewi,
> Ac am gylch y chlawt y chlas gofri,
> Ac amgyrn o dyrn, adurn westi,
> Ac amgant lliant yn llenwi—aber,
> Ac amser gosber gosbarth weini.

> And neither is there want therein,
> but beautiful things and poets and poetry,
> but peace, and mead in vessels,
> but easy discourse, exchange with a poet,
> and fine men without shame, without hardness,
> and a store of gold and talent and goodness,
> and a properly arrayed relic as excellent as itself,
> and craft and song and cheerful singing,
> and our hangings are superior to Llanddewi's,
> and around its dike its honorable community,
> and drinking horns in fists, adornment of the lodge,
> and the circle of the tide filling the river-mouth,
> and at vespers the order of service.

The Godhead shaped a choice residence for him
when he came from Brittany to the community of Christendom.

Because of God's favor toward him and his foundation, Cadfan received
the strength he needed to maintain possession of Tywyn and its revenues:

Kedwis gwir y dir a'e deyrnged,
Kedwis gwr arwr arwymp drefred. (lines 9–10)

He upheld the claim to his land and its tribute,
the heroic warrior maintained the fair dwelling.

Moreover, he continues to exercise that power to protect his foundation:
kadyr y keidw Kaduan glann glas weilgi 'powerfully Cadfan protects the
bank of the blue sea' (line 123), the poet asserts. It is undoubtedly
because of the continuing influence of Cadfan that Tywyn is a place
whose

[G]wyrtheu goleu gwelhator beunyt, (line 83)

[M]anifest miracles are seen daily,

and one

Myn na lleueis treis trasglwy uyned
Myn na lleueis dyn dwyn eishywed — o'r llann
Ger glann glas dylann, o'e dylyed,
Men na leuessir dir o'e daered. (lines 18–21)

Where violent plots dare not go,
where no one dares take any necessity from the church
near the bank of the blue sea, because of its due,
where no one dares constrain its revenues.

Llywelyn Fardd says further of the security of St. Cadfan's that,

Ny chollir o'e thir nac o'e thewdor — annhet
Troeduet yr dyhet, dihawt hepcor. (lines 71–72)

There is not lost a foot of its land nor of the dwelling-place
        of its strength,
because of war, difficult to avoid.

The security of Tywyn appears to be insured by the martial prowess of
the abbot Morfran. For the poet, however, a willingness to defend
Tywyn and its rights by force when necessary is part of a tradition that
stretches back to its foundation, when such use of force was justified by

God, the ultimate source of strength both for Cadfan the founder and for Morfran, his heir.

The same sort of approach to the issue of an ecclesiastical foundation's territorial rights is common in the *vitae* of saints. In the *vitae* of Dewi, for example, St. David gains possession of Vallis Rosina or Glyn Rhosyn, where he would establish his principal monastery, later known as St. David's, as the result of a decisive confrontation with the Irishman Boia. Boia is undone by miracles that manifest God's alliance with David and, by implication, his heirs. He sets out with his retinue to attack David and his companions, but they are all seized with fever *en route*, and are unable to deliver anything more than *spurcissimis opprobriorum blasphemiis* 'the filthiest and most blasphemous taunts'. When he returns home, he discovers that all of his cattle have died suddenly. Only when he cedes to David *in sempiternam* the land upon which he and his companions have settled are the cattle restored to him. And when he and his wife later provoke the monks by sending maidens to comport themselves lewdly in their sight, Boia is decapitated by an enemy and his fortress destroyed by heavenly fire.[16] The story of David and Boia is more than an episode in David's life, and more than an account of how St. David's was founded. It is a warrant for the security of the place in perpetuity, a warning to any who might think to threaten that security and an assurance to all who inhabit it: God's power protects this place, it tells us, and as that power was made manifest to Boia through David, it can be made manifest through his heirs, to whom the place was granted *in sempiternam*. Divine ordination of the site of an ecclesiastical foundation, then, and the protection afforded by that divine interest, are themes by no means characteristic of a eulogy of place only, but belong to the saint's *vita* as well.

If a preoccupation with power, manifest in miracles, to protect the integrity of a religious foundation is one concern that *Canu Cadfan* shares with prose *vitae* and other more conventional forms of medieval hagiography, its interest in relics is another. Aron Gurevich opens an essay on the medieval cult of the saints with several citations of cases in which rival groups not only argued, but actually fought over the mortal remains of a saint — his relics.[17] Insular hagiography preserves a similar story

---

16 J. W. James, ed. and trans., *Rhigyfarch's Life of St. David* (Cardiff: University of Wales Press, 1967), pp. 9-12; D. Simon Evans, ed., *Buched Dewi* (Caerdydd: Gwasg Prifysgol Cymru, 1965), pp. 6-9.

17 Aron Gurevich, "Peasants and Saints" in *Medieval Popular Culture: Problems of Belief and Perception*, János M. Bak and Paul A. Hollingsworth, trans. (Cambridge: Cambridge University Press, 1988), pp. 39-77, at pp. 39-41. He describes the argument between the people of Poitiers and those of Tours over the relics of St. Martin, as recounted by Gregory of Tours in the *Historia Francorum*, and another conflict described by Gregory in his *Vitae Patrum* over the relics of St. Lupicinus.

about the body of Patrick, contended for by the Uí Néill and the Ulaid.[18] A saint's mortal remains were his principal relics, but other objects associated with him were venerated as well. These relics were regarded as the sign and the source of the continued presence of the special favor and powers granted to a saint. It was one of the functions of narrative hagiography to explain the origins of objects venerated at a given cultic site, or to describe miracles in which they had been involved.

Llywelyn Fardd offers no such history in his *Canu Cadfan*, but he celebrates the relics of Tywyn, and does so in order to document the continuing immanence of the divine power granted to Cadfan. St. Cadfan's church is one *y chreiryeu bangleu bann glyhwitor* 'whose renowned relics are bruited about' (line 81). He speaks specifically of a miraculous crozier,

> [Y] fagl ferth werthfawr wyrthau newydd,
> A ludd i'r gelyn ladd ei gilydd. (lines 51–52)

> The fair precious crozier of new miracles,
> which prevents an enemy from killing his opponent.

A crozier called *Cirguen* or *Cyrwen* figures in the *vita* of St. Padarn, written towards the end of the first quarter of the twelfth century. Like that of his cousin, Cadfan, Padarn's crozier is associated with bringing peace where there is discord, and is regarded as having protective powers.[19] The incidence of a shared motif like this, well-documented as a feature of the *vitae*, is in itself an eloquent statement of the common nature and purpose of the prose *vita* and the hagiographic poem. Even more intriguing, perhaps, is the existence of a quatrain in Old Welsh praising Padarn's staff, written in a margin of Corpus Christi College Cambridge MS. 199, at some time in the last quarter of the eleventh century, by Ieuan ap Sulien.[20] Whether or not it served as a source for the *vita*, this quatrain certainly indicates that hagiographic material existed in different forms at Llanbadarn, where Ieuan ap Sulien resided and where the *vita* of Padarn was compiled.

Besides Cadfan's crozier, whose preservation at Tywyn is at least suggested by the poem, Tywyn is home to three distinctive and perhaps miraculous altars, one of which may be the repository of Cadfan's remains:

---

18 Kathleen Mulchrone, ed. *Bethu Phátraic: The Tripartite Life of Patrick*, vol. 1: Text and Sources (Dublin: Royal Irish Academy, 1939), pp. 150–51.

19 See Henken (1987), op. cit. n.13, pp. 121–22.

20 See Ifor Williams, *The Beginnings of Welsh Poetry*, ed. Rachel Bromwich, 2nd ed. (Cardiff, 1980), pp. 181–89.

Allawr Ueir o'r Peir, hygreir hygred;
Allawr Bedyr y'w uedyr yd yr uolhed;
A'r drydet allawr a anlloued — o nef:
Gwynn y uyd y thref gan y thrwyted. (lines 25–28)

Mary's altar from the Lord, trustworthy and sacred relic;
the altar of Peter in his authority which should be praised;
and the third altar which was bestowed by heaven:
its dwelling place is blessed because of its hospitality.

And finally, there is a suggestion that there is a treasured gospel book at Tywyn, *uchel euegyl uwyl ouyt* 'the noble gospel of the gentle lord' (line 50), although the reference may be to the preaching of the gospel rather than to a specific object.

Power, manifest in miracles and intrinsic to sacred objects, is an overriding concern of *Canu Cadfan* as of prose *vitae*, despite its non-narrative structure. So too is pedigree. The poem participates simultaneously in panegyric and hagiographic traditions in its use of the idea of lineage, or *ach*. Descent is always important in bardic eulogy, of course, because it is the source of the patron's essential nobility. Thus, for example, Gwalchmai ap Meilyr opens each of a series of *awdlau* to Owain Gwynedd with the citation of a different ancestor — Gruffudd, Iago, Rhodri, Aeneas, and so on.[21] Some of these are historical, others legendary. It is common for the *vitae* of saints, too, to begin with a pedigree, one which serves to establish spiritual and sometimes temporal nobility as well. The opening lines of the *Buchedd Dewi*, for example, trace St. David's ancestry back to Euddoleu, son of the Virgin Mary's sister.[22] The corpus of Welsh genealogies includes similar lineages, with no narrative context or embellishment, for nearly one hundred saints.[23] The genealogical tracts complement the information about lineage in the prose *vitae*, just as they do the information in bardic praise poetry.

In *Canu Cadfan*, the saint's fleshly ancestry goes back no further than his parents, Eneas and Gwen, mentioned in lines 12–13.[24] There is not much more in the twelfth-century *Bonedd y Saint*, which offers *Catuan sant yn Enlli m. Eneas ledewic o Lydaw, a Gwenn teirbron merch Emyr*

---

21 J. E. Caerwyn Williams, ed., *Gwaith Meilyr Brydydd a'i Disgynyddion*, Cyfres Beirdd y Tywysogion I (Caerdydd, 1994), pp. 172–91.

22 "Dauyd uab Sant, vab Keredic, vab Kuneda, vab Edyrn, vab Padarn Beisrud, vab Deil, vab Gordeil, vab Dwvyn, vab Gordwvyn, vab Amguoel, vab Amweryt, vab Omit, vab Perim, vab Dubim, vab Ongen, vab Auallach, vab Eugen, vab Eudoleu, vab chwaer Veir Wyry, vam Iessu Grist." Evans, *Buched Dewi*, p. 1. For a collection of Welsh saints' pedigrees from Latin and Welsh lives, see P. C. Bartrum, ed., *Early Welsh Genealogical Tracts* (Cardiff, 1966), pp. 22–31.

23 See *Bonedd y Saint* and *Achau'r Saint* in Bartrum, pp. 51–71.

24   . . . uab Eneas, eurwas uyged.
         Kedwir nenn, uab Gwenn, a uad weled.

Llydaw y vam.[25] The poem seems to make use of nearly all the genealogical data that were available for Cadfan.

The sense of a much more significant line of descent informs the poem, however. Cadfan is represented as one of a series of praiseworthy figures all of whom belong, in a spiritual sense, to the same lineage. That pedigree includes, reading upward: Morfran, abbot of St. Cadfan's church at Tywyn when Llywelyn Fardd composed his poem in the mid-twelfth century; Lleuddad, a saint associated with Ynys Enlli and also one of Cadfan's companions and successors; Cadfan himself; and the primordial progenitor, occupying the position that might be held by Coel Hen or Cunedda Wledig in a secular genealogy, God.

Morfran is exactly what a lord ought to be, from a bard's point of view. He is, first of all, an effective defender of his territory, capable of planning battles when God requires that he do so: *rydylyf kynnyf kan uot Douyt* 'he arranges battle with the Lord's consent' (line 59). He is also the *abad rhoddiad* 'abbot-giver' (line 57) and *rhodd gynan Forfran* 'Morfran flowing with gifts' (line 60), so that he has the generosity required of a praiseworthy lord as well.

Morfran shares these noble qualities with Cadfan, the founder of the church and *clas* at Tywyn — Morfran's predecessor and spiritual ancestor. Cadfan too was a warrior, the *kedwyr noted* 'refuge of warriors' (line 8), *gwr arwr* 'warrior hero' (line 10), and *kadwent nerthnawd* 'the mighty one of the battlefield' (line 14). And Cadfan too was a benevolent ruler who provided for the well-being of his people: *ef a warawd ball a gwall a gwad* 'he drove off plague and want and denial' (line 111).

Lleuddad, whose sixteenth-century *vita* makes him Cadfan's successor not at Tywyn, but at the island monastery of Ynys Enlli,[26] is a fleshly cousin and spiritual twin to Cadfan in the poem. In a series of eight linked lines they are identified in miraculous power, protection of the church, and generosity.[27] Despite the poem's focus on Tywyn, in

---

25 "Saint Cadfan in Enlli, son of Eneas the Breton of Brittany, and Gwen Three-paps daughter of Emyr of Brittany his mother." Bartrum, p. 59.

26 For traditions concerning Lleuddad, see Henken (1987), pp. 168–73.

27   Deu wr a uolaf ual y'm kennyad—Douyt,
           Deu dec, deu dedwyt, deu ryt rotyad,
           Deu doeth y ghyuoeth, y ghyuaenad,
           Deu gu, deu gyueith, deu wynneithad,
      Deu a wna gwyrtheu yr goleuad—racdut,
           Deu dilut eu but yr bot eirchad,
           Deu gefynderw oetynt ny uerwynt urad:
           Kaduan y gadw llann, ef a Lleudad   (lines 115–22)

      Two men I praise, as the Lord permits me,
           two fair ones, two blessed ones, two liberal givers,
           two wise in dominion, in harmony,
           two dear ones, two compatriots, two holy ones,

Meirionydd, Llywelyn Fardd invokes the holy island of Enlli as well;[28] it
is, as it were, another of Cadfan's territories, the naming of which
amplifies his glory as the naming of lands and waters under the sway of
Owain Gwynedd amplified *his* magnificence in the *Arwyrain Owain
Gwynedd* mentioned earlier in this essay. Lleuddad seems to share with
Cadfan the patronage of all of his foundations; in hagiographical terms he
is, like Morfran, an incarnation of the powers and virtues manifested in
Cadfan, and in panegyric terms he is another kinsman whose merits
redound to Cadfan's glory.

At the head of this lineage stands God, like the others a protector
(*diffynnyad*, line 95) who "gives continual gifts" (*ryt rot gygwasdad*, line
96). His patriarchal role in the spiritual pedigree that is constructed by
attribution of the same virtues to each of its four members is accentuated
when Cadfan is said to have "taken heaven in exchange for his [earthly]
patrimony" (*Ef a gymerth nef dros dref y dad*, line 114).

In praise poetry, noble ancestry serves to magnify the prince to whom
it is addressed: the present historical moment is the real focus of attention. In hagiography, the focus is simultaneously on a moment in the
past — the saint's lifetime —and on an eternal present in which God
reveals himself in his saints and in the ongoing sanctity and power of
their foundations. Insofar as it is panegyric, then, it may be fair to say of
Canu Cadfan that it is in one sense "about" Morfran more than it is
"about" Cadfan; but that is only because, conventionally, a bardic eulogy
is "about" the person to whom it is addressed, and the person to whom it
is addressed, conventionally, is a person living and present at the poem's
performance. In fact, however, there is more of Cadfan in the poem than
there is of Morfran, in terms of both biographical detail[29] and reference
to ongoing maintenance and protection of Tywyn.[30] Insofar as it is hagiographical, *Canu Cadfan* is "about" Cadfan and the perpetual self-revela-

---

       two who perform miracles in order to shed forth light,
         two unstinting of their favor for the
         contentment of the suppliant,
         two cousins they were who plotted no treachery:
         Cadfan to protect the church with Lleuddad.

28   Arwyn y drwyted kyn no'e dreghi — ydoet
      Yn cadw rac kyhoet anlloet Enlli.
      Un llogawd yssyt herwyt heli,
      Lleudad a Chaduann yn y chedwi.   (lines 137–40)

      Splendid was his support before he died
      guarding the treasure of Enlli from the people.
      There is a monastery by the sea,
      with Lleuddad and Cadfan guarding it.

29 See especially lines 9–12, 37–40, 43–46, 107–114, 137–38.
30 See especially lines 13–14, 123–24, 139–40, 175–78. Cf. lines 53–66, 75–79,
    which focus on Morfran.

tion of God, and also about the claims that the *clas* of Tywyn may fairly make, because of the age and sanctity of the foundation, to pre-eminence among the churches of North Wales. The conjunction of the structures of praise poetry with the purposes of hagiography here is, in fact, a felicitous one. The characteristically bardic, non-linear, juxtaposition of themes enables the collapse into a single timeless plane of the past moment of Cadfan's life, the present moment of Morfran's abbacy and the poet's act of praise, and the eternal moment of God's favor to Cadfan and his foundations.

To this point, I have examined the hagiographical character of *Canu Cadfan* with the understanding that hagiographical writing is any writing that serves to foster the cult of a particular saint, often at a particular site. There was often, in medieval Wales, a political dimension to this promotion of a saint's cult — the need to assert the legal and pecuniary rights of a given church in the face of challenges from secular authorities and other ecclesiastical foundations, especially, in the twelfth century, new Norman foundations. Concern with the rights and status of particular churches shaped twelfth-century Welsh saints' lives to a considerable extent,[31] and informs *Canu Cadfan* as well.

Concern with the rights of St. Cadfan's church is apparent in the assertion, cited earlier, that Cadfan *kedwis gwir y dir a'e deyrnged* 'upheld the claim to his land and its tribute' (line 9), and that under the direction of Morfran, his successor, there is *achadw croc a ched a choydyt a chor, a mor ac aruor a goruynt* 'safeguarding of the crucifix and the tribute and the woods and the chancel, and the sea and the coast and the highlands' (lines 65–66). Morfran is *aessawr hael orwawr arhawl oruyt* 'a generous, magnificent shield prevailing over counter-claims' (line 56). The joint protection of Cadfan and Morfran insures that *na lleuessir dir o'e daered* 'no one dares constrain its revenues' (line 21), and that *ny chollir o'e thir nac o'e thewdor annhet troeduet* 'there is not lost a foot of its land nor of the dwelling-place of its strength' (lines 71–72).

Throughout the poem, too, as has already been observed, there is an emphasis on the security of Tywyn, *myn na lleueis treis trasglwy uyned* 'where violent plots dare not go' (line 18), and *ny lleueis neb treis tros y ysgor, ny chymwyll nep twyll tyllu y dor* 'no one dares bear violence over its ramparts, no one contemplates the treachery of piercing its gates' (lines 73–74). The martial prowess of the warrior-abbot Morfran, and of

---

31 See R. R. Davies, *Conquest, Coexistence, and Change: Wales 1063–1415* (Cardiff, 1987), pp. 172–75, pp. 183–84; Wendy Davies, "Property Rights and Property Claims in Welsh *Vitae* of the Eleventh Century" in E. Patlagean and P. Riché, eds., *Hagiographie, cultures, et societés IVe–XIIe siècles* (Paris, 1981), pp. 515–33. This aspect of Welsh hagiography is present in the two other *Gogynfeirdd* poems to saints as well, as noted by their editors in the *Cyfres Beirdd y Tywysogion* (see n.1).

Cadfan before him, which might strike some as incongruous in a Christian saint, is integrally related to the security of Tywyn; they are its protectors, even as princes eulogized by the bards are portrayed as the protectors of their lands and the inhabitants thereof. In *Canu Cadfan*, the theme of security may embody obliquely another assertion of the rights of Tywyn, in this case the right to extend *nawdd*, or protection, to anyone within its territory.[32] This prerogative, which is claimed as well in the *vitae* of Saints David and Cadog, gave ecclesiastical institutions considerable leverage *vis à vis* secular authority.

One last way in which the claims of Tywyn make themselves felt in the poem is in the comparisons that are made between St. Cadfan's and other foundations in Wales. The church at Tywyn is said to have been made like St. David's '*ual eglwys Dewi y digoned*' (line 32), and to be in possession of a cloth of some kind that is superior to a comparable object at St. David's '*ac amgen yw yn llenn a Llanndewi*' (line 158). It is impossible to say whether the object, the *llen*, is an altarcloth, a wall hanging, or a relic of the founding saint, but it is noteworthy that a *llenn bali*, a silken *llen*, is one of the praiseworthy features of Llanddewibrefi in Gwynfardd Brycheiniog's *Canu i Ddewi* (line 157). St. Cadfan's is also said to be like Bangor (line 80), the cathedral church of the bishopric in which it was located.[33] These comparisons with other churches encourage devotion to Cadfan and grants to his church rather than to other saints and their foundations, and also suggest a certain resistance to the authority of the bishop of Bangor.

In its celebration of past and present miracles performed by Cadfan and through his intercession, of his sacred relics at Tywyn and the consequent strength and security thereof, of his life and of the replication of his virtues in Abbot Morfran, and above all of the divine favor manifest in all these ways, *Canu Cadfan* serves the same purposes as the prose *vitae* of saints, and should be treated as part of the corpus of Welsh hagiography, as it has been by Elissa Henken.[34] In his 1988 study of medieval hagiography, Thomas Heffernan links the emergence of the *vita* as the paradigmatic hagiographical document to the formalization of the process of canonization under Pope Alexander III (1159–81).[35] Welsh tradition, in which *vitae* evidently made their first appearance in the twelfth century under the double pressure of Vatican and Norman practices, reflects this new demand for texts in a relatively standard form. We ought not to be

---

32 On *nawdd* and ecclesiastical sanctuary, see Huw Pryce, *Native Law and the Church in Medieval Wales* (Oxford, 1993), pp. 165–203.
33 See R. R. Davies, pp. 182–86, on the definition of dioceses in twelfth-century Wales.
34 Henken (1987), op. cit. n.13, p. 23, pp. 174–76.
35 Thomas J. Heffernan, *Sacred Biography: Saints and Their Biographers in the Middle Ages* (Oxford and New York, 1988), pp. 22–25.

surprised, though, to discover traces of other kinds of hagiographical tradition.

Canu Cadfan, regarded in the context of its own time — *ca.* 1147 — is neither a *vita* proper nor a simple eulogy, either of place or person. It is a poem intended both to celebrate and to foster the cult of St. Cadfan, as the *Arwyrain Owain* and other eulogies of princes were valued, not only as moments in the history of an essentially economic exchange between poet and patron, but as means to the end of confirming and enhancing the prince's status among his people, his peers, and his rivals. *Canu Cadfan* shares this kind of perlocutionary intent not only with the secular eulogies of the *beirdd y tywysogion* but also with Latin *vitae* and vernacular lives of saints throughout Europe.

Although we do not know very much about the circumstances under which bardic poetry was recorded, there is good evidence that it was orally performed and that oral transmission coexisted with and often preceded the written record.[36] It is often taken for granted of oral literature that its audience is familiar with its content, so that the oblique allusion to an event or set of events is sufficient to call forth in the audience their traditional memory of the matter. Perhaps it was in this manner that *Canu Cadfan* worked, awakening memories of Cadfan and of the history of Tywyn that were the common heritage of the *clas* there and could be shared conversationally with guests. Or perhaps *Canu Cadfan* and other hagiographic poems were considered to be comprehensively instructive in the same way that the prose *vitae* were, providing all the information that an adherent of the saint's cult needed. The prose *vitae* too, after all, were performed orally, read aloud in monastic refectories and at church services on such appropriate occasions as the saint's feast. Oral performance was the principal medium of instruction, and the *clas* at Tywyn might well have used *Canu Cadfan* for that purpose in the same way that other houses employed *vitae* that they had commissioned.

Are the three poems to Welsh saints vestiges of a hagiographic tradition that the *vita* came to replace during the course of the twelfth century or, to the contrary, an innovative adaptation of the *molawd* inspired by the genre of the *vita*? Although they are, along with the quatrain in praise of St. Padarn mentioned earlier, the first hagiographic poems in the Welsh tradition, they are not the last — poems commemorating saints were composed by the *cywyddwyr* through the fourteenth and fifteenth,

---

36 There is evidence for the oral performance of poetry during this period in the Laws of the Court, a tractate which prescribes that the *pencerdd* (lit. 'chief of song') *a dele dechreu kerd* 'should commence the song'. Aled Rhys Wiliam, ed., *Llyfr Iorwerth* (Caerdydd, 1960), p. 21. There is also a description of an oral performance of bardic panegyric in the *Breuddwyd Rhonabwy*, generally dated to the twelfth or thirteenth century. See Melville Richards, ed. *Breudwyt Ronabwy* (Caerdydd, 1948), p. 20, lines 13–16. In addition, the self-referential vocabulary of bardic poetry, with its reliance on verbs like *canu*, implies oral publication.

and even into the sixteenth, centuries.[37] It is possible that lost poems supplied some of the material employed by the writers of prose *vitae*, but possible too that the poems originated in the adaptation of the tactics of narrative hagiography to the conventions of bardic poetry. But whether it was originary or derivative, *Canu Cadfan* shows the techniques of bardic encomium being turned to precisely the same purposes, purposes that were fundamental to all hagiography, as were served by the prose *vitae* that began to appear at about the same time.

37 For a list of these, see Henken (1987), op. cit. n.13, pp. 23–30.

ON THE ORIGINS OF *LU*'S MARGINAL .r.

Daniel F. Melia

UNIVERSITY OF CALIFORNIA AT BERKELEY

DEPARTMENT OF RHETORIC AND CELTIC STUDIES PROGRAM

In a recent article in *Celtica*,[1] I argued that the somewhat mysterious marginal notation .r., found in various places in the eleventh century Irish manuscript *Lebor na hUidre* (*LU*)[2] probably originated in a common scribal abbreviation in Latin manuscripts, r = *require*, and that it was owing to a scribal misunderstanding that it came to be understood as a special marker for verse, representing Irish *retoiric* 'rhetoric',[3] or *rosc/roscad* 'archaic poem'.[4] My argument was made on the general principle that, however it came to be understood later, the .r. marker appeared in *LU* opposite things demonstrably not verse of any kind, opposite more than one sort of verse, and not consistently opposite all examples of any particular feature. I was unaware when I wrote the *Celtica* piece that a similar line of argument had been followed by Stephen Tranter in his somewhat broader article, "Marginal Problems", in *ScriptOralia* 10 (1989).[5] I was, of course, delighted to find another

---

1 "Further Speculation on Marginal .R.", *Celtica* 21 (1990), pp. 362–67.
2 *Lebor na Huidre: Book of the Dun Cow*, R. I. Best and O. Bergin, eds. (Dublin: Royal Irish Academy, 1929). Facsimile, *Leabhar na h-Uidre* (Dublin: Royal Irish Academy, 1870).
3 Suggested by R. Thurneysen, *Die irische Helden- und Königsage* (Halle, 1921), pp. 54–56.
4 Ernst Windisch, in Windisch and Wh. Stokes, *Irische Texte mit Übersetzungen und Wörterbuch* (Leipzig, 1880), p. 748. Windisch's interpretation was strongly supported by Proinsias Mac Cana in his major review of the matter, "On the Use of the Term *retoiric*", *Celtica* 7 (1966), pp. 65–90.
5 *Early Irish Literature — Media and Communication/Mündlichkeit und Schriftlichkeit in der frühen irischen Literatur*, S. N. Tranter and H. L. C. Tristram, eds. (Tübingen: Gunter Narr Verlag), pp. 221–40. According to the preface, an earlier version of Tranter's article had been presented at a colloquium in June 1987 in Freiburg.

scholar making a comparable cut with Occam's razor, and encouraged thereby to pursue the subject further.

It is particularly appropriate, I think, to present the results of this further pursuit in a book dedicated to the memory of my friend Brendan O Hehir, a true scholar who was never satisfied with the glib or canonical explanation of things and who habitually hunted his evidence to ground.

My interest here, as in my earlier article on the subject, is not to take issue with the arguments already made so well by Mac Cana and Tranter that, by the twelfth century, at least some scribes had identified the marginal notation .r. (or .R.) with a particular kind of archaic verse. My interest is, rather, in the origins of the use of this sign in *LU*, or in its immediate sources. I present here a brief history of the marginal notation .r. (representing an abbreviation for Latin *require*) along with evidence that it was in use in this sense by at least one scribe in eleventh century Ireland. The general background will help to clarify the process by which, as I have argued, a very common medieval scribal notation indicating a scribe's dubiety about a particular reading came to be reinterpreted by some Irish scribes as a designation for an archaic style of verse.

Although generally paying little attention to marginalia of any kind, standard texts on Latin paleography usually mention the frequent use of .r. Bernhard Bischoff, for instance, states in a footnote, "Doubtful passages are most often indicated by the use of .r. or .rq̄. ('require') in the margin."[6] A. C. Clark comments, "I will here mention another critical sign which is very common in mss. viz. ℞ (= *require*)."[7] There is no question that medieval scribes had the same understanding of the uses of .r. Wilhelm Wattenbach cites a marginal explanation of about A.D. 1100 by the author of the St. Gall Chronicle: "Very frequently ℞, *ϒ*, *ꝝ* in the margin, sometimes written out as *require* in the St. Gall Orosius and in the codex Colon. 204, indicates that something is not in order or is doubtful. Ekkehart IV wrote in Codex Saint Gall 174 of the letters of Augustine (s. ix): 'A splendid book, very badly written out, though. Lacking another exemplar, I have tried to correct it, if I could, by my own skill. But when I was not able to, I have put a letter *𝕏* next to it.'"[8]

6 *Latin Palaeography: Antiquity and the Middle Ages*, D. Ó Cróinín and D. Ganz, trans. (Cambridge: Cambridge Univ. Press, 1990), p. 43, n.39.
7 *The Descent of Manuscripts* (Oxford: The Clarendon Press, 1914), p. 35.
8 "*Sehr häuftig zeigt* ℞, *ϒ*, *ꝝ* *am Rande an, dass etwas nicht in ordnung oder zweifelhaft ist, ausgeschrieben im Sanctgaller Orosius* require, *und im cod. Colon. 204. Ekkehart IV schrieb im Cod. S. Gall. 174 der Briefe Augustins (s. ix): Liber optimus, nimis autem vitiose scriptus. Hunc ego quidam corrigere per me, exemplar aliud non habens, si poteram temptavi. ergo ubi minus potui litteram* 𝕏 *apposui.*" Wilhelm Wattenbach, *Anleitung zur Lateinischen Palaeographie* (Leipzig:

It ought not to be surprising to find Irish scribes of the eleventh century using such an abbreviation. Whether in the margins or in the text itself, abbreviations are a notable feature of insular hands from an early period. The three major types, Roman suspensions (C = Gaius), tironian notes (⁊ = et) and *notae juris* (ṁ= *mihi*) are all found in profusion, along with a host of other abbreviations. F. W. Hall has theorized that this scribal style originated in an Irish foundation: "In the continuous hands contractions are rare. They are common in the insular hands where the separation of words is fairly consistent. It has been suggested that the practice began in the Irish monastery of Bobbio in Italy. Parchment was scarce and to save space the scribes adopted contractions from all the sources mentioned above."[9] The use of marginal .r. as an abbreviation for *require*, r̄/, by an insular hand in a seventh century Bobbio ms. can be seen in a reproduction in Franz Steffens' *Paléographie latine*.[10] The text is of Orosius' *Historiae adversum paganos* (Chap. 2, Bk. 1) and Steffens identifies the handwriting as "Irish". In his commentary on the passage, Steffens says that the *r(equire)*, "seems to have here the sense of *nota*, and to be intended to draw the attention of a reader to this passage."[11]

In discussing the frequency of medieval marginalia of all kinds, A. C. Clark remarks, "I should say that classical mss. of the Caroline and post-Caroline period are not a good hunting-ground for such evidence. On the other hand, theological mss. at all periods are much more instructive, and sometimes present a veritable *embarras de richesses*. One particular collection I found to be of extraordinary interest. This consists of mss. from the Irish foundation of St. Killian at Würzburg, given to the University of Oxford by Archbishop Laud. Most of these form part of the Laud Misc. in the Bodleian Library."[12] In the same passage, Clark reports that he has seen marginal .r. [for *require*] used "more than nine times on one page in the ninth-century Laud Misc. 120 [Augustine's *De civitate Dei*]."

It seems clear from the above examples that the marginal notation .r. = *require* was known in "Insular" scriptoria from the seventh century on. It is also clear that it was put to more than one purpose, drawing on, in fact, a wide range of the possible meanings of *require*, from "question

---

S. Hirzel, 1886), pp. 93–94. I must here thank my colleague Charles Murgia for vetting my translation and suggesting the emendation of *quidam* to *quidem*.

9   F. W. Hall, *A Companion to Classical Texts* (Oxford: The Clarendon Press, 1913), pp. 166–67.

10   Franz Steffens, *Paléographie latine*, Fr. Remi Coulon, O. P., ed. (Paris: H. Champion, 1910), Pl. 26.

11   *On a, en marge de la ligne 7, r = require, ce qui semble avoir ici le sens de nota et être destiné à attirer l'attention du lecteur sur ce passage.* Commentary opposite Pl. 26.

12   *Descent of Manuscripts*, p. 35.

(this)" to "look into (this reading)" to "have a look at (this)". But do we find it used in Ireland outside the puzzling context of *LU* and related mss.? We do. Oxford, Bodleian Library ms. Rawlinson B.503, known as the "Annals of Inisfallen", contains at least five instances of marginal .r. and one of .s.r.[13] In the introduction to the facsimile, R. I. Best describes the systematic marginal signs thus: "Special signs are: marginal .r. '*require*', .s.r. '*sed require*'. . . ."[14] Examination of the placing of these signs in the ms. seems to bear out this interpretation of the use of .r. to mark questionable or otherwise noteworthy readings. None of these entries contains any verse.

[.r.] A.D. 619 (p. 11) The entry under this Kalend contains a reference to the death of a "son of Comgall"; the Annals of Ulster[15] and the Annals of Tigernach, however, refer to a "bishop Comgall".

[s.r.] A.D. 688 (p. 12) Reports the death of "Diarmait, son of 'In Caech'"; identified as "Diarmait of Mide, son of Airmedach Caech" in the Annals of Ulster.

[.r.] A.D. 690 (p. 12) No known discrepancy here with other surviving texts. The entry reports the death, however, of Congal mac Mael Dúin, mac Aed Bennán. Aed appears to have been a key figure in Eóganachta genealogical lore[16] and since these annals are chiefly concerned with Munster events the entry may have special significance for the scribe.

[.r.] A.D. 694 (p. 12) Entry records the death of Fínnechta son of Dúnchadh, king of Laigin; the Annals of Ulster call him "Rex Temhro", that is "King of Ireland".

[.r.] A.D. 896 and [.r.] A.D. 901 (p. 15) No known discrepancies, but these entries refer to the "taking" of the kingship of Cashel by Cenn Gégáin (Finguine mac Dub-Lachtna) in 896 and his deposition in favor of the legendary Cormac mac Cuilleáin in 901. From the Eóganachta point of view, this represented a return to the "proper" lineage, but the Annals of Ulster report that "Finnguine, king of Caisel, was deceitfully killed by his associates." The Annals of Inisfallen do not mention Finguine's passing, merely the accession of Cormac. At any rate, these were notable events in Munster.

13 For facsimile see *The Annals of Inisfallen*, R. I. Best and E. Mac Neill, eds. (Dublin: Royal Irish Academy, 1933). For printed edition see *The Annals of Inisfallen*, S. Mac Airt, ed. and trans. (Dublin: Dublin Institute for Advanced Studies, 1988).

14 *Annals of Inisfallen*, facsimile, p. 7.

15 *The Annals of Ulster*, Seán Mac Airt and Gearóid Mac Niocaill, eds., pt. 1 (Dublin: Dublin Institute for Advanced Studies, 1983).

16 See M. A. O'Brien, *Corpus Genealogiarum Hiberniae* (Dublin: Dublin Institute for Advanced Studies, 1962) at 149a12, 150b16, 151a1, 3, 5, 13 etc.

We are fortunate with respect to Rawl. B.503 that we are able to use internal evidence to date its original compilation to the end of the eleventh century, probably no later than 1092. "The manuscript up to that date was written out by one scribe, probably Diarmait Ua Flainn Chua, bishop and *fer-léigind* (head of the monastic school) of Emly, Co. Tipperary, the chief church of Munster."[17] R. I. Best describes the hand this way: "The hand extends to f.29c 29, down to the middle of A.D. 1092, occupying just one-half of the entire volume. It is unmistakably a hand of the late eleventh century; one has but to compare hand A of Tigernach's Annals (Rawl. B 502, f. 1–4) and hand A of *Lebor na Huidre* (ed. pl. 1). It is an elegant symmetrical book-hand, clearly that of an expert scribe."[18]

We thus have accumulated evidence that the use of marginal .r. to stand for *require* is a feature of Insular manuscript style throughout the Middle Ages, and that this abbreviation was known and used in the standard way in Ireland by at least one highly trained scribe exactly contemporaneous with the scribes of the main text of *LU*. This evidence strengthens the assertions I made in my earlier article: that "some scribe of one of the sources of *LU* introduced .r. = *require* to mark certain passages which were to get special attention from future copyists or readers because of format (columns), or archaism, or stanzaic structure which might require special copying or performing care or style. Because most of the uses were, in fact, to mark poetry, some of it archaic or archaized, some later scribe (*LU*'s M?) made the association with the native term *roscad* (or *retoiric*) and this identification then solidified."[19] In the absence of some undiscovered scribal confession, this scenario cannot, of course, be proven. It does provide, however, a simple explanation which accords with the known facts. The history of the use of .r. = *require* provides a set of background conditions which can easily lead to the kind of reinterpretation we seem to be seeing in its use in *LU*.

A curious corroboration of the explanation offered above can be found in the use of the alternate or parallel marginal abbreviation .z., the suspension for Greek ζητέι 'ask, seek'. Like .r. = *require*, .z. is found in Latin manuscripts in insular hands in the eighth century at Bobbio. An example, .Ƶ., can be seen in Steffens (Pl. 27), from an eighth century Bobbio ms. of Augustine's *De haeresibus*, in an Irish hand. "It appears that the z is for ζητέι corresponding to Latin *require*; in Latin manuscripts this sign is often to be found written in the margin at erroneous

---

17 F. J. Byrne, *A Thousand Years of Irish Script* (Oxford: Bodleian Library, 1979), p. 12.
18 *Annals of Inisfallen*, facsimile, p. 5.
19 "Further Speculation . . .", p. 366.

passages."[20] .z. is also found no fewer than ten times in the ninth century Book of Armagh and unquestionably is used to mark a doubtful source since in two instances the scribe has added *"incertus liber"*.[21] Also like .r., .z. appears somewhat enigmatically in *LU*. On page 86, in the *Togail Bruidne Da Derga* (the *LU* text other than the *Táin Bó Cuailnge* which shows marginal .r.) .z. appears in the margin, .ꞃ.[22] There seems to be nothing obviously wrong in the line so marked (*mac tire ina fhlaith, acht tárag firend cacha indse o cind*) '[no] wolf [takes] during his [Conaire's] sovereignty but a [single] bull-calf from each byre during [the year]'. On the other hand, we have no way of knowing how this passage may have appeared in the source.

We thus see in *LU* the use of two different marks (.r. and .z.) with a long history of standardized significance in scribal practice in Latin mss. written in "Insular" hands. In each case, we find explicit use of the mark in Irish mss. earlier than or contemporaneous with *LU*. On the basis of such usage, it seems difficult to escape the conclusion that the state of affairs we find in *LU* must have arisen from a misunderstanding about the normal use of these markers by one of the *LU* scribes, or by a scribe of some mss. antecedent to *LU*. We may not be able to say exactly what the mark meant to any of the scribes of *LU*, but we can say, I think, that we know where it came from and why it was there to be misunderstood or reinterpreted.

---

20 *Paléographie latine*, commentary opposite plate 27: *"On suppose que ce z est pour ζητέι correspondent au latin require; dans les manuscrits latins ce signe se rencontre souvent aux passages fautifs, écrit en marge."*

21 *Liber Ardmachus: the Book of Armagh*, John Gwynn, ed. (Dublin, 1913), cited and discussed in Tranter, "Marginal Problems", p. 227 and n.6.

22 *LU*, line 7013; facsimile, p. 86, between columns.

DARING YOUNG MEN
IN THEIR CHARIOTS

Joseph Falaky Nagy

UNIVERSITY OF CALIFORNIA AT LOS ANGELES

In his plenary lecture to the Sixth International Congress of Celtic Studies, the late James Carney dwelt on some of the resemblances between the *Táin Bó Cúailnge* and the *Iliad* that, he claimed, were so close that we must assume in seventh- or eighth-century Ireland either a direct or an excellent indirect knowledge of the Greek epic (Carney 1983, 128). As compelling as some of these resemblances are, our understanding of what lies behind them is perhaps better served by the approach on display in Daniel Melia's article "Some Remarks on the Affinities of Medieval Irish Saga" (Melia 1979). In this piece, Melia outlines a core story pattern shared among the *Táin*, the *Iliad*, and the Indic epic *Mahābhārata* and proposes an analysis of the structural as well as the more specific parallels among these texts in terms of an Indo-European heritage of heroic tale. Melia's project is in effect the rehabilitation of a comparative approach that over the years has accrued both venerability and notoriety. The following study is an attempt to understand one of the resemblances noted by Carney in this comparative light, rather than in the flicker of the will-o'-the-wisp notion of a medieval Irish familiarity with Homer. Admittedly, what I have to offer is only a hesitant biped slyly casting about for that extra Indo-European parallel which will make it into a sturdy tripod. And yet, even if the *comparanda* are only generically and not genetically related, I would argue that bringing them together helps us to understand each better within its own context.

Developing an observation already made by Cecile O'Rahilly in her edition of the *LL Táin* (O'Rahilly 1967, 302, n. on 1680–81), Carney, in the same lecture mentioned above, noted that Fergus mac Róig's treatment of the body of Etarcomol, the fosterling of Ailill and Medb who defies both Cú Chulainn and the rules of war as negotiated by Fergus, is cut from the same savage cloth as Achilles' mutilation of Hector's body (*Iliad* 22.395–404). In both cases, the corpse is pierced through the ankles, tied to a chariot and dragged about messily for the purpose of public display (Carney 1983, 129). Carney whimsically noted a third domain for comparison, that of modern popular culture:

> Apart from the *Táin* the closest comparison I have noticed with the incident in the *Iliad* is found in Wild West films where an unfortunate character is dragged by a horse over rough country. Such instances (based originally on actual happenings) lack the emphasis on the spancelling and the contextual similarities of the *Iliad* and the *Táin*; also, of course, in such films the victim is always alive (ibid., n.2).

While there is to my knowledge no evidence to substantiate the claim that medieval Irish men of letters were familiar with the Homeric specifics of Hector's fate, Carney here was indeed on to something, as he almost always was. The symbolism of the chariot, as well as of abuse inflicted from the chariot, do form common ground traversed by Homeric and Irish hero-tale (as well as Indic, see Hiltebeitel 1982). And there is an even more detailed parallel to be drawn between the Etarcomol episode in the *Táin* and yet another Iliadic demonstration of what men can do and express to other men by way of their chariots. Our attention is drawn to this other possibility when we consider a major difference between the two episodes brought together by Carney, as well as a fascinating technical problem that glares at us from amidst the gruesome details supplied by the Irish text. Etarcomol's body, already sliced up by Cú Chulainn, moves around a good deal during its humiliating ride. In the words of O'Rahilly's translation of the *LL* text: "At every rough rock he met, his lungs and liver were left behind on the stones and rocks (?). Wherever it was smooth for him, his scattered joints came together around the horses" (O'Rahilly 1967, 185). Hector's corpse, on the other hand, is reasonably intact and, despite Achilles' rough treatment, is actually kept in good shape and ready for its funeral, courtesy of Apollo (*Iliad* 24.18–21).

Examining more closely the *LL* account of the spectacle, we even wonder about just how much of Etarcomol was actually dragged back to camp. In this version, Cú Chulainn slices his victim down to the navel and then, with another blow, across. Thus, we are told, Etarcomol ends up in three pieces. Yet two of these would remain attached to nothing if the spancel went through the ankles. This spancelling would work, however, were Etarcomol divided into only two pieces. This is in fact what happens in the *LU* version, according to which Cú Chulainn's *coup de grâce* delivered to Etarcomol goes down from head to navel, and no further dismemberment takes place. Here, the corpse behaves in an even neater alternating way on the road home: "Whenever Etarcomol's body went over rocks, one half would part from the other; when the path was smooth, the two parts would come together again" (O'Rahilly 1976, 163).

It is more than just a ghoulish exercise to dwell on these details of the story. What we come to appreciate is how much even the *LL* account with its tripartition of Etarcomol goes out of its way to make the rough ride of the defeated in the wake of a chariot into what we can call a demonstration of "twoness". The impression left in the wake of Etarcomol's return is that the corpse consisted of only two parts, that it could be dragged by the (two) ankles, and that it responded in one of two contrasting ways to whichever of the two terrains, the rocky and the smooth, it happened to encounter.

Significantly, the dyadism nearly prettifying this descriptive passage permeates the entire episode as we find it in both of these versions of the *Táin* (O'Rahilly 1976, lines 1287–1387; O'Rahilly 1967, lines 1565–1695). Etarcomol, unlike most other characters in the *Táin*, is introduced not only with a patronymic but also a metronymic. He is, according to *LL*, the son of Fid 'Wood' and Lethrind 'One of Two Points' (O'Rahilly 1967, line 1566), or according to *LU*, the son of Id 'Withe' and Lethrind (O'Rahilly 1976, line 1290). Their son's name contains the prepositional prefix element *eter* 'between', while the second part of the name, *comal*, is the verbal noun of *con-lá* 'places together' and means 'bond', and in some cases 'penis', presumably in the sense of something that joins together (*DIL*, s.v. *comal*). Hence the name implies a pair between which a relationship exists. It has even been suggested, we note in passing, that *Etarcomol* as a personal name derives from a reinterpretation of a lost placename containing the term *id erchomail* (*DIL*, s.v. *airchomal*, consisting of *air-* and *comal*) 'spancel', which we actually find in the description of how Fergus tied the remains of the dead hero to the chariot (O'Rahilly 1976, line 1378; Haley 1970, 91).

The brash Etarcomol's decision to disregard his promise to Fergus and attack Cú Chulainn as soon as possible comes, according to *LU*, when his chariot reaches a spot or spots designated by the twinlike place-names Meithe (or Méithe) and Ceithe (O'Rahilly 1976, line 1335; Haley 1970, 92–94), which are cited elsewhere as parts of an obscure proverbial phrase, *is dometu for cette* (*DIL*, s.v. 2 *Méithe*). It is here, at the site of the two mounds (?), that Etarcomol orders his charioteer to turn back and return to Cú Chulainn, contrary to the vow just made to the Ulster warrior that he, Etarcomol, would be the first to meet him in single combat the next day. Finally, when in *LL* the bi- or trifurcated Etarcomol is delivered back at the doorstep of his foster parents, Fergus compounds the irony of the situation with a quip, apparently yet another proverb, pointedly featuring yet another pair of twin words: *Ar cach assec cona thassec is téchta* (O'Rahilly 1967, lines 1685–86), "For every restoration has its fitting restitution" (ibid., 185), that is, Etarcomol's mode of return is a consequence of his actions.

Although the instances of dyadic configuration mentioned so far certainly have their contributions to make to the story, the most important formations into pairs that occur in the episode have to do with behavioral alternatives and alternations. More specifically, these are choices having to do with what a warrior ought, as opposed to wants, to do, and, perhaps even more important, with what he ought, as opposed to wants, to *say*. When at the beginning of the episode Etarcomol proposes to Fergus that he take the younger warrior along for company on his embassy to Cú Chulainn, Fergus draws a contrast (or is it a parallel?) between the arrogance (*sotlacht* and *saisle*, O'Rahilly 1976, line 1293) of Etarcomol and the explosiveness (*luinne*) of his counterpart (*do chéli*, ibid., lines 1293–94), and predicts that trouble will arise from the chemistry of their confrontation. Fergus, upon being pressed further by Etarcomol, relents, agreeing to guarantee the young man's safety, expressly provided, however, that he say nothing provocative to Cú Chulainn. When the latter and Fergus meet, Cú Chulainn's first words to his foster father are the epitome of grace and camaraderie, despite the rather awkward and hostility-racked circumstances. Indeed, Cú Chulainn's publicly announced offer to share with Fergus whatever he has for provision in the wilderness, an echo of what he said earlier to another friend on the other side of the conflict (ibid., lines 1170–74), contrasts with the far cattier assessment of Fergus's scabbard and its contents (or lack thereof), words addressed *sub rosa* by Cú Chulainn to his charioteer immediately before Fergus's arrival. It is only fitting, given the cordiality of the exchange between Cú Chulainn and Fergus, that their negotiations so successfully reach a mutually satisfactory conclusion.

After Fergus leaves, however, Etarcomol emerges out from under the senior warrior's shadow, only to evince his inability to do what he has promised to do, namely, to mind his tongue and bide his time. His impetuosity brings about the next day's rendezvous with death, prematurely realized the same day thanks to yet a further display of Etarcomol's bad timing and poor choices. This takes place after he and his charioteer turn their vehicle around at the site or sites mentioned above. As long as he can, the protector of Ulster staves off the inevitable. Even in the face of the clear signs of Etarcomol's hostile intent and the verbal abuse heaped upon him, Cú Chulainn continues to show restraint as well as respect for Fergus by deferring the death-blow and only playing with his would-be opponent, all the while issuing him repeated warnings.

Tellingly, what Cú Chulainn does to Etarcomol with his deft sword-play is to render him a sign of the fate he is blindly courting. As if he were a corpse, Etarcomol, with a flick of Cú Chulainn's wrist, is buried under the ground on which he is standing. Then he is stripped of clothes, like the hero bereft of reputation that he is about to become. Next, with the scoffing Etarcomol still refusing to change tactics, his hair is shaved clean off, in what can be taken to be a sartorial reflection of his junior status or base nature (J. Nagy 1985, 151–53). Finally, Etarcomol, according to *LU*, is split in two. What Cú Chulainn has now generated is not a sign of things to come but arguably a terrible memorial to his young victim's duplicity, or to the choice that lay before the youth, between the behavior dictated by Fergus or the behavior to which his lust for fame compelled him. The memorial, however, awaits completion in the act of dragging the corpse, when appropriate response is finally aligned with appropriate stimulus. The body splits when it comes in contact with the rough, but comes together in contact with the smooth.

When Fergus learns of the death of the warrior under his protection, but before learning of the details, he returns in fury to Etarcomol's slayer and berates him, running over a still submissive Cú Chulainn three times with his chariot. Thus he inflicts upon the living body of his foster son as much wear and tear as he will inflict upon the corpse of Ailill's and Medb's foster son. Cú Chulainn, with the assistance of Etarcomol's corroborating charioteer, enlightens Fergus as to the facts of the case and poses to him his own dyadic dilemma: Which would you have preferred, my slaying him, or his slaying me? Fergus's anger dissipates, and he admits that, despite the embarrassment he has suffered with the death of Etarcomol, he prefers the outcome as it is. Fergus returns with the body in the fashion we have already noted. And upon witnessing what is being done to the corpse of her foster son, Medb chides Fergus: "That was not kind treatment for a young hound (*moíthchulióin*)" (O'Rahilly 1976, 163). Fergus's rejoinder highlights yet another dyadic and didactic dimension to the incident. It is a comment that serves as a caption to the preceding events, leaving no doubt as to which member of the young heroic pair was truly heroic and which was not: "It is no source of annoyance to me . . . that the mongrel (*at[h]echmatud*) should have waged battle with the great hound for whom he was no match" (ibid.). And so, in Etarcomol's dossier as left for posterity, the image of tender pup is replaced with that of churlish mongrel, after an encounter with the very embodiment of heroic, "canine" qualities, Cú Chulainn, proves a litmus test for Etarcomol's faulty reactions.

To summarize, we have here a story in which a young hero in a chariot is given good advice by an older warrior who is responsible for him, sage words to the effect that it is advisable to act and speak in a restrained manner under restraining circumstances. The youngster, however, discards the advice as he drives by a twin location and recklessly turns back. His ill-chosen words addressed to an ill-chosen opponent bring about his disgraceful, chariot-powered demise. This is also brought about by Etarcomol's inability or unwillingness to read the verbal signs on the wall, namely the prediction of Fergus and the advice that Fergus gives, as well as the more graphic signs that Cú Chulainn inscribes upon Etarcomol's own person.

Seen thus, the story of Etarcomol is reminiscent not just of the disturbingly triumphant episode of the slaying and humiliation of Hector at the hands of Achilles, but even more of another episode from the *Iliad* that in fact features no ignominy or terribly won victory. This is the chariot-race scene from Book Twenty-Three (lines 262–650), following the funeral of Patroklos as the first of the funeral games held in his honor. Etarcomol of the *Táin*, I would argue, is an Indo-European cousin of the winner of the moral victory in the Iliadic race, Antilokhos, the son of Nestor. More specifically, Etarcomol is an Antilokhos gone bad.

In Book Twenty-Three, Antilokhos, aspiring to a fame he does not yet have, is coached before the race by his father as to how he along with Nestor's admittedly mediocre horses should compete against the best of the Achaeans. The formula for winning renown in the race is to concentrate on what happens going around the *térma*, the turning point, where Antilokhos is to hug the curve and pull ahead by speeding up one horse and slowing down the other. All this he is told by Nestor, who, no mean horseman himself, is regularly referred to in Homeric poetry as *hippóta* 'horseman' (Frame 1978, 152, n.72).

The most difficult aspect of this strategy is the ambidexterity required of the driver at the *térma*. He is to engage in two contrasting maneuvers designed to make his horses go at different rates of speed. The difficulty, however, is overcome, and Nestor's advice bears fruit. The up-and-coming young hero wins second place, behind Diomedes, while others with far better horses and reputations are left behind in Antilokhos' dust.

Not only does Nestor's son demonstrate in the course of this race that he can do two seemingly very different things at the same time, like the twin drivers that Nestor mentions as having defeated him in the past (lines 638–42), but Antilokhos also shows off an impressive spectrum of alternating discourses that together guarantee both his showing in the race and the official acknowledgement of his achievement (G. Nagy 1990, 217; Martin 1989, 188). First, Antilokhos proves that he is a good listener, when he thoughtfully takes the advice of his father. Then, during the race, he alternately berates, threatens, and encourages his horses, almost in the style of a Lóeg providing stimulation for Cú Chulainn in the throes of battle. When the great senior Achaean Menelaos (also in the race) angrily tells Antilokhos to give his chariot room, Antilokhos does not hotheadedly sling back an insult, but remains quiet and stays on his course, thereby ultimately driving Menelaos off his.

It is, however, after the race that Antilokhos proves that talking like a winner is half of winning itself. For Achilles, the judge of the race, declares his intention to award second prize to Eumelos, who in fact came in last but was expected to win, and to this declaration Antilokhos boldly but respectfully declares his objection, recalling the fatefully protesting speech of the wronged Achilles to Agamemnon in the first book of the *Iliad* (Martin 1989, 188–89). Responding favorably to Antilokhos' daring plea for equity, the relentlessly depressed Achilles actually smiles (line 555). The young hero similarly turns a potentially explosive situation into one of concord and renewed friendship when, after Achilles has awarded him second prize after all, he is confronted by a verbally abusive Menelaos, who elsewhere in the *Iliad* is assisted in battle by the fledgling hero (Book 5, lines 561–89), but now is furious at him for engaging in what Menelaos describes as cheating. Antilokhos' response is as measured as Cú Chulainn's was to Etarcomol, or as restrained as Etarcomol's was unrestrained. Apologizing for the impetuosity of young men to Menelaos and even going so far as to cede his prize to him, Antilokhos shames his older adversary into backing off and allowing the youngster his time in the limelight. This time will soon be cut short, when, according to Pindar's *Pythian Ode* 6 (lines 28–42), Antilokhos, in an attempt to rescue his father whose chariot has been disabled, will be slain by Memnon, the Trojan's great white hope after the demise of Hector (see also *Odyssey* 4.186–202).

Thus we see a chariot-riding young man who, under the supervision of an older male, not only can engage in seemingly mutually counter-productive activities at the same time, but also can switch from one speech act to another with the greatest of ease and effect. Knowing when to restrain his resources or words as well as when to take risks, albeit with an eye to a reasonable and attainable goal, is the key to Antilokhos's success and to his functioning as what the name of the Irish Anti-Antilokhos, Etarcomol 'Mutual Bond', suggests should have been *his* role as well.

Furthermore, it is at the site of a landmark that serves as a turning point for a spin in the chariot that the fates and the decision-making capacities of these two young men from two separate Indo-European traditions are decided. In the case of Antilokhos, this landmark, the *térma* or *sêma*, is a sign of a sign, as it were (G. Nagy 1990, 209). Negotiating one's way around it proves to be yet another test of the young man's ability to encode and decode traditional signs, including different modes of verbal discourse. In light of the Iliadic parallels between the two stories, can we resist viewing the twin hills or landmarks where Etarcomol exposes his poor judgment as not-too-distant cousins of the stones Blocc and Bluicne that, we are told elsewhere, helped to determine the worthiness of the chariot-borne candidate for the job of king of Ireland (Gwynn 1912, 134)?

This piece is dedicated to a scholar who, in his wisdom, was a Fergus to the current generation of Celticists in this country, as well as an Antilokhos in his bold vision and courage.

REFERENCES

Carney, James. 1983. "Early Irish Literature: The State of Research". In Gearóid Mac Eoin, ed., with the collaboration of Anders Ahlqvist and Donncha Ó hAodha, *Proceedings of the Sixth International Congress of Celtic Studies,* pp. 113–30. Dublin: Dublin Institute for Advanced Studies.

Frame, Douglas. 1978. *The Myth of Return in Early Greek Epic.* New Haven and London: Yale University Press.

Gwynn, Lucius, ed. and trans. 1912. "De Shíl Chonairi Móir", *Ériu* 6:130–43.

Haley, Gene G. 1970. *The Topography of the Táin Bó Cúailnge.* Ph.D. diss., Harvard University.

Hiltebeitel, Alf. 1982. "Brothers, Friends, and Charioteers: Parallel Episodes in the Irish and Indian Epics". In Edgar Polomé, ed. *Homage to George Dumézil,* Journal of Indo-European Studies Monograph 3. Washington, D.C.: Journal of Indo-European Studies, pp. 85–111.

Martin, Richard P. 1989. *The Language of Heroes: Speech and Performance in the Iliad.* Ithaca and London: Cornell Univ. Press.

Melia, Daniel F. 1979. "Some Remarks on the Affinities of Medieval Irish Saga", *Acta Antiqua Academiae Scientiarum Hungaricae* 27:255–61.

Nagy, Gregory. 1990. *Greek Mythology and Poetics.* Ithaca and London: Cornell University Press.

Nagy, Joseph F. 1985. *The Wisdom of the Outlaw: The Boyhood Deeds of Finn in Gaelic Narrative Tradition.* Berkeley, Los Angeles, and London: University of California Press.

O'Rahilly, Cecile, ed. and trans. 1976. *Táin Bó Cúailnge.* Recension I. Dublin: Dublin Institute for Advanced Studies.

———, ed. and trans. 1967. *Táin Bó Cúalnge from the Book of Leinster.* Dublin: Dublin Institute for Advanced Studies.

THE INTRODUCTION OF ALPHABETIC WRITING TO IRELAND: IMPLICATIONS AND CONSEQUENCES

Michael Richter

UNIVERSITY OF KONSTANZ

For the purpose of the present discussion, it is sufficient to state that writing in the Latin alphabet came to Ireland along with Christianity and that alphabetic writing subsequently became the predominant kind of writing.[1] In order to throw into relief the implications of this for the native traditional learned class, it will be necessary to present the introduction of alphabetic writing to Ireland as part of Christianization, which thus will have to be discussed as well.

*

* *

* * *

In receiving Christianity in the way it did, Ireland in the fifth century was not moving with the general trends; this increases the importance of the event. Around A.D. 400, Catholicism, as one must say in distinction to other strong manifestations of the Christian religion, was on the defensive

---

[1] One can detect a renewed interest in *ogam* and its complex relation to Latin alphabetic writing, see e.g. Anthony Harvey, "Early Literacy in Ireland: The Evidence from Ogam", *CMCS* 14 (1987), pp. 1–15; Damian McManus, "Ogam: Archaizing, Orthography and the Authenticity of the Manuscript Key to the Alphabet", *Ériu* 37 (1986), pp. 1–31. A good summary of earlier discussions, as well as a placing of the phenomenon in a wider context, can be found in J. Vendryes, "L'écriture ogamique et ses origines", *Études Celtiques* 4 (1940), pp. 83–116, reprinted in Vendryes, *Choix d'études linguistiques et celtiques* (Paris, 1952), pp. 247–76.

in the world of antiquity. Arianism, that variety of Christianity that had been declared heretical in 325 soon after Christianity had won acceptance within the Roman Empire, was progressing instead and was to make further considerable gains at the expense of Catholicism in the fifth century. But there was more: Christianity lost out likewise to paganism, and nowhere more devastatingly than in Britain, where the Saxon advances since the first decades of the fifth century effected the repaganization of a former Roman Christian province on a scale altogether stunning. This shows clearly, indeed painfully, that Christianity was a delicate plant that could be more easily uprooted than some of its advocates cared to believe. Its implantation, conversely, required great care and a suitable habitat. The gains made by Catholicism in Ireland were in that respect and at that time negligible; it could not be foreseen then that Irish Catholicism would become the most dynamic branch of Christianity in early medieval Europe. That, however, was a later phenomenon outside the time limit of the present discussion.

Historians tend to work with concepts of cause and effect. Here I will take a different approach because the causes of the development to be discussed escape me, indeed, the effects puzzle me, and I intend to emphasize this enigma in order to stimulate its investigation. I will work forward chronologically, concentrating on the societal aspect of religion in general and of Christianity in particular.[2] Christianity was to have a delicate, indeed an ambivalent role in the early centuries. Due to this, I am unhappy about the way Irish historians refer to the historical time before the twelfth century as "early Christian". This phraseology, no doubt meant initially merely as a convenient label of periodization, has gradually taken on the quality of a factual statement. This, in my view, would be a travesty of the situation in Ireland, as I will explain.

Contemporary documentation of Christian activity in Ireland begins in the first quarter of the seventh century, with the writing tablets from the Springmount Bog in Co. Antrim[3] and the earliest Biblical texts. Of the latter I take the *Cathach* to be the oldest; placing it in the first quarter of the seventh century, as many experts do,[4] I suggest that this manuscript is unlikely to be Colum Cille's work. Nor can one make reliable statements concerning the places of origin of the earliest preserved Irish medieval

---

2   Such an approach was brilliantly demonstrated by R. W. Southern, *Western Society and the Church in the Middle Ages* (London, 1970), a book that deservedly has been circulated very widely. See John van Engen, "The Christian Middle Ages as an Historiographical Problem", *American Historical Review* 91 (1986), pp. 519–52, at pp. 526 f.

3   E. A. Lowe, *Codices Latini Antiquiores*, Supplement, no. 1684 (Oxford, 1971). On wax tablets more generally see below, n.14.

4   James Kenney, *The Sources for the History of Ireland*, vol. I, Ecclesiastical, no. 454 (New York, 1929), p. 629; E. A. Lowe, *Codices Latini Antiquiores*, II, 2nd ed., no. 266 (Oxford, 1972).

manuscripts. However, all of them are later than the time dealt with here, which is, thus, unattested by contemporary material from within Ireland. One has to make use, instead, of contemporary material from outside Ireland and, within strict limits, of later material from Ireland which permits reconstruction of what is likely to have happened during the times preceding the oldest documentation that has survived.

The focus of the present discussion will be the establishment of writing in the Latin alphabet in Ireland as a by-product of the spread of Catholic Christianity. This was an innovation of the greatest possible consequences for Irish society. It deserves attention even in fields that at first sight would appear as rather uninspiring. But before turning to that, the origins of Christianity in Ireland must be sketched.[5]

It is in Britain that we must look for the origins of Christianity in Ireland. Roman rule in Christian Britain came to an end between 407 and 409.[6] I would have found it impossible to make such a blunt statement in the past; but having witnessed in 1989 in Europe how regimes collapsed within months or even weeks, I now have to take this way of presenting historical events as occasionally justified. Before the end of Roman rule in Britain, relations with Ireland would have been in the field of trade predominantly; there is reason to believe that raids became more common after 409. In any case, there had been contacts, and through these contacts enough Christians had emerged in Ireland for Pope Celestine I to decide to send Palladius as the first bishop to the Irish believing in Christ in 431. This information provided by the Gaulish historian Prosper of Aquitaine in his *Vita Germani* is not contemporary but is from within the fifth century. It permits fairly palpable conclusions.

Prosper's principal objective was the description and *laudatio* of what Germanus of Auxerre achieved in Britain. He had been sent there in 429 to counteract what was believed to be spreading Pelagian heresy[7] among Catholics. Not just incidentally, this is a most precious piece of information: contacts with the Empire had continued from Britain even after 409. The Saxon invasions may well have been on a devastating scale and lethal to Christianity in the medium term, but the invaders needed time to establish themselves in hostile territory, and the uprooting of

5 For more detail, see M. Richter, "Ireland and Europe — the Early Church" in P. Ní Chatháin, M. Richter, eds., *Ireland and Europe, the Early Church* (Stuttgart, 1984), pp. 409–32; also M. Richter, *Medieval Ireland: The Enduring Tradition* (Dublin, London, New York, 1988), pp. 43–49.

6 See especially E. A. Thompson, "Britain A.D. 406–410", *Britannia* 8 (1977), pp. 303–18; id., "Zosimus 6.10.2 and the letters of Honorius", *Classical Quarterly* 32 (1982), pp. 445–62.

7 See Robert A. Markus, "Pelagianism: Britain and the Continent", *Journal of Ecclesiastical History* 37 (1986), pp. 191–204; also Ian Wood, "The Fall of the Western Empire and the End of Roman Britain", *Britannia* 18 (1987), pp. 251–62.

Christianity in considerable parts of Britain, of necessity undocumented, would take even longer.

When Germanus returned to the Roman Empire, which still survived in both Gaul and Italy, report would have been made of the successful conclusion of Germanus's mission to Britain. Along with that, information would be provided about Christians in Ireland, presumed also to be potentially Pelagians, which was why Palladius was commissioned to go there. He was to ensure that Irish Christians would be Catholics. He would not set out on his own, and he would be provided with the necessary material to perform this task properly. In such missionaries' equipment, manuscripts would have been of prime importance. The Latin Bibles, absolute essentials, would be of the type known summarily as the *Vetus Latina* or the Old Latin text; Jerome's Vulgate had not yet reached the popularity which it was to attain in the subsequent two centuries. In the course of time the Vulgate would supersede the Old Latin Bible on the Continent. This was also to happen in Ireland, but in the short term contacts between Ireland and the Empire as well as Rome weakened considerably, with the result that the Latin Bible in the form of the *Vetus Latina* predominated in Ireland longer than elsewhere. Modern scholars attempting to recover as much as possible of the *Vetus Latina* text are aided in their task by material from Ireland in a very special way.[8]

Even if manuscripts did not arrive in Ireland with the first Christians, they must have been brought at the latest by Palladius. Romans at that time could look back upon a rich civilization characterized by extensive use of writing; their alphabet was an adaptation of the Greek alphabet. At the height of its power, the Roman Empire was organized on the basis of the written word. Though literacy was not general,[9] it was widespread enough to make the administration rely on writing for its successful functioning. Learning among the Romans was a deeply respected social value. Children of the well-to-do were normally taught at home and in the course of their education were initiated into the skill of writing even if later in life they would fall back upon the assistance of professional scribes. They were taught to write, as Quintilian (*ca.* A.D. 35–100) put it, *bene ac velociter* 'legibly and fast'.[10]

Christianity, based on Scripture, could best take root in a literate society. In the Roman Empire, these preconditions were available. In the early fourth century, after Christianity in Rome had turned to Latin rather than Greek as the language in which the religion was to be conducted, it

---

8 A good survey is provided by Martin McNamara, "The Text of the Latin Bible in the Early Irish Church: Some Data and Desiderata" in P. Ní Chatháin, M. Richter, eds., *Ireland and Christendom: The Bible and the Missions* (Stuttgart, 1987), pp. 7–55.

9 The most recent and penetrating analysis has been provided by William Vernan Harris, *Ancient Literacy* (Cambridge, Mass., 1989).

10 *Institutio Oratoria* I, 28.

found acceptance in Roman society and could go public. By the end of the fourth century, it had become the only accepted religion of the state, with forced repression of the previous religious cults.[11] Resistance to this was stronger than is often maintained, and there are enough signs even in the fifth century, arguably the time when the climate was most favorable to Catholicism, of syncretism rather than thorough application of Christian forms of life. Such less than fervent acceptance of Christianity by a quite educated Roman society, with adherence instead, in several fields, to older traditional values, was to accompany the history of Christianity throughout the subsequent centuries, along with more or less strong expressions of regret on the part of fervent Christians that this was so. One is compelled to conclude that to the Roman population Christianity perhaps did not appear as the outright favorite[12] especially if it stood up as intolerant of other opinions, since its message was that "no one comes to the Father but by me" (John 14:6). It will be argued that a comparable, less than enthusiastic, attitude towards Christianity can be detected in Ireland, with the one, important, difference that Christianity in Ireland did not have the massive support of public authority that had helped it in Rome. There simply was not any such powerful authority in Ireland. Here precisely lies the core of the enigma of the success of Christianity in Ireland in the fifth and sixth centuries.

Christianity being based on the Book, I will now turn to some technical aspects of book production in the Roman Empire, which is a necessary backdrop to what was to take place in Ireland in the fifth and sixth centuries.

The development of alphabetic writing has been hailed by modern scholars as one of the greatest achievements of humanity. It emerged in Greece in the eighth century B.C., and it was not long before the Romans used it as well.[13] The relative simplicity of the alphabet, one of its strengths when used for writing Greek and, if only slightly less so, Latin, was maintained with hardly a modification even when the writing of other languages with the help of the alphabet posed greater problems. Conservative as was the medium, so was also the packaging of writing, as it were. One tended to cling to traditional forms; innovations were few

11 A very stimulating concise account of this is given by Ramsay MacMullen, *Christianising the Roman Empire, A.D. 100–400* (New Haven and London, 1984), here particularly p. 100 f.

12 For a sympathetic account of late Roman religion, see Peter Brown, *The World of Late Antiquity* (London, 1971), esp. pp. 49–57. Further illuminating observations on how Christianity was adapted to the traditional Roman mentality are offered by Peter Brown, "The Saint as Exemplar in Late Antiquity", *Representations* 1.2 (1983), pp. 1–25.

13 Jacques Poucet, "Réflexions sur l'écrit et l'écriture dans la Rome des premiers siècles", *Latomus* 18 (1989), pp. 289–311.

and slow to make their weight felt. They seem to have been successful only when their advantages were considerable.

In Roman times (and this is all that concerns us at this point), writing was predominantly done on papyrus sheets which when glued together formed rolls. Papyrus provided a surface on which one could write in the manner expressed by Quintilian, *velociter* even though not always *bene*. Existence of cursive script among the Romans was another indication that writing had been fully embraced. Writing exercises and training as well as drafts were done on wax tablets, which were easy to produce and economical to use; this guaranteed the wax tablet a long life and made it a highly recommended writing implement. Papyrus was very extensively used. Egypt was the main producer and exporter of it, which was fine as long as the Roman Empire controlled the Mediterranean. Furthermore, in the Mediterranean climate, papyrus was a durable material; it enjoyed high professional prestige.[14]

One of the rare substantial changes in connection with the technology of writing in antiquity appears in the second century and gradually spreads in the third and fourth centuries, particularly in association with Christianity.[15] It became more common to write on animal skin instead of on papyrus, on vellum or parchment. Writing on this material involved more labor;[16] it was slower than on papyrus. Calligraphy rather than cursive script would be its main characteristic in the centuries to come. Writing developed increasingly into a craft for specialists. The sheets of parchment or vellum would be bound up to form a codex. Parchment and vellum codices were the norm for Christian material in Rome by the early fifth century, i.e. by the time that Palladius was sent to Ireland. It can be supposed that he was equipped with the most up-to-date of Christian accessories. As it happened, the change in writing material in this respect proved to have distinct advantages. Parchment and vellum were more resistant to the humid conditions which prevail in Ireland. Furthermore, in a cattle-raising society like that of Ireland the raw material for producing a codex was available locally when required. In forgoing the use of papyrus, the Irish became independent of imports from the eastern Mediterranean and from functioning long-distance trade, which in any case is unlikely to have continued to include Britain regularly after the early fifth century, let alone reached beyond Britain to Ireland. So once

---

14 Bernhard Bischoff, *Latin Palaeography, Antiquity and the Middle Ages* (Cambridge, 1990), pp. 7 f.

15 See especially C. H. Roberts, "The Codex", *Proceedings of the British Academy* 40 (1954), pp. 169–204; for more details C. H. Roberts and T. C. Skeat, *The Birth of the Codex* (London, 1983).

16 Cf. the eighth-century marginal note "*qui nescit scribere, putat hoc esse nullum laborem, O quam gravis est scriptura*", quoted by Wilhelm Wattenbach, *Das Schriftwesen im Mittelalter*, 3rd ed. (Leipzig, 1896), p. 283.

the codex was introduced to Ireland, its production could be taken up there without the requirement of links with the outside world.

Before pursuing how this was done, however, we will have to say something about the other Christian teacher whom we know by name besides Palladius, namely Patrick. While he cannot be the central figure of this account, he cannot be passed over either. Rather, I intend to fit him into the picture drawn so far. This will be done with reference to the *Confessio* in the form we believe he left it,[17] trimmed of the accretions and treatments by other writers. Working on the assumption that Patrick was more or less a contemporary of Palladius, he was raised a Romano-British citizen, speaking British as his first language, acquiring Latin later, becoming competent in it though not confident with it. His abduction as a youth by Irish pirates was a personal misfortune that was repeated many times over in the early fifth century when the Irish raided the west coast of Britain while the Saxons were gaining footholds along the east and south. Having returned home from Ireland, before setting out on his missionary activity, Patrick would have improved his grasp of Latin learning and Christian education. While this is likely to have happened after the Roman legions had deserted Britain, he would still have enjoyed the more recent developments in the sphere of writing that had spread among Roman Christian circles. There is nothing to refute the assumption that the equipment and the texts which Patrick took when going as a missionary to Ireland would not have differed in any essential aspects from the material brought by Palladius. There was one major feature distinguishing the two men: Palladius was a native Latin speaker, Patrick was not.

I will now come back to the earliest specimens of alphabetic writing that have survived in Ireland, the wax tablets and the oldest Biblical manuscripts. The tablets are regarded as containing in the texts of the psalms written on them samples of school exercises. The earliest Biblical manuscripts attest that calligraphy had been successfully taught in Ireland. One must regard the oldest surviving manuscripts from Ireland as copies made from material which also had been produced there, ultimately deriving from the manuscripts brought by Palladius and Patrick. It is important to take note of the fact that these two men came from the same civilization; if each of them separately established institutions to teach the production of manuscripts for the use of Christians, as was most likely the case, what they taught would be more or less identical, and eventually the two strands could merge without difficulty. There can be no doubt that in the earliest surviving specimens of alphabetic writing from Ireland we are witnessing the products of a successfully established training for scribes

---

17 The best edition is that of Ludwig Bieler, *Libri Epistolarum Sancti Patricii Episcopi, Classica et Mediaevalia* 11 (1950), pp. 3–150.

and other craftsmen engaged in the production of manuscripts in the first half of the fifth century, and a continuing activity in that field from then onwards. In emphasizing the craft aspect of manuscript production,[18] I want to convey the need for continuity, the passing on of skills necessary for this task over several generations.

The late Julian Brown has shown convincingly that the oldest Irish manuscripts to have survived show in the arrangement of the foliation as well as in the layout of the text those very features which characterize Roman Christian manuscripts in the early fifth century. Whereas on the Continent generally and in Italy in particular changes were introduced in these features over the next two centuries as far as the manuscript appearance is concerned, what had been the trend in Rome in the early fifth century was continued in Ireland with such remarkable faithfulness that it still was recognizable in the seventh century.[19] Two phenomena are thus illustrated: the strength of schooling as established during the first generation of organized mission in the middle of the fifth century in Ireland, and the fact that this schooling took place without the further contacts that left their marks on Continental developments. Internal solidity, but in isolation, would sum up the situation of Christianity in Ireland in the later fifth and the sixth centuries.

The successful establishment of manuscript production in Ireland is a visible sign that the Christian religion had taken root in Irish society. How this happened is, unfortunately, impossible to see. What happened has been discussed more than once, and in a particularly attractive and persuasive manner by Ludwig Bieler, in his beautiful book *Ireland: Harbinger of the Middle Ages*.[20] Bieler presented a many-faceted account of the activity of Christians, offered perceptive insights into their work and thoughts, and conjured up the atmosphere in which the term "early Christian Ireland" seemed a thoroughly appropriate summary of the situation. If Bieler did not show how Christianity was in fact established, this omission was at least shared by virtually all workers in that field.

It is with a sense of deep respect for my former colleague at University College, Dublin, and with gratitude for the many insights that his rich oeuvre has offered me, that I venture to turn in a direction that he did not face. Any characterization of Christianity in early medieval Ireland will necessarily be a reflection of the state of Irish society more generally.

18 Roberts and Skeats underscore the high technical accomplishment required for transforming animal skin into a writing surface (p. 9), quoting with approval R. Reed, "parchment making is perhaps more of an art than a science".
19 J. T. Brown, "The Earliest Irish Manuscripts and their Late Antique Background" in P. Ní Chatháin and M. Richter, *Ireland and Europe*, pp. 311-27.
20 This book was originally published in German in 1961 under the title *Irland — Wegbereiter des Mittelalters* in 1961 and issued in English in 1963, in a translation by Bieler.

This, in turn, will illuminate what was specific to Irish Christianity in those centuries.

The last point to be considered thus concerns the implications of the introduction of the Latin alphabet to Ireland for writing both Latin Christian material and material in the Irish language. The latter, in the early centuries, was partly Christian at best, non-Christian more often than not. This aspect of Irish culture in the early Middle Ages has not found more than passing mention in Bieler's works, but it is arguably of as much importance as are the Christian Latin texts produced in Ireland.

The earliest surviving texts of any length written in Irish date from the eighth century.[21] However, it has been established by a number of Celtic scholars that there are reliable enough indications to suggest plausibly that writing Irish material in the Latin alphabet goes back as far as the sixth, perhaps the mid-sixth century.[22] Its application expanded continually from then so that by the eighth century one has the impression that more was written in Irish than in Latin.[23] In confining myself here to the time before *ca.* 600, I can nevertheless state that in the first two centuries of Christianity in Ireland writing both in Latin and in Irish had been established and continued to be practiced.

It is necessary to come back again to the technical aspects connected with writing. Producing texts written in parchment codices required expertise of various kinds, and investment of not inconsiderable resources. From what was indicated earlier, the Christian religion in order to function required such investment as a matter of course. The continuity of maintaining the required skills has been pointed out. Producing written Latin texts meant handling Latin learning, albeit of a limited, clearly defined nature, in Irish society.

There was, of course, also that other kind of learning in Ireland, at the time of the introduction of Christianity as well as before and after.[24] That other, secular, Irish kind of learning had, until then, existed without alphabetic writing, as a matter of choice more likely than as a consequence of non-familiarity (a point that need not be developed here). From the later sixth century onwards it can be seen that the fruits of the indigenous learning, cast in the Irish language, very gradually found their way into writing, and produced, in the course of centuries, the enormous corpus of Irish literature that forms the daily bread of Celtic scholars and

21 Cambray Homily, *Thesaurus Palaeohibernicus* II, Whitley Stokes and John Strachan, eds. (Cambridge, 1901-1903, repr. Dublin, 1975), pp. 244-47.
22 See especially Calvert Watkins, "Indo-European Metrics and Archaic Irish Verse", *Celtica* 6 (1963), pp. 194-249.
23 For the material written in Latin see Michael Lapidge and Richard Sharpe, *A Bibliography of Celtic-Latin Literature, 400–1200* (Dublin, 1985).
24 This, one of the main themes of my *Medieval Ireland: The Enduring Tradition* (1988), has been vehemently, though inconsistently, questioned by Kim McCone, *Pagan Past and Christian Present* (Maynooth, 1990).

is the unique distinctive feature of the medieval Celtic societies, giving them pride of place in the European context, if only the Europeans knew.[25]

In this paper I have emphasized at several points the technical requirements for the production of written texts. I have further emphasized that these technical resources had been available to institutionalized Christianity, and there only. As we have seen, they were available. Since they were also availed of, for purposes other than writing Latin — namely, for writing Irish — it is very likely that writing in Irish took place, initially and for several centuries to come, by recourse to the available Christian institutions.[26] Writing in Irish thus became one of the significant accomplishments of Irish Christians, and, thus, a distinctive feature of Irish Christian society. This point needs a little elaboration.

The problem we encounter here was of a more general kind. Wherever Christianity came, it encountered societies that had existed without it before, and had their own institutions and ethics that had provided internal stability and cohesion. Jan Vansina has coined the happy phrase "congruence between society and its traditions" respecting institutions.[27] In other words, traditional societies had developed customs and institutions that best served their needs. Existing institutions were subordinated to the overall common good; they were functionally part of the society. Such societies may well be called conservative or backward looking, upholding what had been maintained in the past. By contrast, Christianity, the newcomer to such societies, entailed in almost every respect unfamiliar values. It was conceived as offering something essentially new: "The old has passed away, behold, the new has come" (2 Cor. 5:17). Also, it claimed to have the best solutions to Man's questions, the best way to fulfill Man's needs. It claimed universal validity and exclusiveness. It set out to break with other values that might exist.

It is this aspect which is of greatest relevance to us here as regards Ireland. That Christian values were pursued by Irish people in the period under consideration is shown nowhere better than in the life and works of

---

25 It is symptomatic that the Celtic countries are left out in the survey by Karl Langosch et al., *Geschichte der Textüberlieferung der antiken und mittelalterlichen Literatur*, vol. 2 (Middle Ages) (Zürich, 1964), a work which has not really been superseded. Yet even in the *New History of Ireland*, vol. 2 (Ireland 1169–1534), A. Cosgrove, ed. (Oxford, 1987), just over 1% of the space is given to material written in the Irish language. The most concise and comprehensive survey now available is *Geschichte und Kultur der Kelten. Vorbereitungskonferenz 25.- 28. Oktober 1982, Bonn. Vorträge*, Karl Horst Schmidt and R. Ködderitzsch, eds. (Heidelberg, 1986).

26 "In the earliest period of our written vernacular literature there was a large group of men who combined in themselves the native tradition and the new Christian learning. All our early literature is the result of this complexity." James Carney, *The Irish Bardic Poet* (Dublin, 1967), p. 9.

27 Jan Vansina, *Oral Tradition as History* (London, 1985), p. 114.

Columbanus. It suffices to point to him as a representative of what was most uplifting in early Irish Christianity: his radical determination to follow Christ, the awareness of the difficulty which this entailed, but also the deep conviction that there was no alternative path to salvation.[28] Such an attitude of course required a complete break with values upheld in Irish society; it may be said that, as far as can be seen, Columbanus did this successfully to a remarkable degree.

We have mentioned earlier that this problem was universal, and everywhere men and women like Columbanus are found, but they were exceptional personalities, not the rule. The problem was summed up, better than by many, by Gregory the Great, one of the people with whom Columbanus corresponded.[29] Columbanus behaved towards the bishop of Rome with a curious mixture of respect and self-assurance, in this attitude embodying the proud Irishman. But he would have agreed with the statement of Gregory on the issue in question here. Gregory wrote to bishop Leander of Seville: *In uno se ore cum Iovis laudibus Christi laudes non capiunt.*[30] In a loose way, and surely in the manner intended by Gregory, the phrase may be translated as follows: "It is not appropriate to sing the praises of Christ and at the same time uphold traditional values."

Apparently, such a reminder was appropriate towards the Spanish bishop. Of course, it was likewise applicable to Ireland, even though no comparable utterance can be quoted. However, the available material concerned with traditional Irish beliefs, practices, and ethics is ample proof that Christianity had not transformed (nor was to transform) Irish society in the manner and with the completeness envisaged by the founder and pursued by some of his determined followers. This is the ambivalence I referred to at the beginning of the article.[31] The material written in Irish, to some extent, though by no means exclusively, dealing with matter non-Christian and pre-Christian, shows that traditional values were not abandoned in Irish society even after Christianity had been established. One can thus speak of a certain degree of syncretism characterizing Christianity in early Irish society, a syncretism which, as I have indicated,

---

28 See Richter, *Medieval Ireland*, pp. 56–59. An excellent discussion of early Irish Christian spirituality has recently been provided, professionally, as it were (the author is a bishop) by Paul-Werner Scheele, "Motive altirischer Spiritualität in der Passio Kiliani" *Würzburger Diözesangeschichtsblätter* 51 (1989), pp. 181–219.

29 G. S. M. Walker, ed., *Sancti Columbani Opera* (Dublin, 1957), Ep. I, pp. 2–13.

30 Pierre Riché, *Education et culture dans l'Occident barbare, VI–VIIIème siècles*, 3rd ed. (Paris, 1962), p. 196.

31 One may refer to an extreme manifestation of this in pointing out that, as an expression of respect, Christ is occasionally even called "my druid" e.g. *is é mo·drui Crist mac Dé*. See J. Vendryes, "Druidisme et christianisme dans l'Irlande du Moyen-Âge", in Vendryes, *Choix d'études* (see n 1), pp. 317–32, at p. 331. For a more recent discussion, see Proinsias Mac Cana, "Christianisme et paganisme dans l'Irlande ancienne", in Proinsias Mac Cana, ed., *Rencontres de religions* (Paris, 1986), pp. 57–74.

was irreconcilable with the Christian message *tout court*, but which was the most that could be achieved almost anywhere.[32]

Is there, then, nothing peculiar to the situation in Ireland as I have presented it here? Surely the answer must be more than monosyllabic. If it is the case that in early medieval Europe Christianity could be put into practice at best partially — if old, pre-Christian values remained in force — then Ireland indeed is just one more case showing the limitations of the power of Christian persuasion.

But there is also another dimension to the problem. While in one respect, in the qualified success of Christianity, the Irish situation repeats or foreshadows other cases, in another respect this cannot be maintained. For one of the results of the implantation of Christianity into Irish society, the writing down of traditional learning with the help of the Latin alphabet, has no equivalent in other societies.[33] It is true that basically Christianity brought about the "literalization" of previously unwritten languages in many societies, but nowhere did this produce such a stunning amount of material, nor such great diversity, as in the corpus available in early and medieval Irish.

As far as the Western half of Europe is concerned, Ireland stands out not only in the context of subsequent development, but even when one compares it to the situation of the Roman Empire. Here we must be clear about our terms of comparison. Christianity spread in Roman society at a time when that society had had several centuries of learning fixed in writing, much of it of great antiquity and preserved because it had withstood the test of time. Roman society possessed a fairly advanced level of lay literacy which was, predominantly, built on traditional values, maintained and continued by people of good social standing.

In Roman society Christianity brought new ethics,[34] but no new technology to fix its ideas in written form and thereby spread them. In this respect, Christianity had fewer "fringe benefits" to offer to the Romans than to other societies that had not had literacy before the advent of Christianity.

I have indicated that the "fringe benefits" of Christianity were taken up in Ireland along with parts of the central message. While, speaking very generally, Christianity in Roman society did not in a major way stimulate pre-Christian learning, perhaps because that had long been cast in written form, this does seem to have been the situation in Ireland.

---

32 I have developed this further in "Die Symbiose von Christentum und archaischer Gesellschaft in Irland, 400–800" in Hildegard L. C. Tristram, ed., *Studien zur Táin Bó Cuailgne* (Tübingen, 1993), 159–72.

33 There was no such thing as a "European mainstream" into which Ireland could be fitted as maintained by McCone, *Pagan Past and Christian Present*, pp. ix, 25, 142, 148.

34 See, however, the article by Peter Brown quoted above, n.12.

We must not confine our view of the material produced in written form in Ireland to that cast in the Irish language. Nor is it the case that all material written in Irish presents traditional values from time immemorial conserved in unadulterated form.[35] However, it cannot likewise be maintained that what was produced in written form in the Irish language was all new, of Christian inspiration,[36] and without roots in pre-Christian times.

However, to deal with these special aspects is beyond the brief I have set myself here. It is a subject that has been discussed variously and will continue to attract attention. My aim has been to provide a basis for discussing the suggestion that the coming of Christianity to Ireland, especially the introduction of Latin alphabetic writing, made a considerable difference to Irish society even if the particular manifestations of this difference remain to be determined.

35 See Donnchadh Ó Corráin, Liam Breatnach, and Aidan Breen, "The Laws of the Irish", *Peritia* 3 (1984), pp. 382-438, and the warning note sounded by Thomas Charles-Edwards, "Early Irish Law", *School of Celtic Studies, Fiftieth Anniversary Report 1940-1990* (Dublin, 1990), pp. 110-12.
36 "Die überlieferten Landesgesetze sind . . . das wohlerwogene Werk gebildeter christlicher Rechtsgelehrter, die aus einheimischen und fremden Quellen Recht *für eine christliche Gesellschaft* [italics MR] setzten." Donnchadh Ó Corráin, "Die Kirche in der irischen Gesellschaft. Ihre politische und rechtliche Stellung" in Kilian, *Mönch aus Irland. Aller Franken Patron, Veröffentlichungen zur Bayerischen Geschichte und Kultur* 19 (1989), pp. 39-47, at p. 41.

A NOTE ON
EARLY IRISH PROSODY

Edgar M. Slotkin

UNIVERSITY OF CINCINNATI

In his seminal article "Three Old Irish Accentual Poems" the late James Carney claimed that the earliest and most natural prosodic forms of attested Irish verse were accentual in nature and that "strict syllable counting began in the early seventh century [and] was an upper-class aberration" (Carney, 53). Professor Carney was almost certainly correct in thinking that early Irish poetry was accentual like popular modern verse forms. Accentual verse seems inherent in the rhythmic structure of the language. Every indication suggests that Old Irish was a stress-timed language — that is, in the production of speech, rhythm was characteristically achieved through "the stress-producing process: the stress-pulses, and hence the stressed syllables, are isochronous" (Abercrombie, 97). Stress-timed languages contrast with syllable-timed languages where "recurrence of movement is supplied by the syllable-producing process" (ibid.). Syllable-timed languages include French and Japanese; stress-timed languages include English, German, Irish, and Welsh.

Where the normal production of speech shows a tendency toward isochronous alternation of stressed and unstressed syllables, we normally find a language's natural meters to be accentual ones. Languages which are syllable-timed have naturally syllabic or quantitative meters. Now it is perfectly reasonable for poets to employ further defining characteristics in metrical practice, so that much of post-medieval English verse is accentual-syllabic in nature. But Derek Attridge (1982) has demonstrated the follies of attempting to describe English metrical practice through syllabic meters alone; and his system, surely the most useful devised so far, can account for English classical verse purely through the arrangement of beats and offbeats within the framework of isochronous English stress patterns. Indeed, his system allows for prosodic descriptions of folk and nursery rhymes as well as Shakespeare and Milton, something which "classical" scansions in terms of iambic pentameter, etc., systems founded on syllabic-quantitative meters, cannot accomplish.

To return to Professor Carney's position, he criticizes the now standard position of Calvert Watkins in "Indo-European Metrics and Archaic Irish Verse" as to the status of what Watkins characterized as the Irish archaic long line verse form: a heptasyllabic line with a final cadence of stressed syllable, unstressed syllable, anceps syllable. Professor Watkins' position here, though, takes the meter to be syllabic in part but characterizes its most distinctive feature, the cadenced ending, through a stress pattern. Carney claimed that Watkins' views and his own "seem to be mutually exclusive" (Carney, 53), but such is not really the case.

Let us assume that Professor Watkins is correct, and the verse form he discusses represents a basic, native, archaic meter and not an "upper-class aberration". Let us also assume that Professor Carney was correct as well, and that such an archaic meter was inherently accentual, at least in the Old Irish period and after. Now let us look at a characteristic line, one from the legal text *Din Techtugud*:

> ó modaib marc　　mrogsaite[1]

Using the system developed by Attridge, we could scan this line as follows:

> –s +s –s　　+s　　　+s　–s –s
> **ó modaib marc　　mrogsaite**
> o　B　o　　B　　　B　　ô

Here "+s" stands for a stressed syllable, "–s" for an unstressed syllable. "B" represents a beat, "o" an offbeat, and "ô" a double offbeat. This method graphically represents how stressed and unstressed syllables are realized as beats or offbeats in a verse instance. Another example, from *Longes Mac n-Uislenn*:

> +s –s　　　+s –s　　　+s　–s –s
> **frissa-　mberad　Feidlimid[2]**
> B　o　　　B　o　　　B　　ô

---

1 'Through the labors of horses who extended it' (Watkins, 221).
2 'From which Feidlimid might obtain' (Watkins, 223).

Elaborating examples would only serve to indicate that the meter is a three-beat meter with an obligatory offbeat after the third beat, which is usually a double offbeat.[3]

In the normal course of isochrony, however, what we would expect to find is what is elaborated in the previous examples, stressed syllables followed by unstressed syllables, or vice-versa as in the first example. Given that the final cadence requires three syllables to achieve a beat and double offbeat or a fourth beat and that we require two beats in the first half-line, the norm for this verse is a line with seven syllables. Hence, the line looks to be heptasyllabic and most frequently is in fact heptasyllabic. However, in order to maintain the idea that the *meter* is heptasyllabic, Professor Watkins must resort frequently to explanations of individual lines as either catalectic or acephalic or in some way extra-metrical:

```
+s    -s-s +s  -s +s -s -s
findnaise ban a céttellach4
 B   ô   B   o  B   ô
```

This example from the Laws is octosyllabic and contains an extra offbeat. But the three-beat pattern with the cadence remains intact.

Crucial to understanding this verse is understanding the allowable placement of offbeats, but I am not going to attempt that here other than to note the obligatory cadenced ending offbeat. My purpose has been to indicate a fruitful way of examining early Irish meters and to reconcile what might appear to be a discrepancy between observing that early Irish verse is accentual and the nevertheless archaic nature of the verses Professor Watkins examined. For by considering this archaic verse as accentual, we in no way violate his basic observation that its form resembles that of the gnomic-epic line he demonstrates in Sanskrit, Greek and Slavic. Rather, the question now becomes a more basic one. If the earliest attested Indo-European languages were syllable-timed languages which developed basically syllabic meters, by what process did other Indo-European languages become stress-timed languages, developing accentual meters? Do other stress-timed languages show similar accom-

---

3   Attridge contends convincingly that in English verse there are no three-beat lines; all seemingly three-beat lines contain an unrealized fourth beat:

> Hickory Dickory Dock.
> B ô   B ô   B   [B]

The "natural" English verse meter is a four-beat line. Whether or not this is true for Irish I am not prepared to say definitively, but it may be correct. In that case, three-beat lines would contain an unrealized beat which is actually realized when the anceps syllable is stressed.

4   'With women witness on the occasion of the first entry' (Watkins, 227).

modations to archaic Indo-European metrical practices? These questions would have been of great interest to Brendan O Hehir. I raise them in his memory and hope that further work will add to our understanding of metrical practice to the same extent that his research did.

REFERENCES

Abercrombie, David. 1967. *Elements of General Phonetics*. Chicago: Aldine Publishing.

Attridge, Derek. 1982. *The Rhythms of English Poetry*. London and New York: Longman.

Carney, James. 1971. "Three Old Irish Accentual Poems". *Ériu* 22:23–80.

Watkins, Calvert. 1963. "Indo-European Metrics and Archaic Irish Verse". *Celtica* 6:194–249.

SAILING STRANGE SEAS OF THOUGHT: *IMRAMA*, MÁEL DÚIN TO MULDOON

Robert Tracy

UNIVERSITY OF CALIFORNIA AT BERKELEY

> A man in the wilderness asked me,
> How many strawberries grow in the sea?
> I answered him, as I thought good,
> As many as red herrings grow in the wood.
> (Nursery rhyme)

In 1987 Paul Muldoon left Belfast to settle permanently in the United States. In doing so, he came to live in the country that had long nourished his imagination, and to enact in reality a theme he had already treated in several long poems, the journey or voyage westwards. In Old Irish literature that theme has shaped a small genre, the *imram* or voyage, literally, 'rowing about'. Muldoon has adopted and expanded that genre, beginning with "Immram" (1980), the long concluding poem in his third collection, *Why Brownlee Left* (1980), continuing through "The More a Man Has the More a Man Wants" (1983) and "7, Middagh Street" (1987), appearing respectively in *Quoof* (1983) and *Meeting the British* (1987), and culminating, at least for now, in his book-length *Madoc: A Mystery* (1990). These poems all draw on the *imram*, with its frequent random landfalls and encounters, to explore at once inner and outer reality, recognizing that the geography of the *imram* is a geography of the mind. Muldoon is closest to his Old Irish prototype in his own "Immram", acknowledging his debt to Whitley Stokes's edition and translation of the ninth-century "Voyage of Máel Dúin", and noting that his own name closely resembles that of the ancient voyager.

The *imram* (sometimes spelled *immram*) is a relatively late genre, developed after Ireland had been Christianized. Monks, hermits, themes of forgiveness for injuries or repentance for crimes are typical elements, as are frequent landings to attend Mass. We can perhaps translate *imram* more freely as 'Massing about in boats'.

Of the two major medieval tale lists we have, only one, usually called List A, refers to *imrama*, naming three: *Imram Máele Dúin*, *Imram ua Corra*, and *Imram Luinge Muirchertaig meic Erca*. List A goes on to include as *imrama* four examples of the *longes*, "or exile narrative, only one of which involves a sea narrative" (Mac Cana, 43, 77). *Imram Snēdhghusa agus Mac Ríagla* is unlisted, but nevertheless survives.

This kind of literary classification can be a slippery business, and there is a genuine problem in distinguishing between the *imram* and a pre-Christian genre, the *echtra*, or 'expedition' — literally 'outing', but with a notion of going out of this world and into the other — 'othering'. List A's *Imram Luinge Muirchertaig meic Erca* is called *echtra* in List B, as is the *Echtra Brain*, though a passage within this text refers to it as *Imram Brain*. The *imram* is essentially a Christianized *echtra*, replacing islands of sensual delight with edifying visits to holy men or tormented sinners (Mac Cana, 69–71, 76–79). Although it is written in Latin, we should also include among the *imrama* the *Navigatio Sancti Brendani*.

We arrive, then, at five *imrama*: the Voyage of Máel Dúin, the Voyage of the Uí Chorra, the Voyage of Snédgus and Mac Ríagla, the Voyage of Bran, and the Voyage of St. Brendan. Muldoon has drawn upon all five for his own *imrama*.

The *imrama* have sometimes been seen as exaggerated accounts of real voyages, and sifted to find traces of genuine navigating or recognizable geography. No doubt some of the peculiar landfalls described in these texts recall yarns of Irish sailors who had ventured out into the North Atlantic. Máel Dúin's island of the giant smiths and their fires, also visited by St. Brendan, may record a glimpse of volcanic Iceland; Brendan's "column of crystal" may have been an iceberg.

The *imrama*, however, neither describe nor recall real voyages. They are journeys of the mind, allegorical imaginings, and perhaps, as Alwyn and Brinley Rees suggest, a kind of Celtic Book of the Dead (Rees and Rees, 325), charting, like the Egyptian prototype, the soul's travels in a world of absolutes and archetypes, symbols and metaphors. Bran visits the Island of Laughing, a place where the inhabitants do nothing but laugh endlessly, inanely — at nothing. What a scholastic philosopher would call the accident of laughter, needing a consciousness in which to inhere, has here achieved an impossible independence. In other *imrama*, accidents or properties, which properly must inhere in some object, show a similar independence, and bring us into a bizarre metaphysical playground. The Uí Chorra visit an island of lamenting (44);[1] Máel Dúin

---

1   Stokes, Meyer, and other editors have arranged the *imrama* texts in numbered paragraphs, stanzas, or "chapters". My references to *imrama* are by those numberings rather than to pages.

comes to an island divided by a wall, black sheep on one side, white on the other — a white sheep placed among the black will become black, and vice versa (12). Blackness and whiteness somehow exist independently here, and in a later island of men "black in body and clothing" who lament; one of Máel Dúin's men lands, immediately turns black, and begins to lament (15). Oisín visits islands of dancing, of victories, and of forgetfulness. To "other" is, in Wordsworth's phrase, to sail strange seas of thought alone, to evade the categories of logical thought.

Since the *imram* is a literary form developed after Christianity came to Ireland, it usually reflects the dualistic either/or nature of Christian thought, itself the heir of Greco-Roman philosophy. Máel Dúin finds laughers on one island, wailers on another; black sheep are separate from white sheep. If the *imram* voyager sails among independent accidental qualities, the qualities are rigidly categorized. *Imram Brain*, however, is intriguingly free of this categorization, perhaps because its early date means it is least affected by Christian or Greco-Roman thought.

Like Connla the Fair and Cormac mac Airt, Bran is enticed to journey by a beautiful but otherworldly woman, who suddenly appears in his banquet hall to sing of the wonders out in the sea, in a poem of twenty-eight stanzas — the number of Bran's company, and of the phases of the moon, or days of the lunar month. In the text as we have it, he does not visit any of the wonderful places her song describes, except the island of laughter (21, 61) and the island of women (19, 30, 62).

Unlike the other *imrama*, where the voyagers are always arriving at, nearing, or departing from yet another island, rather than sailing the open sea, Bran's chief adventures are passive and literary: his listening to two poems. That sung by the mysterious woman becomes true when he does reach the island of women, where he and his twenty-seven companions, in three companies of nine, are sexually and gastronomically entertained. The other poem is sung by Manannán mac Lir, as he rides in his chariot beside Bran's ship. Manannán's song, also in twenty-eight stanzas, denies the evidence of Bran's senses, or rather suggests the simultaneous presence of alternate realities. For Manannán, the sea over which Bran sails is a plain of flowers:

MANNANÁN MAC LIR'S SONG TO BRAN MAC FEBAIL[2]

Caíne amrae lassin mBran
ina churchán tar muir nglan;
  os mé, im charput ca déin,
  is mag scothach imma-réid.

His ship on the shining ocean
Delights and amazes Bran,
Where the flowering plain spreads wide
For the chariot I ride.

Is muir nglan
don noí brainig i tá Bran;
  is Mag Mell co n-imbud scoth
  damsa i carput dá roth.

Shining ocean
For the prowed ship bearing Bran:
Mag Mell's broad flowering fields
Are under my chariot-wheels.

Ad-cí Bran
lín tonn tipri tar muir nglan;
  ad-cíu ca-déin i mMaig Mon
  scotha cennderga cen on.

Before Bran
Waves break on bright ocean.
Flawless flowers are in scarlet bloom
For me on the Plain of Games.

Taitnet gabra lir i ssam
sella roisc ro shiri Bran,
  bruindit srotha srúaim di mil
  i crích Manannáin maic Lir.

In summer sea-horses gleam
Wherever Bran's eyes roam.
Flowers' sweet nectars stream
In Manannán mac Lir's realm.

Lí na fairgge fora taí,
geldath mora imme-raí,
  ro sert buide ocus glas,
  is talam nád écomrass.

The shining sea beneath you,
The dazzling ocean you row,
Where yellows and greens extend;
It is solid ground.

Lengait iich ass di brú
a muir finn forn-aiccisiu,
  it loíg, it úain co ndagdath,
  co cairdi, cen immarbad.

You see speckled salmon leap
From the womb of the white sea;
They are lovely-hued lambs, they are calves
Living peaceful harmonious lives.

---

2 Manannán's twenty-eight stanza song (Meyer/Mac Mathúna, §§ 33–60) shifts
   after twelve stanzas (at 45) into a description of Adam's fall, and a prophecy of the
   conception and birth of Mongán (unnamed), who is clearly a version of the re-
   deeming Christ, though fathered by a trick on a mortal woman by a pagan god.
   The poem looks both ways, combining two more contraries, pagan and Christian
   beliefs. I include above the text and my translation of the poem's first twelve
   stanzas (M/M, §§ 33–44), those dealing with the two realities and describing the
   sinless land undersea. Irish text from David Greene and Frank O'Connor, ed. and
   trans., *A Golden Treasury of Irish Poetry* (London: Macmillan, 1967), there
   adapted from A. G. van Hamel, ed., *Immrama*.

Ce ad-cetha oínchairptech
i mMaig Mell co n-imbud scoth,
  fil mór di echaib ar brú
  cen suide, nád aiccisiu.

Mét in maige, lín int shlóaig,
taitnet líga co nglanbóaid,
  findshruth arcait, dreppa óir,
  fáircet fáilti cech imróil.

Cluiche n-aímin, indel áig,
aigtit fri findimmarbáig
  fir is mná míni, fo doss,
  cen pheccad, cen immorbus.

Is íar mbarr fedo ro sná
do churchán tar indrada,
  fid fo mess i mbí gnöe
  fo braini do beccnöe.

Fid co mbláth ocus torad
for mbí fíno fírbolad,
  fid fil cen erchra, cen bath,
  fors fil duille co n-órdath.

Fil dún ó thossuch dúile
cen aís, cen coirbthi úire;
  ní frescam di meth angus;
  nín táraill in immorbus.

The lone charioteer you sight
On the many-flowered Plain of Delight
You cannot see the host of steeds
On its bosom, to all sides.

Lovely gay colors shine
From the vast crowd, the broad plain;
Golden stairs, silver streams are bright
Making every feast a delight.

Gentle men and women play
A sweet and pleasant game
Under boughs, in fair competition,
Sinless, without transgression.

Your curragh voyages
Across tree tops, over ridges;
Beautiful orchards grow
Under your vessel's prow.

Trees are in blossom, yet bear,
True scent of vines on the air
In that wood without blemish or blight
Whose leaves are golden bright.

Here, since creation began
We neither age nor weaken;
We do not grow old or die;
Sin has passed us by.

The poem dissolves, or at any rate questions, the logical distinction between sea and land, and questions what Bran sees and experiences as he sails. It is not just a challenge to his senses. It asserts that two realities can exist simultaneously in the same place at the same time. Contraries can be tolerated rather than reconciled. Richard Kearney has argued that the Irish mind thinks in terms of both/and rather than either/or:

> From the earliest times, the Irish mind remained free, in significant measure, of the linear, centralising logic of the Graeco-Roman culture. . . . This . . . culture was based on the Platonic-Aristotelian logic of non-contradiction which operated on the assumption that order and organisation result from the dualistic separation of opposite or contradictory terms. Hence the mainstream of western thought rested upon a series of fundamental oppositions — between being and non-being, reason and imagination, the soul and the body, the transcendentally divine and the immanently temporal, and so on . . . .

In contradistinction to the orthodox dualist logic of EITHER/OR, the Irish mind may . . . favor a more dialectical logic of BOTH/AND: an intellectual ability to hold the traditional oppositions of classical reason together in creative confluence . . . [T]he symbolic systems of neolithic Newgrange or Celtic mythology . . . testify to an alternative order and organisation . . . not meaninglessness but another kind of meaning, not confusion but another kind of coherence . . . . I would insist that this be understood as a CULTURAL phenomenon which develops and alters as history progresses, and NOT as some innate racial characteristic.

(Kearney, 9–11)

Kearney cites Joyce's neat encapsulation of both/and thinking: "two thinks at a time" (*Finnegans Wake* 583.7).

Irish folklore and earlier Irish mythology present a world of men and women sharing Ireland with the other world of the *sí* (Middle Irish *áes síde* 'folk of the fairy mounds'). Sometimes the two worlds interact. Manannán's double vision, where sea is land and land sea, recurs in some of the other *imrama*. Máel Dúin comes to a part of the sea that is like cloud, so thin he fears it cannot support his boat; undersea are forts, a broad landscape, herdsmen and flocks, an armed man, a monster in a tree that seizes and devours an ox (23). In *The Calendar of Oengus*, St. Scothín, walking on the sea, encounters Barra of Cork in his ship. Scothín insists he walks on a flowery meadow, and tosses Barra a flower to prove it; Barra insists they are on the sea, and, reaching down, pulls a salmon from the waves and throws it to Scothín (*Oengus* xxxii).[3]

The interpenetration of two realities, sea and land, is neatly reversed in an experience of the monks of Clonmacnoise, the subject of a poem by Seamus Heaney:

The annals say: when the monks of Clonmacnoise
Were all at prayers inside the oratory
A ship appeared above them in the air.

The anchor dragged along behind so deep
It hooked itself into the altar rails
And then, as the big hull rocked to a standstill,

A crewman shinned and grappled down the rope
And struggled to release it. But in vain.
'This man can't bear our life here and will drown,'

The abbot said, 'unless we help him.' So
They did, the freed ship sailed, and the man climbed back
Out of the marvellous as he had known it.

(*Seeing Things* 62)

3   For an alternate version, see Appendix.

"The folk tradition of the insular Celts seems to present to the mind a half-aquatic world . . ." David Jones remarked; "it introduces a feeling of transparency and interpenetration of one element with another, of transposition and metamorphosis" (Jones, 238–39). The other world shares space and time with this one. Contraries can be united, yet remain dual. If this reflects aspects of Celtic or pre-Celtic cosmology, it also anticipates modern scientific thought. Einstein's theory of relativity as developed by his successors sees the universe originating in a mathematical point of infinite density and zero extent, but the laws of quantum physics declare such a point to be impossible. Theoretical physicists have to act as if these mutually contradictory concepts are both true. The physicist Niels Bohr recognizes art's ability "to remind us of harmonies beyond the grasp of systematic analysis" (Bohr, 79), but science, for all its dependence on logic, must do the same; J. Robert Oppenheimer points out that "an electron must sometimes be considered as a wave, and sometimes as a particle" (Oppenheimer, 69), two mutually contradictory positions.[4] Manannán's song presents us with an expanded provisional reality, and so enables us, like Bran and his companions, and all the other *imrama* voyagers, to experience mystery, the most profound of religious — or artistic — sentiments.

Paul Muldoon's *imrama* retain that mystery. They are not simply narratives of journeys westward, though they are shaped by the act of journeying. They preserve the spirit, indeed the paradox, of the traditional *imram*, its uncertainties and amazements. If the first of them, "Immram", closely parodies *Imram Máel Dúin*, it shows how thoroughly Muldoon has understood the genre's characteristic guilt/penitence and the characteristic randomness of the encounters it portrays. In each subsequent *imram*, Muldoon shows greater boldness, and a deeper understanding of the genre's defiance of linear patterns and categories of thought. With *Madoc: A Mystery* (1990) he explores Manannán mac Lir's vision of mutually existing contraries, and even connects the poem's contradictory realities, if not with theoretical physics, at least with advanced cybernetic theory and technology. In his modern *imrama*, Muldoon has re-worked a traditional Irish genre, as Joyce before him combined the *Odyssey* and the *imram* in *Ulysses*, and elaborated the *imram* in *Finnegans Wake*.

The searcher in "Immram" searches for his father, not his father's murderer, but most of his adventures have their parallels in *Imram Máele Dúin* — though Muldoon does not encounter Máel Dúin's gigantic ants or the mysterious beast that can turn itself inside out (*Máel Dúin* 2, 8). In "Immram" Muldoon — let us call him — decides to look for his father,

---

4   I am indebted to Norman Rabkin, *Shakespeare and the Common Understanding*, for directing me to these passages by Bohr and Oppenheimer.

vanished like the expected *ball* of the opening couplet: "I was fairly and squarely behind the eight / That morning in Foster's pool-hall." He undertakes the search because a billiard player, "Dressed to kill, or inflict a wound," knocks him out with a billiard-cue after a brief lesson in genealogy:

> 'Your old man was an ass-hole.
> That makes an ass-hole out of you.'
> My grand-father hailed from New York State.
> My grand-mother was part Cree.
> This must be some new strain in my pedigree.

Máel Dúin's adventures begin when, competing at games, a jealous comrade tells him his parents are in fact foster parents ("Foster's pool-hall"); he learns that his mother is a nun, raped by his father, and that his father was later killed by "Marauders of Leix". Muldoon drives "west to Paradise", not exactly a convent, but a religiously run hymn-singing home for the elderly; on his first visit there his mother is unable to speak, but a second visit is more productive: "my father owed Redpath money. / Redpath. She told me how his empire / Ran a little more than half-way to Hell / But began on the top floor of the Park Hotel."

Muldoon's journey takes him through Raymond Chandler's Los Angeles, sometimes described in the language of Philip Marlowe: "I suppose that I should have called the cops / Or called it a day and gone home. . . . She was wearing what looked like a dead fox / Over a low-cut sequinned gown. . . . I did a breast-stroke through the carpet." Like Marlowe, he encounters various thugs and temptations on his way to Redpath, the Mr. Big who controls the narcotics trade.

Not surprisingly, some of Muldoon's adventures take place in and near the Atlantic Club, others at "that old Deep Water Baptist Mission / Near the corner of Sixteenth and Ocean", where hymns have given way to "the strains of Blind Lemon Jefferson." Both are outposts of Redpath's drug empire. The music, like the hymns at the rest home, recalls the psalm-singing birds Máel Dúin finds (18). Máel Dúin visits an island containing a comfortable and well-provisioned house uninhabited save for a small playful cat; when one of the travelers takes a necklace, the cat "leapt through him . . . like a fiery arrow, and burnt him so that he became ashes" (11); the "Immram" counterpart is "a solitary black cat / Who would have turned the heads of Harlem . . . I watch him trickle a fine, white powder / Into his palm . . . angel dust." Muldoon has already been sent on a drug-induced trip. "When I was hit by a hypodermic syringe. / And I entered a world equally rich and strange," to be seduced by a woman who invites him to share her morgue slab. He wakes up outside, "under a steaming pile of trash / In the narrow alleyway" behind the Baptist Mission. Máel Dúin and his men are drugged, or made drunk, by a woman who listens to proposals that she sleep with him, but when they awaken, "they were in their boat on a crag; and they saw not the island, nor the fortress, nor the lady, nor the place wherein they had been" (18).

Muldoon seeks help from a police lieutenant named Brendan, who turns out to be in Redpath's pay, corrupt as Chandler's police often are. When he returns to the Mission, it has been transformed into a church for "a wholly new religion" based on surfing: "He called it *The Way Of The One Wave* / This one wave was sky-high, like a wall of glass, / And had come to him in a vision. / You could ride it forever, effortlessly." Máel Dúin comes to places (24, 25) where the water behaves in a similar way, though it never occurs to him to break out his surfboard.

Muldoon finally discovers that his father was a "mule", a carrier of drugs from South America for Redpath's syndicate. He is now hiding from the syndicate, having lost a shipment of cocaine stashed inside a hollow statue of Christ of the Andes — he dropped the statue in Lima airport, and it shattered. Muldoon is taken finally to see Redpath, who turns out to be the late Howard Hughes:

> He was huddled on an old orthopaedic mattress,
> The makings of a skeleton,
> Naked but for a pair of draw-string shorts.
> His hair was waistlength, as was his beard.
> He was covered in bedsores.
> He raised one talon.
> 'I forgive you,' he croaked. 'And I forget.
> On your way out, you tell that bastard
> To bring me a dish of ice-cream.
> I want Baskin-Robbins banana-nut ice-cream.'

So forgiveness is achieved at last, and Muldoon leaves us, to make "my way back, like any other pilgrim, / To Main Street, to Foster's pool-room." Máel Dúin long ago spoke with the hairy Hughes: on four different islands he met hermits clothed only in their own hair (19, 20, 30, 33); the last of them, the hermit from Torach, tells Máel Dúin he will find his father's murderer, but adds "slay him not, but forgive him, because God has saved you from manifold great perils, and ye, too, are men deserving of death." If Máel Dúin's is a journey of the imagination, a romp among qualities and concepts, Muldoon enters the hallucinatory world of drugs, or perhaps dreams it all after being struck with the billiard-cue. His is a very private eye — though he notes an unmarried couple registering at the Park Hotel as Mr. and Mrs. Alfred Tennyson, a graceful reminder of Tennyson's "The Voyage of Maeldune" (1880) exactly a century earlier.

Madoc: A Mystery (1990) represents Muldoon's most complex re-working of the *imram*, both as imagined journey and as philosophic voyage through strange seas of thought. Though perhaps technically excluded from the *imram* genre because its journeying is mostly on land — there are river journeys — Muldoon's voyagers move through a shifting and fluid landscape. As they do, they explore North America to the Pacific, and also explore the concept of exploring: exploring as surveying and mapping, exploring as quest, exploring as exploiting, exploring as random wandering, as drug trip, as hallucinatory or imaginary journey, as engagement with mystery. In one sense, *Madoc* is a poem about itself, about the act of reading poetry.

Muldoon's title commemorates Robert Southey's long heroic poem *Madoc* (1805), which in turn celebrates the discovery and conquest of America by the twelfth-century Welsh prince Madoc, or Madog. Madoc's legendary achievement was sometimes cited in Tudor times as justifying English claims in the New World (Deacon, 60). Madoc sailed to America around 1170, and established a colony in the Mississippi Valley near Aztlan, then the home of the Aztecs; in 1953 the D.A.R. erected a memorial tablet at Mobile, Alabama, to mark his landing place. Madoc defeated the Aztecs in battle, overthrew their idols, and converted them to Christianity. But when he returned to Wales to recruit more settlers, the Aztecs lapsed. Madoc defeated them again, killing their serpent god. The Aztecs were forced to leave Aztlan, and wandered until they eventually settled in the valley of Mexico. Southey's preface notes the presence of Madoc's "posterity . . . to this day, on the southern branches of the Missouri."

Southey learned about Madoc from the Welsh poet Edward Williams (1740–1826), also known as the bard Iolo Morgannwg, who wrote about Madoc, and forged a medieval account of his journey, early in the nine-teenth century (Deacon, 56–59). Eighteenth-century travelers reported a tribe of Welsh-speaking Indians, presumably descendants of Madoc's colony, who had rosaries, crucifixes, and Welsh Bibles: perhaps the Mandans, perhaps the Modocs. The Welsh speakers shyly retreated west-wards as Europeans advanced. At Williams's suggestion, John Evans (1770–1799) went to find them, and spent a winter among the Mandans. "In respect of the Welsh Indians," he wrote in 1797, ". . . I think you may with safety inform our friends that they have no existence" — a statement that at least one modern enthusiast considers evidence that they *did* exist. Lewis and Clark used Evans's map of the Missouri; they, too, tried to find the Welsh Indians. In 1815, Southey reviewed Lewis and Clark's account of their expedition; in a new edition of *Madoc* he sadly conceded "that no Welsh Indians are to be found upon any branches of the Missouri" (*Madoc* 1:viii). To enjoy Southey's story of Prince Madoc, we must believe what we know is not true, balance our sense of American history against his, live for a time in Manannán's realm of simultaneous contraries.

Southey and Coleridge are Muldoon's principal characters in *Madoc*, and they too introduce us to the play of contraries. In 1795, according to Muldoon, the two poets and their wives, the Fricker sisters, sailed from Bristol to Philadelphia to establish their long-projected Pantisocracy — "equal rule by all" — on the banks of the Susquehanna, between Athens and Ulster. The colony began well, but Cinnamond, their guide, abducted Sarah Coleridge and sold her to the Senecas, a tribe of philosophers. Coleridge went to the rescue. Through a telescope he watched Chief Red Jacket rape her. He was never able to catch up with her as various tribes traded her westwards. During his quest he was captured by Lewis and Clark, who took him for a British spy. He escaped to reach the Pacific, where he lived with a Spokane Indian woman tattooed with the name "Evans" — perhaps a Welsh Indian, perhaps inscribed by John Evans, perhaps the Mary Evans whom Coleridge had loved in early youth. Coleridge died in 1834, en route back to the Pantisocracy. His ghost made it back, frightening Southey badly.

After Coleridge had gone west, Southey became increasingly reclusive, introspective, tyrannical. He made the Pantisocracy into Southeyopolis, with himself as dictator, enslaving the Cayuga Indians. Edith (Fricker) Southey lapsed into "a succession of incoherent dreams" (R. S. to Lightfoot, 11 May 1836; Simmons, 196). She died in 1837; her last word was "sentiment", or possibly "Cinnamond". Southey was senile when the Cayugas, with the help of the Iroquois False Face Society, revolted, destroyed Southeyopolis, and killed him in 1843.

But the Pantisocracy was never real, it was only a dream project that Southey and Coleridge never attempted and soon abandoned. In reality, Southey settled in the Lake District, providing a home for Sarah Coleridge and her children. Coleridge avoided his family, gave brilliant lectures, and became addicted to laudanum. He placed himself under a doctor's supervision at Highgate in 1816, and died there in 1834. Southey eventually became Poet Laureate, to Byron's scorn. He wrote constantly until his death in 1843. In his last years, he published successive volumes of *The Doctor* (1834–47), a kind of novel based on *Tristram Shandy*, full of digressions and long quotations from other books. In *The Doctor* he frequently quotes approvingly from the clerical controversialist Robert South (1634–1716).

Coleridge and Southey did not sail to America; Coleridge and Southey sailed to America. Coleridge abandoned his wife; Coleridge sought her in vain across a continent. Southey died in his bed; Southey died in an Indian rebellion. We bring to *Madoc* our own knowledge of the two poets' careers, which we must keep in mind as we watch them in America, their adventures placed among other events that we know occurred: the Lewis and Clark Expedition, Aaron Burr's conspiracy, the career of Handsome Lake, the Iroquois prophet. As in Manannán's song, we must accept and play among contraries, abandon traditional categories of either/or. "Two thinks at a time" (Joyce, *Finnegans Wake* 583.7).

Muldoon's *Madoc* is about traveling, and the reader becomes a voyager, erranding into the wilderness as Coleridge does, to move among the apparently random episodes which comprise the poem's wilderness. *Madoc* employs the simultaneous frames of advanced cinematic technique to present alternate realities. Muldoon heads each episode with the name of a philosopher, from Thales, who believed that everything was water, to Stephen Hawking, who can tolerate contraries. "I love to keep the story flowing on in one unbroken tide of time if possible," said Southey of his *Madoc*. He considered Lewis and Clark hopelessly unimaginative when they named new places ("Big-Muddy . . . Little-Shallow"), and jeered at their naming the Jefferson River's three tributaries: Philosophy River, Wisdom River, Philanthropy River (Southey, *Quarterly Review* 335, 346). Muldoon's *Madoc* is Philosophy River. The reader moves from philosopher to philosopher as the *imram* moves from island to island. Lewis and Clark describe buffaloes leaping from ice-cake to ice-cake to cross the thawing Missouri; Muldoon requires a similar agility from his readers. If some of the philosophers can be related to the events in their sections, others seem unrelated, random, but they all add to the poem reminders of a tier of abstract thought, present if often unexplained.

Scotus Eriugena considered Hell "a fantasy which torments the mind" (Kearney, 92, 94), an imagined place, and so it appears among the imagined islands of the *imram*. Muldoon provides a provocatively contemporary equivalent for the visionary experiences of the *imrama*. Since "Immram" his characters often find themselves on drug trips, and Coleridge was notorious for his opium habit; here he enters a hashish paradise which is at once Kubla Khan's pleasure dome and "the summer palace / of the Old Man of the Mountains" (61), he who put the hashish into assassins. But in fact *Madoc* takes place in cyberspace, a computer-created "virtual reality", now available as "Virtuality 1000CS", an interactive computer game which gives the helmeted player the sensation of three-dimensional activity. Cyberspace has been defined as "an infinite artificial world where humans *navigate* [italics mine] in information-based space" (Benedikt), that is, an artificial environment created by computer. Drugs alter the mind; cyberspace alters reality.

Cyberspace as technological concept has its literary counterpart in the writers variously labeled Cyberpunks, Mirror-shades, or Neuromantics. William Gibson and Haruki Murakami are perhaps the best known among them. Gibson explores alternate or simulated realities in a world governed by all-powerful international organizations specializing in cybernetics. Computers can generate tactile realities: men, women, their surroundings. They can be talked with, eaten with, made love to. They are realities that co-exist with the often sordid reality of the protagonist: Cyborgs — or, for Gibson, "simstims", simulated stimulations. Sometimes characters have circuitry implanted in their brains. Science fiction has always favored the fantasy voyage. In a sense, the *imrama* were the science fiction of their day, imagining an inner world as if it were an outer world. In Cyberpunk writing, the inner world cannot be distinguished from the outer, and the voyage is indeed through strange seas of thought alone.

Though the whole continent of North America is its stage, *Madoc: A Mystery* actually takes place entirely inside Unitel Corporation's Dome, where one South — who quotes from "Kubla Khan" and Southey's *Thalaba the Destroyer* (1801) — has intruded into the wrong sector, to be captured by armed Geckoes. Kubla Khan's pleasure dome is imagined by the Mongol Emperor before Coleridge re-imagines it; Southey's Thalaba destroys the sinister Domdaniel, a submarine cavern inhabited by sorcerers.

South has "'xferred the motto / from the Roanoke Rood . . . CROATAN'" and glossed it: "'C[*oleridge*] RO[*bert Southey The S*]ATAN[*ic School*].'" Elsewhere, CROATAN flows into CROATOAN, the single mysterious word Captain White found carved on a tree when he returned to Raleigh's Roanoke colony in 1591; and into CROTONA, the Calabrian city where Pythagoras established for a time his own Southeyopolis. Raleigh believed in the Madoc voyage, and later, Welsh-speakers from Roanoke were an alternate explanation for the alleged Welsh-speaking Indians (Deacon, 66). Words will not always hold their shapes in *Madoc* — which can liquefy into the Médoc Jefferson sips at Monticello.

The captured South is Southey deprived of his "ey". The Geckoes harness him "to a retinagraph / . . . though one of his eyes / was totally written-off." Section *Heraclitus* almost immediately follows:

> So that, though it may seem somewhat improbable,
> all that follows
> flickers and flows
> from the back of his right eyeball.

"All that follows" are the 228 sections/philosophers after Heraclitus, who comes in fifth, after Thales (all is water), Anaximander, who invented maps and divided contraries, Anaximenes (all is water), and Pythagoras. Hakluyt, who also believed in Prince Madoc (Deacon, 66), Darwin,

Edison, and Chomsky are in. So is Coleridge, though under a version of the alias he assumed when he joined the cavalry: "Silas Tomkyn Comberbache".

One of South's eyes is "totally written-off", but the other is totally written on, for the whole poem is written or impressed on "the back of his right eyeball", an implant. "What Tiresias *sees* . . . is the substance of . . . . *The Waste Land*," Eliot long ago told us, commenting on his own fluid *imram* (Eliot, 52). South's back of the eyeball mote is to trouble the mind's eye, inscribed as it is with 233 philosophers, Lewis and Clark, Jefferson, Coleridge and Southey, Chief Cornplanter, John Evans, the Cayugas, Senecas, and Modocs, Burr and Blennerhassett and Handsome Lake, together with Pennsylvania and the Louisiana Purchase. South's retina, a net, a net bag, infinitely expandable, is the first of many bags, satchels, portmanteaux, valises, and medicine bags that are carried, lost, mislaid, or stolen throughout *Madoc*, their contents hidden, *A Mystery*.

Southey once compared *The Doctor* to the quill he was using to write it: "The story running through like the stem or backbone, which the episodes and digressions fringe like so many featherlets, leading up to that catastrophe, the gem or eye-star, for which the whole was formed, and in which all terminate" (*The Doctor* 10). Southey never finished *The Doctor*, so we never reach that "eye-star". But perhaps Muldoon does. The inscribing continues until South's eyeball explodes, taking with it Southeyopolis and the Unitel Dome.

Like the traditional *imram*, Muldoon's *Madoc* features random encounters, contraries that exist simultaneously, a subversive attitude towards the tradition of Western philosophy and its logical categories, a willingness to let the current decide the route, a tolerance for mystery, and an awareness of both sin and redemption. Southey commits the primal American sin by introducing slavery into the New World, by exploiting the Indians. Coleridge undertakes an errand into the wilderness to enact the American dream of an unspoiled and unexploited West. Unlike Lewis and Clark, who travel to survey and map, his journey is a quest, initially to find Sarah, eventually for its own sake, ending in an attempted return home, presumably to describe what he has seen, a poet's report to set beside the scientific report of Lewis and Clark. *Madoc* is that poet's report, of an America that is both visionary and cruel, a repository of yearnings, a hallucination that is virtual reality.

The western voyage, whether of Bran and the other Old Irish voyagers, or of Coleridge and Southey, has something to do with redemption, social as well as personal. The *imram* voyagers must tell their stories, bring something back to redeem the lives of those at home. The voyage westward, after all, is a voyage to the land of the dead, and such voyages — Odysseus's, Aeneas's, Christ's descent into Hell —

precede renewal: the purification of Ithaca, a new Troy, resurrection.

An errand can be a journey with a specific purpose, or an erring, a wandering — perhaps a straying from the right path, perhaps a relinquishing, a readiness for whatever may come next. Southey wanders morally by repeating the sins of slavery and exploitation. Coleridge's wandering quest intersects with the purposeful travels of Lewis and Clark. Muldoon's reader at once travels purposefully, seeking to comprehend the poem, and wanders, accepting the enigmatic development of the narratives, the abrupt appearances and disappearances of characters, the elusive themes. The reader moves through a wilderness more trackless than that of Lewis and Clark, or, as in the *imram*, over uncharted seas, like Bran and Máel Dúin. That wilderness/ocean is a virtual reality, which we can enter and wander as Bran and Máel Dúin wandered their island-dotted idea-tormented seas, each island a new revelation, a new philosopher, a new adventure, and presumably a new stage in imaginative growth.

APPENDIX
AN ENCOUNTER

How did Scothín get his name?
Not hard to say.
Once he traveled from Ireland to Rome
And back in a single day;

He met Barra of Cork in his ship
As he marched along the deep.
Asked Barra: "Why walk on the sea?"
"I walk flowering meadows," said he,

And he tossed a *scoth* on the deck,
A purple flower just picked,
Asking, "Why do you sail on land?"
Barra stretched out his hand

And plucked a fish from the waves,
A fine fresh squirming salmon,
And threw it in Scothín's way.
In those days, such encounters were common.

Robert Tracy, after a passage
in the *Martyrology of Oengus*

PRIMARY REFERENCES

Hamel, A. G. van, ed. 1941. *Immrama*. Medieval and Modern Irish Series, vol. 10. Dublin: The Stationery Office.

Mac Mathúna, Séamus, ed. and trans. 1985. *Immram Brain: Bran's Journey to the Land of the Women*. Buchreihe der *Zeitschrift für celtische Philologie*, Bd. 2. Tübingen: Max Niemeyer.

Meyer, Kuno, ed. and trans. 1893. "The Voyage of the Huí Corra", *Revue Celtique* 14 (January): 22–63.

———. 1895. *The Voyage of Bran Son of Ferbal to the Land of the Living*, vol. 1. London: David Nutt.

Muldoon, Paul. 1977. *Mules*. Winston-Salem: Wake Forest University Press.

———. 1980. *Why Brownlee Left*. Winston-Salem: Wake Forest University Press.

———. 1983. *Quoof*. Winston-Salem: Wake Forest University Press.

———. 1987. *Meeting the British*. Winston-Salem: Wake Forest Univ. Press.

———. 1990. *Madoc: A Mystery*. London: Faber.

Oskamp, H. P. A., ed. and trans. 1970. *The Voyage of Máel Dúin*. Groningen: Wolters-Noordhoff.

Stokes, Whitley, ed. and trans. 1888. "The Voyage of Mael Duin", *Revue Celtique* 9.4 (October 1888): 447–95; 10.1 (January 1889): 50–95.

———. 1889. "The Voyage of Snedgus and Mac Riagla", *Revue Celtique* 10:1 (January): 15–25.

Webb, J. F., trans. 1973. "The Voyage of St. Brendan", *Lives of the Saints*. Harmondsworth: Penguin.

SECONDARY REFERENCES

Benedikt, Michael, ed. 1991. *Cyberspace: First Steps*. Cambridge: MIT Press.

Bernhardt-Kabisch, Ernest. 1977. *Robert Southey*. Boston: Twayne.

Bohr, Niels. 1958. *Atomic Physics and Human Knowledge*. New York: John Wiley.

Carney, James. 1955. *Studies in Irish Literature and History*. Dublin: Institute for Advanced Studies.

Cross, Tom Peete and Clark Harris Slover, eds. 1936. *Ancient Irish Tales* (Repr. New York: Barnes and Noble, 1969).

Curry, Kenneth. 1975. *Southey*. London: Routledge.

Deacon, Richard. 1967. *Madoc and the Discovery of America*. London: Frederick Muller.

Eliot, T. S. 1952. *The Complete Poems and Plays*. New York: Harcourt, Brace.

Gibson, William. 1984. *Neuromancer*. New York: Ace Books.

———. 1987. *Count Zero*. New York: Ace Books.

———. 1988. *Mona Lisa Overdrive*. New York: Bantam.

Harbison, Peter. 1991. *Pilgrimage in Ireland: The Monuments and the People*. Syracuse: Syracuse Univ. Press.

Heaney, Seamus. 1991. *Seeing Things*. London: Faber.

Jones, David. 1959. *Epoch and Artist: Selected Writings*, ed. Harman Grisewood. London: Faber.

Joyce, James. 1939. *Finnegans Wake*. New York: Viking [1958].

Kearney, Richard, ed. 1985. *The Irish Mind: Exploring Intellectual Traditions*. Dublin: Wolfhound.

Kinsella, Thomas, trans. 1970. *The Táin*. London: Oxford University Press.

Löffler, Christa Maria. 1983. *The Voyage to the Otherworld Island in Early Irish Literature*. Salzburg Studies in English Literature: Elizabethan and Renaissance Studies 103, 2 vols. Salzburg: Institut für Anglistik und Amerikanistik.

Mac Cana, Proinsias. 1980. *The Learned Tales of Medieval Ireland*. Dublin: Institute for Advanced Studies.

McCaffery, Larry, ed. 1991. *Storming the Reality Studio: A Casebook of Punk and Postmodern Fiction*. Durham, N.C.: Duke University Press.

Mooney, James. 1891. "The Growth of a Myth", *American Anthropologist* 4 (October): 393–94. [on the Welsh Indians]

Murphy, Gerard, ed. and trans. 1955. *Saga and Myth in Ancient Ireland*. Cork: Mercier, n.d. (c. 1971 72).

———. 1955. *Early Irish Lyrics*. Oxford: Clarendon.

Opie, Iona and Peter, eds. 1951 [1983]. *Oxford Dictionary of Nursery Rhymes*. Oxford: Oxford University Press.

Oppenheimer, J. Robert. 1954. *Science and the Common Understanding*. New York: Simon and Schuster.

Rabkin, Norman. 1967. *Shakespeare and the Common Understanding*. New York: Free Press.

Rees, Alwyn and Brinley. 1961. *Celtic Heritage: Ancient Tradition in Ireland and Wales*. London: Thames and Hudson.

Simmons, Jack. 1945. *Southey*. London: Collier.

Southey, Robert. 1805. *Madoc*, 4th ed. 1815, 2 vols. London: Longman, Hurst.

———. 1815. "Lewis and Clarke's *American Travels*", *Quarterly Review* 12 (January): 317–68.

———. 1851. *Southey's Common-Place Book*, ed. John Wood Warter, Fourth Series. London: Longman.

———. 1834–1847. *The Doctor*. Ed. 1853 John Wood Warter. London: Longman.

Sterling, Bruce. 1988. *Mirrorshades: The Cyberpunk Anthology*. New York: Ace Books.

Stokes, Whitley. 1880. *The Calendar of Oengus. Transactions of the Royal Irish Academy, Irish Manuscript Series* 1. Dublin: Royal Irish Academy.

White, Michael, and John Gribbin. 1992. *Stephen Hawking: A Life in Science*. New York: Viking.

A POETRY OF MASKS:
THE POET'S PERSONA IN EARLY CELTIC POETRY

Maria Tymoczko

UNIVERSITY OF MASSACHUSETTS, AMHERST

In *A Portrait of the Artist as a Young Man*, Stephen Dedalus — a rather rigid and naive young artist who has not yet written a work like *Ulysses* with its blurring of literary forms — makes the following distinctions between lyric, epic, and dramatic literature:

> The lyrical form is in fact the simplest verbal vesture of an instant of emotion, a rhythmical cry such as ages ago cheered on the man who pulled at the oar or dragged stones up a slope. He who utters it is more conscious of the instant of emotion than of himself as feeling emotion. The simplest epical form is seen emerging out of lyrical literature when the artist prolongs and broods upon himself as the centre of an epical event and this form progresses till the centre of emotional gravity is equidistant from the artist himself and from others. The narrative is no longer purely personal. The personality of the artist passes into the narration itself, flowing round and round the persons and the action like a vital sea. . . . The dramatic form is reached when the vitality which has flowed and eddied round each person fills every person with such vital force that he or she assumes a proper and intangible esthetic life. The personality of the artist, at first a cry or a cadence or a mood and then a fluid and lambent narrative, finally refines itself out of existence, impersonalises itself, so to speak. The esthetic image in the dramatic form is life purified in and reprojected from the human imagination. The mystery of esthetic like that of material creation is accomplished. The artist, like the God of the creation, remains within or behind or beyond or above his handiwork, invisible, refined out of existence, indifferent, paring his fingernails.
>
> $(214-15)^1$

---

1   Cf. Joyce's 6 March 1903 entry in the Paris Notebook: "There are three conditions of art: the lyrical, the epical and the dramatic. That art is lyrical whereby the artist sets forth the image in immediate relation to himself; that art is epical whereby the artist sets forth the image in mediate relation to himself and others; that art is dramatic whereby the artist sets forth the image in immediate relation to others . . ." (*Critical Writings*, 145).

There are many ways of taking issue with Stephen's definitions here, ranging from the observation that etymologically *lyric* is simply 'poetry accompanied by the lyre', thus allowing for a very broad range of verse types, to a sophisticated deconstruction of examples of all literary forms including drama to lay bare the point of view inherent in any text. The theory is nonetheless useful as a touchstone in assessing the early Celtic poetic tradition, for it encapsulates in a somewhat eccentric and Joycean manner contemporary views about lyric, epic, and dramatic forms that command common assent because they accord with our ordinary-language uses of these terms. These definitions are compelling in part because they permeate Western views of literature, being not only wide-spread in the nineteenth and twentieth centuries, but deriving ultimately from Aristotle and the foundations of Western analysis of literature.

What is startling about native Irish and Welsh literature in the early period is the absence of lyric in the sense that Joyce defines lyric in *A Portrait of the Artist*. There is an almost total lack of direct personal expression — an absence, as Joyce puts it, of the "verbal vesture of an instant of emotion, a rhythmical cry" of a poet who is "more conscious of the instant of emotion than of himself as feeling emotion." Despite all of the poetic instruction in early Celtic society, the quantity of poets trained in the niceties and complexities of literary form and in the content of the tradition, the number of poets respected and supported by the society whose names and works have survived, and the relatively large corpus of early Celtic poetry that has been carefully preserved in medieval manuscripts, there is very little lyric poetry of the type that Joyce has defined, the type of lyric that is widespread in Western tradition in other languages.

Where are the love lyrics of early Celtic literature? Did none of the poets feel enough passion about wife or lover to compose lyrics celebrating that feeling? Where do we find an early Irish equivalent of Bernart de Ventadorn's spiritual love poetry? Where are the poems that celebrate the more earthy feelings of a Guillaume IX? Where is the early Celtic poetry celebrating love of a child, or loss of a parent, or grief at the aging of the body, or any of the myriad emotional experiences that poets compose lyrics about because they are part of the universal human developmental cycle, part of the pattern of human life, and yet the most intense moments of any particular life? Where are the lyrics about particular experiences that poets sought out, endured, survived: fear or glory in battle, dismay at the disintegration of culture, joy or awe in the natural world? The fact is that the early Celtic poets did not often compose poems about their own *personal* experiences in this way: poems that are simple rhythmic cries about their own feelings, poetry that memorializes their individual lives, poetry that is lyric in the sense that the term is most frequently used in Western tradition. Our task is to understand this phenomenon.

We can put this line of questioning another way. Why have Irish poets like Flannacán mac Cellaich (ninth century) left us virtually nothing of their own life experiences? One could argue, no doubt, that asking for lyric poetry from such figures is more like asking for lyric from professors and scholars than from poets in the ordinary modern sense of the word. And yet the curious fact is that their near contemporaries, the wandering Irish scholars who went to the Continent, have left us some notable lyrics. Sedulius Scottus comes immediately to mind, and his *Apologia* is a good example that would fit Joyce's definition of a lyric rather well:

> Aut lego vel scribo, doceo scrutorve sophiam:
>   obsecro celsithronum nocete dieque meum.
> vescor, poto libens, rithmizans invoco Musas,
>   dormisco stertens: oro deum vigilans.
> conscia mens scelerum deflet peccamina vitae;
>   parcite vos misero, Christe Maria, viro.

> I read or write, I teach or wonder what is truth,
>   I call upon my God by night and day.
> I eat and freely drink, I make my rhymes,
>   And snoring sleep, or vigil keep and pray.
> And very ware of all my shames I am;
>   O Mary, Christ, have mercy on your man.

> (Waddell, ed. and trans., 122–23)

An argument could perhaps be put forward that the lack of early Celtic poetry celebrating personal emotion reflects recording practice: such poems existed in the tradition, but were not written down because they were not valued by the scholars and monks who controlled manuscript production. Even if this were true — which the widespread literacy among the secular classes and the relative availability of vellum suggest is not the case — the very absence of personal lyric from the manuscript record would itself be worth consideration, particularly in connection with the recording on the Continent of lyrics by Irish writers in both Latin and Irish.

The paradox is, of course, that some of the most splendid early medieval poetry celebrating emotions like love and grief is to be found in Irish and Welsh literature. Almost invariably, however, as even a cursory inspection of the many anthologies of Celtic poetry will show, such poems are attributed to or set in the mouths of well-known fictive or historical characters who are associated in narratives or history with experiences that epitomize the emotions celebrated; they are not presented as emanating from the experience of the historical poets who composed the poems.² To put it another way, in order to express most of the range of human affective experience to be shared intersubjectively in poetry, rather than present such emotions directly through a persona particular to the self, Celtic poets assumed the persona of a traditional fictional character. This assumption of a persona associated with a pre-existing or established character from history or literature we can call a "traditional poetic mask". In proposing the concept of a "traditional poetic mask" I am not suggesting that the "I" of lyrics in other literary traditions is to be equated with the poet himself. Though Stephen's definition of a lyric quoted above identifies the first-person voice of lyric with that of the poet, most contemporary theories sharply distinguish the author from the persona of a poem.³ The lyric poet in most literary traditions creates a mask, but the mask is, paradoxically, usually a mask of the poet's own face. Such is the lyric mask of Catullus and Horace, of Jaufre Rudel and Petrarch, of Robert Frost and Adrienne Rich.⁴ Thus, it is not masking per se that distinguishes Celtic lyric from other lyric traditions, it is the poets' assumption of traditional, pre-established masks that marks the poetics.

Let us return for the moment to a definition of lyric — this time to a contemporary definition by Robert Scholes and Robert Kellogg, who consider the same literary field discussed by Stephen Dedalus:

> By narrative we mean all those literary works which are distinguished by two characteristics: the presence of a story and a story-teller. A drama is a story without a story-teller; in it characters act out directly what Aristotle called an "imitation" of such action as we find in life. A lyric, like a drama, is a direct presentation, in which a single actor, the poet or his surrogate, sings, or muses, or speaks for us to hear or overhear. Add a second speaker, as

2 Discrepancies between the linguistic dating of poetic texts and the dates of the speakers to whom the poems are attributed in the manuscripts indicate that the historical composers are distinct from the first-person speakers of the poems; the historical composers are generally unknown, their own identities subsumed by the identities of the fictive first-person voices of the poems themselves. In Irish literature many of these poems are preserved in the context of sagas and they are excerpted in anthologies of Celtic lyrics; the excerpting is, however, not necessarily deceptive, as textual analysis usually can demonstrate that the poems are extrinsic to the prose settings.

3 See, for example, discussions in Hošek and Parker, 16 ff., 38 ff., 48–50, 55 ff., 239–41, as well as references cited in those essays.

4 The problems resulting from extrapolating from the mask to the poet are graphic in the *vidas* of the Provençal troubadours, where fictive biographies were constructed out of the "latent narratives" in the surviving poems.

Since the mid-nineteenth century the lyric genre of the dramatic monologue is also associated with the masks of traditional characters from history and literature; such masking is found in some modern poetry as well. See Hošek and Parker, 226 ff., esp. 239. It is possible that the assumption of traditional masks in the last century should be associated with models taken from medieval literature, and it may be a feature of Victorian medievalism.

Robert Frost does in "The Death of the Hired Man", and we move toward drama. Let the speaker begin to tell of an event, as Frost does in "The Vanishing Red", and we move toward narrative.

(4)[5]

If the words of the speaker of a lyric poem can at times be seen as a sort of presentation by a single actor, then the poet's assumption of a traditional poetic mask in lyric — particularly when poetry is performed aloud before an audience, as was the case in early Celtic cultures — has analogues to the use of masks in other sorts of performances including ritual, dance, and theater. We can turn to studies of masking in these other types of activities to illuminate the purpose of the traditional poetic masks in early Celtic poetry.

The phenomenon of masking takes many forms worldwide; some scholars include such disparate activities as the body painting of Australian bushmen (Lommel, 55) and the use of dolls, both large and small, or the figures of traditional puppet theater (Lommel, 219). Thus to suppose that the Celtic tradition of poetry about emotions is a form of masking does not distort the notion of masks. A traditional Celtic *poetic* mask is both like and unlike masks in other traditional contexts. The most significant difference, of course, is that a poetic mask is not a material object evoking a visual response. Instead, the poetic mask is in effect a poetic voice, a voice presumed to be distinct from that of the poet. But the gulf is perhaps not as wide as might first appear, since the physical masks of other enactments often have an auditory correlative: the mask brings with it a voice, and in many cases even determinate words of the persona associated with the mask. Indeed, the word 'persona' is from the Latin *persōna*, 'mask': the term refers to the mask which the actor sounded through and which was used by the actor to amplify his voice (*American Heritage Dictionary*, s.v.; Lommel, 198), suggesting that elsewhere in Western tradition the voice was the primary feature of the mask. Moreover, though a poetic mask cannot be the object of natural vision since it is not a material object, the imagery of the poetic utterance appeals to the inner eye and, thus, to the visual sensibility that goes by the term imagination. Still, it must be acknowledged that in the case of poetry, as opposed to drama or dance or ritual, the voice is the tangible

---

5 For other critics who also stress the dramatic character of lyric see Hošek and Parker, 17, 38-40, 49, 226 ff., 239-41, and sources cited; limitations of this definition of lyric are discussed 31 ff., 38 ff., and passim.

It is interesting that Scholes and Kellogg see lyric as the "direct presentation" of "a single actor", for one theory of the origin of Greek tragedy traces it to the performance of lyric odes, the dithyrambs of the devotees of Dionysus. This theory, based ultimately on Aristotle's view of the origin of tragedy, is widespread; see, for example, Gascoigne, 23 ff. and Bieber, ch. 1. For a critique and an alternative, see Else.

constitutive component of the traditional mask, while in most masked enactments the voice is only one of several components.

The similarities between the traditional masks of Celtic poetry and the traditional masks of other enactments are extensive and complex. Here I will concentrate on four primary features of masking which in turn offer insights into the character of masking in early Celtic poetic tradition.

1. *A masked enactment is symbolic rather than mimetic.* The poetic mask like other traditional masks is associated with a persona, a character — and hence with personality, deeds, a fictive history. Whether a player wears the physical mask of a character like Oedipus or speaks with the voice of a character like Deirdre, in virtue of the mask the artistic expression is to a large extent pre-defined. Thus, a mask restricts the activity and at the same time allows for powerful abstraction and epitomization. Susan Harris Smith elaborates on this paradox in masked theater:

> Masked, the character is both narrowly defined by, and often confined to, the part the mask confers on him. If the character is restrained by the device, the playwright, nonetheless, is freed to simplify his characters and underscore his text with concrete images. The mask allows for efficient, visual expression of abstract ideas.
>
> (2)

A mask offers a single clarified image embodying a single emotion, and through the mask the artistic moment is fixed on an idea rather than on personality (Smith, 54). Even when they are satiric, representing what is low or degraded in human life, masks involve magnification: they at once schematize and reduce human experience to its essentials even while intensifying and removing the action to the realm of the superhuman (Smith, 50). In masked rituals the spectator watches characters greater than the self, the beings of mythos, both gods and heroes (Smith, 10). Often, as in Greek theater, physical masks are also literally oversize, with the larger-than-life features making things more visible and at the same time suggesting by a sort of sympathetic magic the large metaphysical dimension of a masked performance.

In theater and other masked enactments, in part because of the larger-than-life quality and the greater visibility (in a cognitive sense as well as a perceptual sense), with concomitant simplification and intensification, masked figures become symbolic and ultimately archetypal. It is thus no accident that in traditional rituals, dance, and theater, masks are typically stylized rather than naturalistic: the mask becomes an icon. The iconic and symbolic quality of masked action is one reason that in theater the use of the mask separates "the presentational stage from the representational stage of realism and naturalism" (Smith, 4).

2. *Enactments with traditional masks are communal and ritual enactments*. The function of ritual enactments — the most common locus of masking worldwide — is complex and beyond the scope of this discussion; nonetheless, the significance of ritual must be invoked as it touches on masking as a general phenomenon. Ritual recreates humanity's place in the accepted order; through the imitation of an ordered universe, the ritual expresses and maintains the cosmic order. In ritual the natural world is also formalized. The actors in ritual are priests or celebrants undertaking the ritual on behalf of the audience, which is a participatory audience.[6] Masked figures in ritual enhance these various aspects of ritual; Andreas Lommel notes that in certain African contexts, for example, ". . . a mask is the embodiment of a tradition and a guarantee of the continuity of an order hallowed by tradition" (9), while in Melanesia masks "are the image and embodiment of a traditional concept of order" (55).

There are other communal dimensions of masking to be noted as well. The use of traditional masks presupposes the sharing of a common tradition between audience and actors. Thus, masked ritual enactment addresses a community that shares (with the artist and with each other) a social and moral order; such enactment functions to validate and recreate community (Smith, 52). Masks are an important vehicle of this feature of ritual, for they "are an expression of both the characteristic features and the moral values inherent in the figures they represent" (Lommel, 43). These communal features of ritual and the significance of masks in particular are not always perceptible to those outside the community or, indeed, to the uninitiated within the community, as Lommel observes:

> Uninitiated spectators see only an uncanny or comic figure, but to the initiated, according to the degree of their awareness, the mask is a personification of cosmic powers or laws. The secret societies, which are associations of the initiated, practise jurisdiction over their group; they uphold the cosmic laws and portray them through their masks. These two functions of the mask — as representations of cosmic laws and as instruments for social correction — have survived in Europe only in a fragmentary form. . . .
>
> (198)

The onlooker of a masked performance participates only to the extent of his knowledge of the mask and of the tradition (Lommel, 44), and, moreover, the rules for interpreting performance content, including "contextualization cues", may be implicit. Speakers may presuppose defined patterns of response which enable members of the traditional audience to work out the bearing of the content on the "current setting" (cf. Bauman and Briggs, 70). Finally, because they generalize and simplify, masks,

6 On these points and the ways in which they relate to the use of masks in the modern theater, see Smith, 3, 49 ff. See also Turner, *From Ritual to Theatre*.

particularly traditional masks, facilitate audience identification: by presenting one simple state that can be recognized and shared by the audience, a mask thus speaks for the audience (cf. Smith, 4, 50).

3. *A mask is a form of liberation.* Roger Caillois has argued that the basic aim of masking is not deception but freedom, the liberation of the true personality. The masker is transformed. By conferring the freeedom of anonymity and by enabling projection, the mask liberates the wearer to express emotions such as pain or anger, as well as to express ideological positions such as social criticism or violation of taboo without incurring for the speaker social or religious restraint or censure. The mask facilitates various forms of socially chaotic behavior, and it allows the wearer to mimic or mock with impunity those with social power, the guardians of social sanction and control.[7] This is the function of masks behind Oscar Wilde's paradox: "Man is least himself when he talks in his own person. Give him a mask, and he will tell you the truth" ("The Critic as Artist", 1045).

Thus, through a masked performance, that which is normally sealed up or inaccessible is drawn forth and made accessible, allowing cultural materials to be moved into a reflexive arena where they can be examined critically.[8]

4. *A masked enactment is an ecstatic enactment.* Whether it is the masked representatives of the kachinas in Hopi enactments or the Greek satyrs and maenads, the masked participants in ritual are thought to become the gods or heroes whom they embody during the sacred period of the enactment. Joseph Campbell summarizes this phenomenon:

> . . . [T]he mask in a primitive festival is revered and experienced as a veritable apparition of the mythical being that it represents — even though everyone knows that a man made the mask and that a man is wearing it. The one wearing it, furthermore, is identified with the god during the time of the ritual of which the mask is a part. He does not merely represent the god; he *is* the god.
>
> (21)

Such enactments are typically undertaken on behalf of the community: the masker shares a moment with a deity or legendary hero of the community and, thus transformed, effects a mystical union and acts out a struggle or a sacrifice on behalf of the community (cf. Smith, 50). As

---

7   See Smith, 2, where some of these ideas are summarized.
8   See Turner, *From Ritual to Theatre*, 13 and passim; Turner's ideas in turn are derived from those of Wilhelm Dilthey. The liberating use of masks is related to the way in which ritual as a whole may facilitate cultural innovation (Turner, 85 and passim).

Bamber Gascoigne (13) observes, primitive ritual involves sympathetic magic, and how better to become the character than to speak with his voice? The masking in such ecstatic rituals has a counterpart in shamanism, for like the maskers of a communal ritual the shaman is also an ecstatic masked figure; though the masks the shaman assumes are personal to him rather than traditional,[9] the rituals he enacts are also for the welfare of members of the community.

While there are many other features of masking that could be brought to bear on textual masking, these four characteristics will be used to develop the following perspective on the use of masks in early Celtic poetry.

Early Irish and Welsh lyric poetry about emotions is a poetry of traditional masks. Once the concept of a traditional poetic mask is articulated and the reader is sensitized to this aspect of the poetics, poetic masks are everywhere apparent. The lyric expression of love in early Irish poetry is associated with traditional characters like Deirdre, Líadan and Cuirithir, and Gráinne who also figure in love narratives; in singing of love the poets do not project their own love experiences, they assume the masks of characters such as these and sing in their voices. Sorrow for the death of the loved one is associated with the famous lovers already named (since so many good love stories end in sorrow), and also with historical personages like Gormlaith in Ireland; to sing about sorrow after the death of a beloved one the early poets put on the masks of these bereft figures. Old age is epitomized by characters like Llywarch Hen, and lyrics lamenting age — and its complications in terms of power and polity — are spoken in their voices. The function of expressing grief over social disaster and loss is also associated with masks; the loss of Powys is not expressed through the personal voices of Welsh poets but through the mask of Heledd.

A sign of a *traditional* poetic mask in early Irish or Welsh literature is evidence that a mythic, legendary, or heroic figure has been used over a considerable span of time as the vehicle for affective poetry associated with a limited but determinate range of feeling. Thus a traditional poetic mask can be distinguished on the one hand from the occasional use of a historical or legendary character for masking purposes and on the other hand from the speaking of poetry by a narrative-bound character.[10] Oisín is a clear example of a traditional mask, since this figure is associated with a large body of poems with a similar thematic and affective range spanning a considerable period of time; the speaker of the poem "Aithbe

9 On the masks of the shaman see Eliade, passim; Campbell, 231, 241 ff.; Lommel, 126–29.
10 The latter is essentially a narrative act or a lyric moment within narrative, rather than lyric per se.

damsa bés mora" may represent the second type, where a mythic character, Buí or the Caillech Bérri, is used effectively as a mask in a particular
poem.[11] Fedelm banfáith, who speaks the poem beginning "Atchíu fer
find firfes cles" addressed to Medb in *Táin Bó Cúailnge* (O'Rahilly, ll.
67 ff.), is an example of the third type, whose poetry is primarily a
narrative act within a specific tale.

To compare Celtic lyric poetry with masked rituals and theater takes
us deep into performance theory and opens many questions,[12] yet it is
apparent that the characteristics of masks and masked performances
considered above illuminate the nature and functions of poetic masks in
early Celtic poetry. While we will return to the communal functions of
masks in Celtic lyric, we should observe initially that all early Celtic
poetry extant was public poetry, as the evidence regarding the production
and patronage of poetry in Celtic cultures indicates. Early Celtic poetry
was public, as well, in being a performance genre: poetry was performed
aloud by poet or reciter, rather than read silently or privately.

When a poet dons a traditional poetic mask in an affective poem, he
presupposes — indeed depends on — the audience's knowledge and
recognition of the traditional character and the emotional situation
evoked; the poet assumes that the audience will have a background of
mythos or history for the persona, thus supplying a considerable context
for the poem itself as it is performed.[13] As a consequence, the presence of
traditional poetic masks in this body of poetry implies a specific relationship between poet and audience: a poet shares with the audience a field of
imaginative experience that the poet evokes and reanimates, but does not
essentially define or create. It follows that there is a climate of expectation on the part of the audience, and the poet in such circumstances is
constrained by the audience's expectations regarding the traditional
character if his poetry is to be received and understood. These traditional
aspects of Celtic lyric should be kept in mind in assessing the poet's task
and the poet's creative process.

As with masking in other human art and ritual, it is obvious that a
poetic mask of a traditional character like Gormlaith defines a poetic
moment; and as in other types of masked performance, the mask distills a
particular sort of human passion even while casting a larger-than-life
image of that same experience:

11 See Murphy, 74 ff. For a different interpretation of this poem see Carney, xxiv ff.
12 See Bauman, and Bauman and Briggs for a current theoretical framework for per-
    formance theory as it relates to literary texts.
13 Even the occasional use of a traditional figure like the Caillech Bérri as a poetic
    mask depends on a shared tradition between the poet and the audience.

Ro charas trĩcha fo thrí,
  ro charas a náoi fo náoi
gē no charfuinn fiche fear
  nocho n-eadh do mheallfadh mnáoi.

Do thréigios íad sin ar Níall,
  dob é mo mhían bheith dã réir,
cidh nach ttrēiccfinnsi gach fear . . .

I have loved three times thirty,
  I have loved nine times nine;
though I should love twenty men,
  that is not what would beguile a woman.

I forsook them all for Niall;
  it was my desire to do his will.
Why should I not forsake every man? . . .
          (Bergin, ed. and trans., 212–13)[14]

Cú Chulainn lamenting the death of his foster-brother Fer Diad exaggerates and hence epitomizes the human experience of being unable to deter one's comrades or kin from a self-destructive course as well as regret at being forced to contribute to the downfall of a friend and more than friend.

Cluithe cách, caíne cách
co Fer Diad isind áth
dursan úaitne óir
forfuirmedh for áth.

Cluichi cách, caíne cách
co Fer Diad isind áth
indar limsa Fer dil Diad
is am diaid no biad co bráth.

All was play and pleasure until I met with Fer Diad in the ford. Alas for the noble champion laid low there at the ford.

All was play and sport until I met with Fer Diad at the ford. I thought that beloved Fer Diad would live after me for ever.
          (O'Rahilly, ed. and trans., ll. 3134 ff.)[15]

14 Lineation in the translation is mine.
15 Kinsella translates:

      All play, all sport,
      until Ferdia came to the ford.

This distillation and magnification of character, emotion, and situation associated with poetic masks in early Celtic poetry — as well as the constraint posed by the traditional configuration of the first-person speakers — indicate that such poems, like masked enactments in other cultures, are symbolic rather than mimetic or representational, a quality that can be traced in other aspects of Celtic art as well.[16]

Like traditional masks in many cultures, Celtic poetic masks are not only symbolic, they are hieratic; the artistic intent is to impress, to impress upon the mind, rather than to describe or represent. Poetic masks are similar in their esthetic, thus, to the portraits in the Book of Kells as well as to various character types found throughout Celtic narrative: they are decorative and geometric more than figural, symbolic and iconic rather than naturalistic, intended to inspire awe and contemplation. Like other aspects of early Celtic art, early Celtic poetry about emotional states is essentially symbolic and non-representational, rather than individualized and naturalistic, in large measure because of the use of poetic masks. This is the case even when there are striking naturalistic motifs or details invoked in the poems themselves.[17]

The presence of traditional poetic masks in early Celtic poetry about emotion is related to masks associated with other types of early Celtic poetry. One can, for example, identify the use of masks related to "nature poetry" in Ireland: seasonal poems, particularly those of a mantic variety, are generally attributed in the manuscripts to characters who are themselves mantic poets, even when such poems are found outside a narrative context. Most of the finest poems of this type are presented as the production of fictional poets such as Finn, Athirne, or Amairgen, rather than attributed to the historical medieval poets who actually

---

Misery! A pillar of gold
I have levelled in the ford. . . .

All play, all sport,
until Ferdia came to the ford.
I thought beloved Ferdia
would live forever after me . . . (204–5)

16 Thus, the magnification associated with poetic masks fits with the exaggeration and larger-than-life quality found elsewhere in the literary tradition — in, for example, the gigantism that pervades both early Welsh and Irish tradition. One thinks of Oisín juxtaposed against the paltry Patrick, for example, or the Arthur of the *mirabilia*, not to mention Bendigeidfran and all the mythic and legendary figures of the Irish *dindšenchas*. Not unrelated is the grotesque quality of many of the literary characters: Mac Cecht, to whom the gnawing of a hairy wolf is like the biting of a gnat, or Cú Chulainn, who can have hunks of flesh the size of baby-heads hacked off and return to fight another day, or Ysbaddaden Chief Giant, whose eyelids are so heavy that they must be propped up with forks.

17 As there are, for example, in Deirdre's laments now found at the end of the earliest version of *Loinges mac nUislenn*.

composed them.[18] An example is the Middle Irish poem on winter attributed to Finn in the commentary on *Amra Choluim Chille:*

> Scél lem dúib:
> 　dordaid dam;
> snigid gaim;
> 　ro fáith sam;
>
> Gáeth ard úar;
> 　ísel grían;
> gair a rrith;
> 　ruirthech rían . . .
>
> I have tidings for you:
> 　the stag bells;
> winter pours;
> 　summer has gone;
>
> Wind is high and cold;
> 　the sun low;
> its course is short;
> 　the sea runs strongly . . .
> 　　　　(Murphy, ed. and trans., 160–61)[19]

Similarly in Welsh tradition prophetic poems are associated with masking: the vaticination poems that have survived from the tenth and following centuries are generally associated implicitly or explicitly either with legendary poets or with historical poets of another era who had come to be known for their prophetic powers — most notably the figures of Myrddin and Taliesin. Thus, in Wales the tenth-century poet who assumed a mantic role may also have assumed the mask — the voice — of one of these traditional prophetic poets.[20]

Recognition of the phenomenon of poetic masks, in particular the use of a mask as a vehicle for expressing communal grief and loss, opens a perspective on the *Canu Aneirin.* Celtic scholars have had a vested interest in seeing the Aneirin poems as the creation of a historical sixth-century poet not only because of the prestige accruing from the antiquity of such a body of poetry. Equally important is our sense of genre: if the *Gododdin* can be identified as the production of a historical Aneirin, the

18　See Tymoczko 1983 on Irish seasonal poetry. Again, linguistic dating of the poems indicates the dates of the historical poets.

19　Lineation in the translation is mine.

20　The problems associated with the entextualization of actual mantic utterances of historical poets and their reattribution to famous legendary seers is discussed in Tymoczko 1994.

poems can be perceived as court elegy or the personal outcry of a poet lamenting historical loss, either way confirming our modern generic sensibilities. Yet Brendan O Hehir, Eve Sweetser, and Kathryn Klar have suggested that these poems are the product of disparate poets over a considerable span of time.[21] They are in effect suggesting that Aneirin was used as a traditional poetic mask, a mask seen, in the perspective being developed here, as a metonymic vehicle for expressing elegiac sentiment, social grief as a whole, or grief over the loss of territory, even while it was a means of shoring up the value system of the culture. If one takes this point of view, then an "Aneirin" elegy, composed by a poet in the centuries after Aneirin himself had died, was a performative that was efficacious at the moment of composition; in evoking Catraeth and the dead heroes of the North the poet was speaking metaphorically or metonymically of other losses that occurred later and elsewhere. The contextual clues for applying the poems to later situations were implicit,[22] and the modern difficulty in interpreting the use of the Aneirin mask is reminiscent of Lommel's observation that the significance of a mask is correlated with the knowledge of the observer:

> The details of a mask, which are understood in all their significance only by the initiated, are related to mythical events, expressed in artistic language. The mythical element is hidden, and at the same time given expression, by the artist's skill, for the symbolism of the mask exists on several levels.

(42)

Early Celtic poets do, of course, speak in their own voices, but what they speak is rarely personal in the strict sense of the word. There is seldom an ostensible mask when the poet either praises or satirizes, nor is a traditional mask generally assumed in most surviving eulogies or elegies, though the case of Aneirin strikes a cautionary note. Yet it can be argued that in composing these types of poems, the poet had already assumed a traditional role or function, which came in a sense with a traditional persona. Thus, many poems in which the poet seemingly speaks with his own voice are limiting cases of the phenomenon of masking, for the poet's voice in certain types of poems was already determined by training and cultural tradition. When the Welsh poet composed a *marwnad*, for example, he was not simply expressing personal grief, he spoke on behalf of the community; moreover, his grief was channeled and constrained, defined as it were, by both genre and the

---

21 See in particular O Hehir, 74 ff.
22 Cf. Bauman, 9 ff., 27 ff. Any performance may have implicit contextualization cues. Thus it was immediately apparent to the original audiences how they were to "apply" Jean Anouilh's *Antigone* or Arthur Miller's *Crucible* to contemporary events, while even Beethoven's Fifth Symphony had implicit contextualization rules during World War II in occupied France.

traditional formulas of the poetic tradition. Even on the level of the performatives of language — metaphor, for example — the voice of such poems is highly regulated. Thus, for example, in the late lament of Gruffudd ab yr Ynad Coch for Llywelyn ap Gruffudd (d. 1282), a poem often praised for the intensity of its personal sentiment, there are conventional metaphors and similes, as well as a range of emotion that is conventionalized, in a poem that is nonetheless a masterpiece, as the following excerpt illustrates:

Oer gallon dan vron o vraw allwynin
  am vrenhin derwin dor Aberffraw.
Eur dilyf yn a delit oe law,
  eur daleith oed deilwng idaw.
Eurgyrn eur deyrn nym daw llewenyd
  Llywelyn, nyt ryd ym rwyd wisgaw.
Gwae vi am arglwyd, gwalch di waratwyd,
  gwae vi or aflwyd y dramgwydaw.
Gwae vi or gollet, gwae vi or dynghet,
  gwae vi or clywet vot clwyf arnaw.
Gwersyll Katwaladyr, gwaessaf llif daradyr,
  gwas rud y baladyr, balawc eur llaw,
gwascarawd alaf, gwiscawd bop gaeaf
  gwisgoed ymdanaf y ymdanaw. . . .
Llawer deigyr hylithry yn hwylaw ar rud,
  lawer ystlys rud a rwyc arnaw;
llawer gwaet am draet wedy ymdreidyaw,
llawer gwedw a gwaed y amdanaw,
llawer medwl trwm yn tonnwyaw,
llawer mab hed dat gwedy y adaw,
llawer hendref vreith gwedy llwybyr godeith
  a llawer diffeith drwy anreith draw;
llawer llef druan ual ban vu Gamlan,
  llawer deigyr dros rann gredyr greinyaw. . . .

The heart is cold under a breast of pitiful fear
  for a king, the oaken door of Aberffraw.
Fine gold was paid to us from his hand
  and he deserved the golden chaplet.
Golden horns of a golden king do not bring me the joy
  of Llywelyn; I am not free to arm as I would.
Woe to me for my lord, the unshamed hawk,
  woe for the calamity of his bringing down.
Woe for the loss, woe for the destiny,
  woe for the news that he has a wound,
Cadwaladr of defence, protection's sharp piercer,

he of the red spear, golden-handed ruler,
he shared out wealth, every winter he dressed me
  in the garments he had worn. . . .
Many a sliding tear runs down the cheek,
  many a flank is red and torn,
much blood has soaked about the feet,
many a widow shrieks for him,
many a sad mind now breaks down,
many a son's left fatherless,
many a homestead stained in the fire's path
  and many a wilderness left by the plunderer,
many a piteous cry, as once at Camlan,
many a tear has fallen down the cheek!

(Gwyn Williams, ed. and trans., 80–83)

It is the artistry of the poem rather than the personal emotion in it that creates the effect of the poem in the first instance (cf. Matonis, 189 ff.); symbolic elements dominate the elegy, rather than particularized, individualized feeling. It is a lament that gives voice to the grief and loss of the community; as Higley says (259), the narrative "I" "becomes the voice of the grieving nation."

While the public roles of early Celtic poets are recognized in the case of praise poetry, satire, inaugural poems, eulogy, and elegy, implicit in the previous argument is that the poet speaks on behalf of the community even in poetry that seems primarily to express personal emotion, and that the masking in such poems is a major vehicle of the effect. As in rituals which enact myth, early Celtic lyric poems in which the poet assumes a traditional mask and speaks in the voice of a traditional character are direct presentations or mythic enactments. Such utterances contribute to formalizing the natural and social world, not the least by formalizing emotional response, and, hence, have some ritualistic functions. Like the eulogies and elegies, as well as the praise poetry and satires, of the Celtic poets, lyrics utilizing a traditional mask presuppose, articulate, and underscore a traditional social and moral order, thereby maintaining or even recreating both the community and the cosmic order. In this ritual process of recreating the moral universe and articulating the place of humanity in it, the early Celtic lyric poet acts as a kind of celebrant.

Though they come from cultures in which the historical practitioners of poetry were overwhelmingly male, many of the Celtic poetic masks are female, and this phenomenon may also be elucidated by the comparative perspective on masks considered above. The temptation is to read these masks as a sign of female empowerment in Celtic society, associated perhaps with patterns of poetic patronage by powerful women. It is of course notoriously difficult to extrapolate from literature to

culture and vice versa (cf. Preston, Introduction), and while women did
have important roles in early Irish and Welsh societies, it is also clear
that the cultures were patriarchal ones. A comparative perspective on
masking helps resolve the dilemma, suggesting that in ritualistic utterances aimed at the entire community — a community that included
women as well as men — female masks would have facilitated the identification of an important segment of the culture and, thus, contributed to
the poet's ability to speak for the audience as a whole; Celtic poets may
have assumed the traditional masks of female characters just as in other
cultures traditional masked male dancers or actors assume the masks of
female figures, goddesses as well as humans. While the prevalence of
female masks may be a concomitant of the high status that in some
respects women held in Celtic societies, it is nonetheless obvious that
even if the audiences of early Celtic poetry were entirely male, there
would be imperatives resulting in the use of female masks. In the ritual
re-establishment of a social and cosmic order, obviously women must
find a place and women's voices must be heard.[23]

At the same time, if masks liberate, the prevalence of female masks
may indicate that through female voices the Celtic poet was enabled to
express for himself and his audience feelings, emotions, or views that in
normal circumstances were either repressed or socially censured in male
members of the culture. Masking as a form of liberation is to be expected
in cultures where there is a good deal of social control, particularly
informal control, as there was in early Welsh and Irish culture. Where
the heroic ethic hung on and was slow to die, feelings of love, grief,
dismay over societal disintegration and defeat, fear of aging, and self-pity
were charged; by putting on a mask and projecting these feelings outward, particularly onto women, the poet and his audience remained safe
in their social identities — in their own personal masks, one might say.[24]
By projecting problematic emotions outward, particularly onto females,
the poet could free himself — and his audience — to consider and
express aspects of life that were, if not forbidden, then at least difficult.
A study of masks in other cultures suggests all these functions and more
for the female masks in Celtic poetry, and the naive modern reader who
does not understand the various functions of masks will go astray if

23 Still another cautionary note is in order here: feminist analysis suggests that the
presence of women's voices cannot prima facie be assumed to indicate female
empowerment. What is said as well as the voice in which it is said must be
considered. The female voices of early Celtic poetry can be read (or heard)
essentially as supporting rather than challenging a patriarchal and male-dominated
worldview; indeed, some of the female voices can be heard as gratifying male
desire and narcissism.

24 In a private communication Nerys Patterson has suggested that in early Celtic literature as a whole there is a pattern of distancing of emotion; projection onto female
masks may be part of the pattern.

the poems in women's voices are read simply as naturalistic and descriptive.[25]

Lyric poetry without a poetic mask or a conventionalized persona is comparatively rare in early Celtic tradition, and where it occurs, it is the exception that proves the rule. Some early Irish monastic poems seem to fit Joyce's definition of lyric as "the simplest verbal vesture of an instant of emotion" where the poet is "more conscious of the instant of emotion than of himself as feeling emotion." In such poems there seem to be no traditional masks and the poets speak ostensibly in their own voices, as for example in the following:

Dom-farcai fidbaide fál
  fom-chain loíd luin, lúad nād cél;
hūas mo lebrán, ind línech,
  fom-chain trírech inna n-én.

Fomm-chain coí menn, medair mass,
  hi mbrot glass de dingnaib doss.
Debrath! nom-Choimmdiu-coíma:
  caín-scríbaimm fo roída ross.

A hedge of trees overlooks me;
a blackbird's lay sings to me
(an announcement which I shall not conceal);
above my lined book
the birds' chanting sings to me.

A clear-voiced cuckoo sings to me (goodly utterance)
in a grey cloak from bush fortresses.
The Lord is indeed good to me:
well do I write beneath a forest of woodland.

(Murphy, ed. and trans., 4–5)[26]

In "Pangur bán" the poet's persona has the same immediacy:

---

25 To ignore the ritualistic function of the masking may lead to overreading the poems as indicators of female status in the hierarchy of Celtic culture. See Carney, xxiv ff. and references cited for some interesting speculation about aspects of the female masks in the poetry. His discussion of the poet as "king-lover" and hence identified with the female function is certainly germane to the question, though this role does not cover the affective range of the poems using female masks.

26 Lineation in the translation is mine.

Messe ocus Pangur bán
cechtar nathar fria śaindán:
 bíth a menmasam fri seilgg,
 mu menma céin im śaincheirdd.

Caraimse fos, ferr cach clú,
oc mu lebrān, lēir ingnu;
 nī foirmtech frimm Pangur bán:
 caraid cesin a maccdán. . . .

I and white Pangur
practise each of us his special art:
 his mind is set on hunting,
 my mind on my special craft.

I love (it is better than all fame)
to be quiet beside my book, diligently pursuing knowledge.
 White Pangur does not envy me:
 he loves his childish craft.

(Murphy, ed. and trans., 2–3)[27]

Yet I would argue that these poems are governed by a different set of conventions and norms from the lyrics already considered. Though in the Irish language and in Irish meters, they are aimed at a different social context; they are more European and have an international religious sensibility. The use of the "I" here is more typical of classical lyric than of early Celtic lyrics as a whole, and the poems seem to be influenced by Latin poetics. It is no accident that both these poems are preserved in Continental Latin manuscripts (see Murphy, 172) rather than Irish manuscripts, and it is even possible that they were composed in the context of an entirely different literary environment — one influenced by Latin literary conventions — and were aimed at the private reader rather than public performance. Ironically, these offshoots of the native tradition are the poems fastened upon as exemplars of the early Celtic lyric genius. In part this occurs because the poet's persona in a poem like "Pangur bán" feels congenial and modern; the persona is an individualized, self-reflective voice. Yet even in early Celtic religious poetry the mask is more typical, as can be seen in the ninth-century dialogue poem between Gúaire and Marbán (Murphy, 10 ff.), a poem preserved in Harleian 5280, or as is indicated in "Ísucán", attributed to Saint Íte (*ca.* 900, Murphy, 26 ff.) and preserved in the Middle Irish commentary to the *Félire Óengusso.* The latter two poems, like poems from the eleventh and twelfth centuries attributed to Saint Columba (Murphy, nos. 20, 29–33),

---

27 Lineation in the translation is mine.

are projections backward onto sixth- and seventh-century religious figures by later poets, and they emanate from an insular religious environment, indicating that in Ireland religious poets also typically operated within the traditional poetic of masks.

With shifting valences, performative and ritual, liberating and ecstatic, the mask was normative in poetry of emotion for Irish and Welsh poets operating strictly within the native Celtic tradition, and the operation of this norm is consistent with other aspects of the role of the Celtic poet. Celtic poets were shamanistic figures: originally a seer, to a very late date the Celtic poet remained a mantic figure, as scholars like Ifor Williams and Calvert Watkins have documented. Both the Welsh *awenydd* and the Irish *éices* or *fili* were possessed of inspiration, able to prophesy, to see afar across time and space. The poets had access to hidden knowledge, knowledge both secret and prophetic; and the poets were associated with rituals intended to induce sight, to confer visions, and to reveal knowledge of the otherworld. From descriptions of the "ravings" of the Welsh *awenyddion*, as well as late descriptions of the trance-like state of some Irish poets, it is clear that the poets were ecstatics. The mantic associations of poetry are signaled as well in the process of composition: as late as the eighteenth century Irish and Scottish poets composed in the dark, relying on their inspiration, a practice that can be traced in early Welsh poetry as well. With the collapse of native religion, upon the poets had also devolved the vestiges of the roles of priest, as the Irish evidence makes particularly clear, and it was the poet who officiated at the inaugural of the prince or king. Like shamans, the poets were wielders of sympathetic magic; they possessed the power of satire which could maim or kill.[28]

By donning a poetic mask, the Celtic poet, even in lyric or poetry of emotions, could see with another's eyes across time and space, and speak mystically with another's voice.[29] Assumed for the sake of the voice, the poetic mask is akin to the physical mask of rituals: with it as a vehicle the poet for the moment becomes the other. The presence of a poetic mask marks the utterance of a lyric poem as a type of ecstatic experience, not unlike rituals in other cultures, in which maskers become the figures whose masks they wear. When the Celtic poet becomes a masked figure, speaking with another's voice, he in effect re-enacts an experience, deed, situation from the tradition. Thus the speaking of a lyric poem is a direct presentation, and the poem uttered with the poetic mask is a ritualistic re-

---

28 On these various aspects of early Celtic poetry see Carney, Flower, Ford, O Hehir, Robinson, Watkins, Ifor Williams.

29 Lyric poems are, thus, related to poetic speech produced under the influence of the poet's inspiration, the poet's *awen* or *aí*, in which the poet's personal voice was subsumed in mantic utterance.

enactment, undertaken on behalf of the community. The use of poetic masks marks the Celtic poet as priest.

By the twelfth century, of course, the influence of Continental courtly lyric is patent in both Ireland and Wales; and in Welsh and Irish poetry of the later Middle Ages there are fewer traditional masks, though the poets continue to assume their conventional personae for certain professional functions like elegy and eulogy, and courtly love lyric brings with it a highly artificial persona imported from the Continental tradition. In the later poetry the poets speak more often through an individualized persona, as in most Continental lyric. Thus in Welsh poetry, the lyric poems of the *cywyddwyr* take their dominant poetic from French and Provençal tradition, a tradition in the main line of European lyric, within which Dafydd ap Gwilym is justly famous as one of the most pleasing lyricists of later medieval literature.

While there is a minor strand of Western tradition that includes poetic masks — a strand that threads through some early English and Old Icelandic poetry — this is not the highroad of European literature. Yet the tradition of the poetic mask, however minor a strand it may be in Western poetry as a whole, has remained vigorous in Irish tradition right down to the present: liberating, symbolic, the essence of ritual ecstatic poetic performance, poetic masks were slow to die. It is an aspect of the tradition that surfaces in Yeats's work, and he shows his indebtedness to Irish traditional literature, as well as to other sources, in using this form. As is clear from Richard Finneran's notes to the most recent edition of Yeats's poems, notes to which Brendan O Hehir's contributions were central, Yeats had a very wide knowledge of early Irish literature; it can hardly be a coincidence that Yeats's lyric, like early Irish lyric, is so often a poetry of masks, a lyric of assumed personae, where Yeats dons mask after mask. Some of these personae are traditional poetic masks; others, like Crazy Jane, are masks that Yeats creates, though his creations are frequently modeled on mythic configurations that antedate his work. His poetry is in turn related to the multiple layers of masking in his drama and to the personae he cast in life, and it is often the masking — in both his plays and poems — upon which the ceremonial quality of Yeats's writing turns.

REFERENCES

American Heritage Dictionary.

Bauman, Richard. 1977. *Verbal Art as Performance*. Prospect Heights, Ill.: Waveland Press (1984).

Bauman, Richard, and Charles L. Briggs. 1990. "Poetics and Performance as Critical Perspectives on Language and Social Life". *Annual Review of Anthropology* 19:59–88.

Bergin, Osborn. 1970. *Irish Bardic Poetry*. Dublin: Dublin Institute for Advanced Studies.

Bieber, Margarete. 1961. *The History of the Greek and Roman Theater*. Princeton: Princeton University Press.

Campbell, Joseph. 1959. *The Masks of God: Primitive Mythology*. Vol. 1. New York: Viking.

Carney, James. 1967. *Medieval Irish Lyrics with 'The Irish Bardic Poet'*. Portlaoise: Dolmen (1984).

Eliade, Mircea. 1964. *Shamanism: Archaic Techniques of Ecstasy*, Willard R. Trask, trans. Bollingen Series 76. Princeton: Princeton University Press (1972).

Else, Gerald F. 1965. *The Origin and Early Form of Greek Tragedy*. New York: W.W. Norton (1972).

Flower, Robin. 1947. *The Irish Tradition*. Oxford: Oxford University Press.

Ford, Patrick. 1987. "The Death of Aneirin". *Bulletin of the Board of Celtic Studies* 34:41–50.

Gascoigne, Bamber. 1968. *World Theatre: An Illustrated History*. Boston: Little, Brown.

Goldin, Frederick. 1983. *Lyrics of the Troubadours and Trouvères*. Gloucester, Mass.: Peter Smith.

Higley, Sarah Lynn. 1988. "Forcing a Gap: The Stylistics of "Amputation" in *Marwnad Llywelyn* by Gruffudd ab yr Ynad Coch". *Viator* 19: 247–72.

Hošek, Chaviva, and Patricia Parker, eds. 1985. *Lyric Poetry: Beyond New Criticism*. Ithaca and London: Cornell University Press.

Joyce, James. 1959. *Critical Writings*, Ellsworth Mason and Richard Ellmann, eds. New York: Viking.

———. 1977. *A Portrait of the Artist as a Young Man*, Chester G. Anderson, ed. Harmondsworth: Penguin.

Kinsella, Thomas, trans. 1969. *The Táin*. London and New York: Oxford University Press (1970).

Lommel, Andreas. 1970. *Masks: Their Meaning and Function*. New York and Toronto: McGraw-Hill (1972).

Matonis, Ann. 1979–1980. "The Rhetorical Patterns in *Marwnad Llywelyn ap Gruffudd* by Gruffudd ab yr Ynad Coch". *Studia Celtica* 14/15:188–92.

Murphy, Gerard, ed. and trans. 1956. *Early Irish Lyrics*. London: Oxford University Press (1962).

O Hehir, Brendan. 1988. "What Is the *Gododdin*?" In *Early Welsh Poetry, Studies in the Book of Aneirin*, Brynley F. Roberts, ed. Aberystwyth: National Library of Wales, 57–95.

O'Rahilly, Cecile, ed. and trans. 1976. *Táin Bó Cúailnge, Recension I*. Dublin: Dublin Institute for Advanced Studies.

Preston, James J., ed. 1982. *Mother Worship: Theme and Variations*. Chapel Hill: University of North Carolina Press.

Robinson, Fred Norris. 1912. "Satirists and Enchanters in Early Irish Literature". In *Studies in the History of Religions Presented to Crawford Howell*, David Gordon Lyon and George Foot Moore, eds. New York: Macmillan, 95–130.

Scholes, Robert, and Robert Kellogg. 1966. *The Nature of Narrative*. London, Oxford, and New York: Oxford University Press (1968).

Smith, Susan Valeria Harris. 1984. *Masks in Modern Drama*. Berkeley, Los Angeles, and London: University of California Press.

Turner, Victor. 1982. *From Ritual to Theatre: The Human Seriousness of Play*. New York: PAJ Publications.

Tymoczko, Maria. 1983. "'Cétamon': Vision in Early Irish Seasonal Poetry". *Éire-Ireland* 18:4.17–39.

——. 1994. "Inversions, Subversions, Reversions: The Form of Early Irish Narrative". In *Text und Zeittiefe*, Hildegard L. C. Tristram, ed. Tübingen: Gunter Narr, 71–86.

Waddell, Helen. 1977. *Mediaeval Latin Lyrics*. New York: Norton.

Watkins, Calvert. 1963. "Indo-European Metrics and Archaic Irish Verse". *Celtica* 6:194–249.

Wilde, Oscar. 1966. *Complete Works of Oscar Wilde*, Vyvyan Holland, ed. New Edition. London: Collins.

Williams, Gwyn, ed. and trans. 1956. *The Burning Tree*. London: Faber and Faber.

Williams, Ifor. 1944. *Lectures on Early Welsh Poetry*. Dublin: Dublin Institute for Advanced Studies (1954).

Yeats, W. B. 1983. *The Poems: A New Edition*, Richard J. Finneran, ed. New York: Macmillan.

A NOTE ON THE ART
OF THE SYLLABLE

Calvert Watkins

HARVARD UNIVERSITY

I take this opportunity to offer to Brendan O Hehir's memory a little observation on the mastery of verse technique shown by the Archaic Irish poet Bécán mac Luigdech, author of the magnificent poem *Fo réir Choluimb céin ad-fías*, edited by Fergus Kelly.[1]

As argued by Kelly, surely rightly, Bécán was two generations later than Columb Cille (*ca.* 522–597), and thus is likely to have lived in the seventh century. The poem belongs to a critical turning point in the development of Early Irish poetry.

Stylistically the poem shares certain features with the *Amra Coluimb Chille* (*ACC*), the eulogy or threnody written shortly after St. Columba's death, which marks the beginning of vernacular literature in Europe. *Fo réir Choluimb* is in fact closely modeled on *ACC*.[2] A shared feature is notably the conscious perturbation of normal Irish word order tolerated for the ends of versification. This appears to function as a *renvoi* or recollection of the sort of "non-configurational" word order characteristic of the elevated poetry of most early Indo-European languages; but it was more likely familiar to sixth- and seventh-century Irish poets from some acquaintance with Vergil or Ovid.

The poem contains some of the finest lines in Irish, as in the recurrent images of Columb's voyage over the sea to found the monastery on the island of Iona off the west coast of Scotland:

---

1 "A Poem in Praise of Columb Cille", *Ériu* 24 (1973), pp. 1–34, from which my citations are mostly taken. I have at times preferred the version in D. Greene and F. O'Connor, *A Golden Treasury of Irish Poetry* (New York: Macmillan, 1967).

2 A systematic comparison of the two is the only lacuna in Kelly's admirable edition, and would considerably further our understanding of both poems. The shared vocabulary alone is striking.

cechaing noïb   nemeth mbled

He crossed in ships the whales' sanctuary,

with the kenning for 'sea' (like the later Old English *hronrād* 'whale's road') showing the semantically charged Celtic word for 'hallowed place, object, or being', first attested on an Old Etruscan grave marker from near Genoa in the first half of the fifth century B.C.[3] The verse concludes with four constituents in the reverse of prose order:

fairrge al druim dánae fer

A bold man over the sea's ridge.

And again with scrambled order and an otherwise unattested verb form,[4]

curchaib tar sál sephtus cló

a whirlwind swept them over the sea in curraghs.

The poem is described in the manuscript as a *laíd imrind* 'poem with rimes all around'. Each verse has four lines of seven syllables, with end-rime *ac, bd*. Each line of each verse typically has a fixed caesura (break, word boundary), normally after the fourth syllable (for the exceptions see immediately below). There is concatenating or chain alliteration between the last word of each verse and the first (stressed) word of the next (6d–7a being the only exception); concatenating or chain alliteration between the last word of every line and the first (stressed) word of the next; and bridging alliteration between the words on either side of the caesura. Absence of the latter two types is compensated for by linkage of grammatical figures (parallelism) or by alliteration elsewhere in the line. Using G. Murphy's notational conventions (*Early Irish Metrics*, p. vi) of boldface italic or roman for end-rime and italic for chain alliteration, plus boldface italic for bridging alliteration, | for caesura, and capitals for *dúnad* or closure ("ring composition"), the first quatrain is

---

3 The text reads *mi nemetieś* 'I [am the tomb] of Nemetie'. See my "Language, Culture, or History?" in *Papers from the Parasession on Language and Behavior*, Chicago Linguistic Society (1981), pp. 238–48, esp. pp. 241–43.
4 Cf. *rodom-sibsea sech riaga*, ACC §141.

FO Réir *Ch*oluimb | *c*éin ad-*fías*
*f*ind for *n*imib | *sn*áidsium *s*echt
*s*ét fri *hú*athu | *ú*air no-*tías*
ní cen *t*oísech | *t*áthum *n*ert

Obedient to Columb, as long as I speak,
may the fair one in the seven heavens protect me;
when I walk the path to terrors,
it is not without a leader, I have strength.

The initial syllable is repeated for a perfect *dúnad* by the last syllable of verse 24:

*R*ígdae *b*ráthair | *b*úadach *r*íg
rathmar *f*íado | *f*eib ron-*a*in
gétait goiste | *nd*emnae *d*ím
*d*úbart a *b*ard | *b*és don-FOIR

May the royal victorious kinsman of kings,
the gracious lord protect us with goodness.
I will remove(?) the snare of demons from me;
the supplication of his poets may perhaps help us.

Here the stressed FOIR /for'/ repeats the pretonic first syllable of the poem FO R /fo r'/, 24 verses, 96 lines, and 671 syllables later.[5]

In 24c the double alliteration *g*était *g*oiste | *nd*emnae *d*ím compensates for the lack of alliteration across the caesura and between the end of 24b and the beginning of 24c. Similarly in 1b the alliteration *snáidsium secht* compensates for its absence across the caesura, as Kelly notes, though we may probably see a secondary bridging alliteration in *nimib snáidsium* and in 14a *línmar sláin* beside *lessach línmar*.

It is evident that Bécán is a master of his art. The very first verse establishes the metrical scheme, the patterns of alliteration, and boldly stretches the limits of word order deviation. Now Kelly states (p. 4) that "In all verses but 2, 3, 4, 5 and 25 there is a regular caesura between the 4th and 5th syllable of each line." We may ignore 25, which is a later addition (n.5 above). Are we then to conclude that Bécán presented his metrical scheme in the great quatrain 1, then floundered until he found it again in 6, from which point he maintained it through 24? Surely not.

---

5   Verse 25 is with Kelly almost certainly a later addition, since it is unglossed and shows a different rime and alliteration scheme. The motivation for its addition must have been precisely to provide a more salient (and less sophisticated) *dúnad*, repetition of the whole first line.

A second look at verses 2 through 6 shows that Bécán is systematic-ally playing with several of the parameters of the verse scheme he presented so forcefully in 1, while holding others constant. The param-eters of isosyllabism and rime remain constant, as does the chain alliter-ation binding both verses and lines, which is always present save in 4b–c and c–d. But the line-internal alliteration can be either present, as throughout 3 and 5, or absent, as throughout 2 and 4ab; and it may either bridge the caesura or flank it. Furthermore, the position of the caesura can be varied from quatrain to quatrain, but not within the quatrain. Using the notation [4|3] (as in *Celtica* 6 (1963), pp. 220 ff.) for the 7-syllable line with caesura after the 4th syllable, [5|2] after the 5th, etc., and assigning a + or – feature for presence or absence of internal alliteration, quatrains 1 through 6 show the clearly intentionally varied pattern

$$
\begin{array}{lll}
1 & [4|3 & +] \\
2 & [5|2 & -] \\
3 & [6|1 & +] \\
4 & [6|1 & -] \\
5 & [5|2 & +] \\
6 & [4|3 & +],
\end{array}
$$

which systematically illustrates each variable before returning to the "default setting" [4|3 +].

Stanzas 2–6 follow, with metrical commentary in the notes.

2. *N*íbu fri coilcthi | *tincha*   [5|2 –]
  *t*indscan ernaigdi | *c*assa
  *c*rochais — níbu i | *cinta*
  a *ch*orp for tonna | *g*lassa.[6]

It was not on soft beds
he undertook elaborate prayers;
he crucified — it was not for crimes —
his body on the green waves.

---

6 The absence of the adornment of internal alliteration may be iconic to the content of this quatrain.

3. *G*abais a n-*a*damrae | n-*aí*   [6 | 1 +]
   *i*s coïr Mo **Ch**ummae i | n-**Í**
   *i*s mó imbrádud cach | *aí*
   a ndo-**r**igni airi in | **r**í.[7]

   He made the marvel of a claim,
   it is right that Mo Chummae should be in Iona;
   greater than anyone could think
   what the King did for him.

4. *R*o-fes i n-ocus i | *céin*   [6 | 1 –]
   *C*olumb coich boí acht ba | *o*ín
   tindis a ainm amail | gr*éin*
   ba lés i **c**omair cach | *oín*.[8]

   It was known near and far
   whose Columb was, but he belonged to the One;
   His name shone like the sun,
   he was a light before everyone.

5. A n-*ó*en as **d**ech di | *rétaib*   [5 | 2 +]
   *r*o-sóer a **m**anchu | *m*oinib
   *m*ár thendál íarna | *éccaib*
   a n-*ai*nm as úaisliu | *d*oínib.[9]

   The one [thing] which is best of things:
   he has freed his monks of riches;
   a great blaze after his death,
   is the name which is nobler than [other] people['s].

7   In *acd* we have alliteration bridging the caesura, so final monosyllables with vowel initial alliterate "twice", both within the line and with the initial of the next line. In *b* the alliterative pair is to the left of the caesura. Note that unstressed words may be fully integrated into the system of alliteration, unlike later Irish (and Germanic) practice.

8   The initials of lines *cd* lack chain alliteration. The lack is compensated for by the internal alliteration, which is non-bridging. On account of this I class the whole quatrain as structurally [6 | 1 –]. In *i n-ocus i céin, coich boí — ba oín* we may have grammatical figures. Cf. *coich boí coich bia ACC* §65?

9   Lines *b* and *c* have bridging alliteration, *a* and *d* non-bridging: *moínib, éccaib,* and *ainm* therefore each count twice, for linking and internal alliteration.

6. Is *d*ín[10] úathaid | is dín *slúaig*   [4|3 +]
  *s*lán cach eslán | asa *d*ún
  is *d*ún n-ínill | is caín *mbúaid*
  *b*uith íar Coluimb | Chille cúl.

   He is the protector of few, he is the protector of many,
   safe is every unsafe one whose fort he is;
   it is a safe fort, it is a fair advantage
   to be under the protection of Columb Cille.

With quatrain 6 we are back in the original verse scheme [4|3 +],
still with some ambiguities since in *a* and *c* it is not clear whether the
grammatical parallelism *is dín úa. | is dín sl., is dún n-í.| is caín mb.*
should take precedence over the weak bridging alliteration.

There is no alliteration linking the end of quatrain 6 *cúl* with the beginning of 7 *Ní séim n atach* 'He is no slight refuge'. The latter topos
serves as a discourse initial figure in one of the poems of Colmán mac
Lénéni, also of the seventh century: *Ní séim anim* 'It is no slight
blemish . . . ' (*ZCP* 19 (1932), pp. 196–207). It is therefore at least
possible that quatrain 7 begins a new sub-section of *Fo réir Choluimb*,
and that 6d *buith íar Coluimb* forms a little ring closing the first sub-
section 1–6, with the saint's name in the same syllable slot before the
caesura in both lines.

In any case, the first six quatrains of this poem in their handling of
meter, syllabism, rime and alliteration must be regarded not as an irregularity but as an artistic *tour de force*, a paradigm of the art of the
syllable in early medieval Ireland.

10 Cf. *Ba dín do nochtaib, ACC* §85, and perhaps read *Ba dīn do bochtaib* with *LH*
  for the continuation in view of the double figure in our poem here.

THE CELTIC BARD

J. E. Caerwyn Williams

CENTRE FOR ADVANCED WELSH AND CELTIC STUDIES
THE UNIVERSITY OF WALES

The word that springs to mind in thinking of the Celtic poet is 'bard', Latin *bardus*, Greek βάρδος.[1] Gaulish-Celtic *bardos*, whence Welsh *bardd* and Irish *bard*, although in Irish the usual word for poet is *file*, older *fili*, but *bard* was used at one time to denote one of the inferior grades of poets. A Latin writer tells us that *bardus* was the Gaulish name for 'the singer who sings the praises of brave men', *bardus Gallice cantor appellatur qui virorum fortium laudes canit, i.e., cantor . . . qui . . . canit*, i.e., 'the singer . . . who sings'. The Latin *cano*, Irish *canaim*, Welsh *canaf* are cognate words, i.e., they are derived from the same root, and though they can be translated 'I sing', they do not have, nor should we expect them to have, exactly the same meaning. After all, 'singing' does not have the same connotation for us as for our children, and 'sing' in Modern English has not the same meaning as Old English *singen*. However, people have always, it seems, distinguished between 'talking' and 'singing', and oral poetry seems always to have been in song. It is interesting to note that the Welsh word *cân* can mean 'poem' as well as 'song', that one of the oldest Welsh poems, the *Gododdin*, is introduced in the oldest manuscript in which it is preserved, the *Book of Aneirin*, with the words *Hwn yw e gododin*,

---

[1] This lecture was delivered as the first Hallstatt Lecture, 1991, for Tabernacl Trust, Machynlleth, Wales. For the classical sources of our knowledge of the Celtic bard see J. J. Tierney, "The Celtic Ethnography of Posidonius", *Proceedings of the Royal Irish Academy*, vol. 60 (1959–60), Section C, pp. 189–275. Cf. W. Dinan, *Monumenta Historica Celtica*, vol. 1 (London, 1911); John T. Koch (ed. in collaboration with John Carey), *The Celtic Heroic Age: Literary Sources for Ancient Celtic Europe and Early Ireland and Wales*, Celtic Studies Publications I (Malden, Massachusetts, 1995).

aneirin ae cant 'this is the *Gododdin*. Aneirin sang it', and that the Welsh formula *a'i cant* 'who sang it', just as the Irish *ro-chan*, has been used from time immemorial to conclude poems and to attribute their authorship. Still more remarkable is the fact that a study of Welsh *canaf* and Irish *canaim* and their derivatives reveals that the Welsh and Irish singer or chanter-poet was thought to have magical powers. Thus the Welsh word *darogan* shows that he could chant a prophecy and the Welsh word *dychan* shows that he could chant a satire, and in olden times it was thought that a satire could bring harm not only to the person satirized but also to his land. A verb-noun for the Celtic verb based on **kan-* was **kantlon*. This gave Welsh *cathl*, Breton *kentel*, and Breton *kentel* means 'lesson, instruction' and is a useful reminder that the Celtic chanter-poet was regarded probably above everything else as an instructor. **Kantlon* gave Irish *cétal*, and the compounds formed from *cétal* indicate what the chanter-poet could do in old Irish society: he gave instruction (*forcetal*), he uttered prophecies (*tairchetal*), he recited satirical insults (*aeraiccetal*), he cast spells (*tinchetal*), even extemporaneous spells, *díchetal di (do) chennaib*, literally, 'a chanting from heads'.

Some of you, some of the oldest perhaps, will remember that Virgil began the *Aeneid* with the words *arma virumque cano* 'I sing of arms and the man'. One of the early commentators on the *Aeneid* tells us that *cano* 'I sing' in such a collocation as *regem cano* meant 'I praise the king', and that in other contexts it could mean 'I prophecy' or 'I sing what has to be sung', e.g. in a religious rite.

All this serves to remind us that in olden times words in certain contexts had magical powers. If God could say, "Let there be light and there was light", so, it was thought, could his priests, his professional worshipers, and his hymn-chanters, the poets. But it was necessary for priest and poet to distinguish between their use of words in ordinary everyday conversation and their use of them in discharging their professional duties. This they could do by chanting their words and by organizing them in a different way through alliteration, consonance and rhythm, what we would call the architectonics of poetry.

Excavations at Uruk, the Biblical Erech, modern Warka in Iraq, have yielded a few tablets on which have been written epithets, adjectives applied to the gods, and dating to around 3000 B.C. On the basis of other and later finds illustrating Sumerian civilization it has been deduced that at the temples in Uruk priests and professional singers used to chant in worship of the gods and that their congregation joined with them, responding just as later congregations have done in liturgical services. Here we have the beginnings of oral literature, just as we have in the tablets the beginnings of written literature. The best known of Sumerian heroes was the eponymous hero of the epic of Gilgamesh, which is interesting to Biblical students because of its account of the Deluge, and interesting to students of comparative literature because the story, current in Asia Minor in the Hittite and Hurrian languages, may have influenced the Greek *Odyssey*.

Thanks to the researches of Milman Parry, A. B. Lord, and others we know a great deal more than our fathers about the *Odyssey* and the *Iliad* and the way they came into being.

A. B. Lord has reminded us that oral poetry was oral song and that the *Odyssey* and the *Iliad* were oral songs. In this context 'song' can mean the actual singing, the actual words used in the performance, and even the theme, which we may assume was the subject of similar songs. We can also distinguish between the new and the old elements in the song. In one way each performance is old insofar as it contains old elements, and new insofar as it contains new elements.

To quote A. B. Lord, Homer, assuming that he was the author, was a singer of tales or an oral poet, but "singer, performer, composer, and poet are one under different aspects *but at the same time*; singing, performing, composing are facets of the same act."[2]

It is significant that the Greeks used ἀοιδός 'singer' to describe Homer. It was later that the need was felt to give the name ποιητής to the poet-composer, and Homer in the strictest sense was not the poet-composer of the *Odyssey*, or perhaps it would be more correct to say that he was the last in a long line of poet-composers.

We can regard it as established that the Celtic *bardos* was an oral poet. If he was, was he such in the same sense as Homer? This is a question which does not in one way admit of an easy answer. We assume that the earliest insular Celtic poets of whom we have any knowledge, Aneirin and Taliesin in Britain and their counterparts in Ireland, composed their poems some time before they rose to deliver them orally in the presence of their patrons. It is an assumption that we make on the basis of our knowledge of the practice of Welsh and Irish poets in later ages.

According to the *Memoirs of the Right Honourable the Marquis of Clanricarde* (1722, 1744), the late but only comprehensive account that we have of an Irish bardic school, the practice there was to give the pupils a subject and details of the requirements of the meter to be used. They then "work'd it apart each by himself upon his own Bed, the whole next Day in the Dark, till at a certain Hour in the Night, lights being brought in, they committed it to writing."

Apparently it was the practice not only of the pupils but also of fully qualified poets to compose their poetry in the dark, and any departure from it provoked comment if not censure. According to Professor Bergin,

2 *The Singer of Tales* (Cambridge, Massachusetts: Harvard, 1960), p. 13.

It looks very like a relic of some rite or ceremony handed down from pagan times, long after its original purpose had been forgotten. We know that in early times the functions of the poet and the druid were very similar, and both practised magic.

It may very well be that Taliesin and Aneirin in Britain and their counterparts in Ireland composed their poems in the dark; it is extremely unlikely that they wrote them down at such an early date.

Granted, then, that they did not compose their poems orally or in the process of singing them as did Homer and his Greek contemporaries, we can say that they differed also in another respect. Homer and the earliest Greek poets sang narrative poems; they recited the mighty deeds of heroes in days long past. In Celtic literature the normal medium for narrative tales was prose, not verse, although verse was used for the expression of strong emotions and in dramatic situations. The late Professor Ifor Williams explained the structure of the so-called Llywarch Hen and Heledd poems as the survival of the verse parts of a now lost prose narrative. He quoted Irish parallels. The great Irish and Sanskrit scholar Windisch had shown that the Irish and the Hindus in ancient times held this tradition in common and it has been suggested that it is a tradition they derived from their Indo-European ancestors. The old Irish poets recited tales in prose. Welsh scholars are not of the unanimous opinion that the Welsh poets also were reciters of prose tales. The author or authors of the Llywarch Hen and Heledd poems and their prose-tales must have been poets.

We know that Taliesin and we assume that Aneirin composed poems in praise of royal patrons and that they recited their poems to them in their courts. That is why we call them court-poets. There is every reason to believe that Homer also sang to a royal audience in royal courts but as his subject was the feats of past heroes, he was not a court-poet in the same sense as Taliesin and Aneirin, who sang the praises of heroes who were present or recently departed.

Nevertheless, Homer and the Greeks knew of court-poets like Taliesin and Aneirin, for the *Odyssey* tells us that Demodocos in the court of Alcinous and Phemios in the court of Odysseus were there to praise their lords in their presence and that they themselves were held in great honor.

Cicero tells us that the Greek poet Simonides was once invited to a feast by a wealthy nobleman called Scopas at Cranon in Thessaly and that he chanted a lyric poem which he had composed in honor of his host and in which he had included for decorative purposes a long passage referring to Castor and Pollux. If we can take the poems of Pindar as normative, connecting the achievements of heroes with the gods was no empty convention devoid of any relevance to their praise.

Cicero also tells us that Cato in his *Origines* stated that it was the custom of the Romans in olden times for the guests at table to sing one after another in praise of the merits of illustrious men to the accompaniment of music from a flute. Varro mentions something similar at a later date: boys sang at banquets old songs of ancestral deeds; sometimes a flautist accompanied them.

The question arises: is there a connection between the tale-songs of Homer and the praise-songs of Demodocos, or to give them their convenient German names, between the *Heldenlieder* and the *Fürsten-Preislieder-Zeitgedicht*?

There is an obvious similarity in their social contexts and we can presume a common source. Indeed, on the basis of parallels taken from the literatures of the ancient Hindus and Persians in the East and of the Romans and Scandinavians in the West, Professor F. R. Schröder has argued that two kinds of hymns were composed in Indo-European societies, one praising and glorifying a single mighty act by a god, the other celebrating a number of such acts, that the first kind was sung to those remote deities who were far removed from men and their affairs, the other to those hero-deities who had taken an active part as saviors, dragon-slayers, etc., in the world of men. To the second type of hymn he gives the name *Aufreihlied* and one of his examples is the Virgilian praise-song to Hercules in Book VIII of the *Aeneid*, which was based, apparently, on an earlier hymn. In the *Aufreihlied* he finds, with good reason, the origin of the *Fürsten-Preislied*, the praise-song of the court-poet.

There can be no doubt that Taliesin and Aneirin in Britain and their bardic contemporaries in Ireland were practicing the same poetic art as that practiced by the *bardī* among the Celts on the Continent.

Although we have no examples of their work, we do have references to these Continental Celtic poets.

Athenaeus tells us that in order to court popular favor Louernius made a great feast, that as he was leaving at the end of the feast, he was met by a Celtic poet who had arrived too late and who composed a song magnifying Louernius's greatness and lamenting his own late arrival.

> Louernius was very pleased and asked for a bag of gold and threw it to the poet who ran beside his chariot. The poet picked it up and sang another song, saying that the very tracks made by his chariot on the earth gave gold and largesse to mankind.[3]

As you see, there is here no support for the view that the Continental Celtic poets composed their poems in the dark!

---

3 Tierney, "Celtic Ethnography of Posidonius", p. 248.

We are told by Appian of Alexandria that Bituitus, king of the Allobroges, sent an ambassador followed by attendants to try to appease the wrath of a Roman commander and that

> a musician too was in the train who sang in barbarous fashion the praises of Bituitus, and then of the Allobroges, and then of the ambassador himself, celebrating his birth, his bravery, and his wealth, and it is for this reason chiefly that ambassadors of distinction take such persons along with them.

Although the person who extols Bituitus, his people, and his ambassador is called a musician, there can be no doubt that he was a Gaulish or Celtic bard, especially in view of Athenaeus's testimony and that of Diodorus Siculus, who tells us that the Gauls had bards who sang sometimes a eulogy, sometimes a satire to the accompaniment of a musical instrument.

It is rather strange, but Julius Caesar does not mention the Gaulish bards, although he describes fairly fully their druids. They and the *equites* were the two important classes among the Gauls: the *plebes* did not count. We gather that the druids were the religious leaders and the legal administrators and that as such they wielded great power: they could ban persons from the public sacrifices and that was considered to be very grievous punishment.

It appears also that the druids were the educators; i.e., they knew and maintained and transmitted the tribal traditions by which people lived in those far-off days. They attracted many students: quite a number as recruits to their Order, but not all.

Caesar tells us two other things which are noteworthy. The Gaulish druids derived their rule of life (*disciplina*) from Britain and some of them still repaired there to perfect their knowledge of it. They had set their faces against committing their teaching to writing. They did not wish it to become common property nor those who learnt it to rely on writing and so neglect the cultivation of memory. Caesar's explanation is probably too simplistic. Dumézil, writing in 1940, suggested the possibility that the druidic aversion to writing stemmed from the belief that the spirit which renders sacred words powerful in themselves would die if they were committed to letters and thus fossilized. A similar aversion was attributed by Plutarch to Pythagoras, to Numa and Lycurgus, and this belief, attested elsewhere, may well be Indo-European.[4]

Some classical authors say that the Celts had another class of people called *vātēs* 'priests, prophets, magicians', and since they delivered their messages in verse, also poets. The name *vātēs* itself is most interesting on account of its cognates, Old English *wōþ* 'song', Old Norse *ōðr* 'poetry',

---

4 G. Dumézil, "La tradition druidique et l'écriture: le Vivant et le Mort", *Revue de l'Histoire des Religions* 122 (1940), pp. 125-33.

Old Irish *fáth* 'prophecy', *fáith* 'prophet' and Welsh *gwawd*, which now means 'mockery' but used to mean 'song, a song of praise'.

I would love to be able to tell you that we have an example of a vatic pronouncement in one of our Gaulish inscriptions. Unfortunately, all that I can say is that Professor Wolfgang Meid has argued, very cogently to my mind, that the Chamalières inscription, which is a magic text, begins with a decidedly rhythmic section.

If Caesar was right in stating that the druids were the only important class of people apart from the *equites* among the Gaulish Celts, and that they were the priests, the legislators and the educators, then the *bardī* and the *vātēs* must have been branches or offshoots of their Order, and we must think of the druids in the same terms as J. MacCulloch in his book *The Religion of the Ancient Celts*: "They were a great inclusive priesthood with different classes, possessing different functions — priestly, prophetic, magical, medical, legal and poetical."

The Romans also had their *vātēs*: indeed, Varro tells us that they used to call their ancient poets *vātēs*. From the word *vātēs* are derived *vaticinatio* in Latin and 'vaticination' in English.

At the beginning of this century *vātēs*, if not taken as a borrowing by the Romans from the Celts, would have been one of the words used to prove that there was a close relationship between Celtic and Latin or rather Italic, a closer relationship than among most of the other languages in the Indo-European family of languages. Nowadays very little credence is given to that relationship, but I need not tell you that it is an article of faith among linguists and philologists that Celtic, Italic, Greek, Persian and Sanskrit and many other languages are derived from Indo-European and that Indo-European comprises one of the great linguistic families of the world.

We know a great deal more than our fathers about Indo-European and the group of linguistic families that are derived from it as well as about Indo-European culture and those elements of it that have survived. Much of our new knowledge is the result of the researches of the late Georges Dumézil.

He studied the social and mythological forms presented by the Indo-European-speaking world and drew the following conclusions:

(1) that the parent Indo-European society before it broke up had a tripartite ideology;

(2) that elements of this tripartite ideology were carried by the inheritors of that society throughout the length and breadth of the area which was to become their domain;

(3) that some of these elements can be discovered in most but by no means all of the early Indo-European epic and mythic literatures, from

the Vedas of ancient India to the Eddas of pre-Christian Iceland, from the *Mahābhārata* to the *Heimskringla*;

(4) that neither this ideology nor anything like it can be found outside the Indo-European domain nor even in that area prior to its occupation by Indo-Europeans or their descendants.

The basis of this ideology was the tripartition of society best seen in early India in the division of the people into *Kṣatriyas, Brāhmana*, and *Vaiśyas*; in early Rome, in their division into *milites, flamines, quirites*; in early Gaul and other Celtic countries, in their division into *equites, druides, plebes*; in other words into the three classes: warrior nobility, the priests and the learned, and the farmers or food-providers.

The significance to us of all this is that we can equate the *druids* with the *brahmans* and the *flamines* as the representatives or descendants of the Indo-European priestly caste. It explains the tremendous power that they wielded and it explains why Dio Chrysostom could affirm with pardonable exaggeration that "the kings were not permitted to do or plan anything without the assistance of these wise men [i.e. the druids], so that in truth it was they who ruled, while the kings became their servants and the ministers of their will."[5]

It may be that Dio Chrysostom had heard that it was the Gaulish druids, like their counterparts in Ireland, who pronounced whether certain days were auspicious or inauspicious for certain actions and that the kings always considered it wise to consult them before embarking on any important course of action. As the representatives of the gods, the druids could demand to be heard, and it should be remembered, of course, that the kings and their warrior-aristocracy were aware that they exercised their power by the will of the gods, and that they could not afford to turn a deaf ear to the representatives of those gods.

I have emphasized the authority and power of the druids because the poets were originally a branch of the druidic order, and because the shadow of the druids lay heavily on the poets of both Ireland and Wales even at a much later date when both countries had rejected paganism.

As I have said, the Irish word *bard* and the Welsh word *bardd* come from the Celtic *bardos* and *bardos* is derived from the IE root *$g^u er(ə)$*- — which meant 'to raise the voice, to praise, to extol, to welcome'. The same root yielded Avestan *(aibi-)jarətay*- 'laudator' and Sanskrit *jaritár*- 'singer, praiser'.

From the same root apparently came the Latin *grātēs* 'thanks' and *grātia*, and the realization that Latin *grātia* gave English 'grace' will help us to realize that the Indo-European and Celtic poet, in welcoming, celebrating and extoling a virtue like 'bravery' in his patron, was acknowl-

---

5 *Orations* 49.

edging that it had come from the gods, and was adding confirmation to it as a gift from the gods, even if not bringing it into existence with their permission.

As poet and prophet, as diviner and magician the Celtic bard was inspired, literally 'breathed into'. The Welsh word *awen* 'muse, poetic genius' is from the same root as Welsh *awel* 'a breeze' and as English *wind*, and it is cognate with the Irish *aí (*aui)* 'poetic art'. Ultimately it is the same root which has given Welsh *gwawd*, Irish *fáth* 'prophecy', *fáith* 'prophet'. Another pair of words which testify to the inspiration of the Celtic poet are W. *anant*, an old Welsh word for 'poets', and Irish *anamain cetharreach*, an old word for a metrical measure: both contain the same root as Welsh *anadl* 'breath' and Ir. *anam* 'soul'.

As I said at the beginning, the usual word for poet in Irish is *file*, Old Irish *fili*. The word has the same root as Welsh *gwel(ed)* 'seeing'. Originally the Irish poet was a 'seer', and because he saw, he also *knew*, with the result that great store was set on his knowledge, which originally, like that of the druid, extended beyond knowledge of this world alone. It was mainly by reason of his knowledge that the Irish *file* was superior to the Irish *bard*.

Our Welsh ancestors could speak of *awen milwriaeth* 'the spirit of fighting', and no doubt the military nobility of the Indo-Europeans, and the military nobility of the ancient Hindus, the Romans, and of the Celts after them knew of this 'spirit', this 'in-spir-ation'. There is reason to believe that one of the names for it in Indo-European was **menes*, which has been defined as 'inward stimulus for action', for the gods could give to men a good **menes*, an exceptional **menes*, a manly **menes*. Its Greek cognate μένος meant 'spirit', its Sanskrit cognate *mánas-* meant 'mind'. Another glimpse of it is caught in the Greek word κῦδος which means 'the magical power the possession of which gave superiority especially in battle, and ensured victory'.

A Greek synonym for κῦδος was κλέος 'honor, fame, glory'; from the same root come W. *clod*, Ir. *cloth*, and the W. *clyw-ed*, the Irish *ro-cluinethar* 'hears', but originally κλέος 'honor' was not something to be heard — it was something to be found in a person, something which could manifest itself and be measured, which could be lost and restored. Welsh *wyneb* and Irish *enech*, both meaning literally 'face', were used as synonyms for 'honor', and for 'honor-price' we have W. *wynebwerth*, Ir. *enechlog*. The honor-price set for the king of Aberffraw in one legal text was a hundred cows from each cantref in his lordship and on top of that a gold rod and plate of specific dimensions.

But if κλέος 'honor' was something in man, it was somehow dependent on being acknowledged by other men. That is why κλέος was not only 'honor' but also 'fame'.

To help you to understand this I invite you to remember an incident in the life of the Irish hero Cú Chulainn.

One day he heard the druid Cathbad say: "This is an auspicious day. Whoever takes up arms today, his name will be above the men of Ireland for feats of valor forever and the story of his fame shall last forever." As was to be expected, Cú Chulainn demanded to be given arms. But then Cathbad had to add: "Yes, he who takes arms today will be famous and renowned, but he will live for only a short time." "No matter," said Cú Chulainn, "so long as I shall be famous, I shall be content with only one day in the world."

It will be seen that Cú Chulainn was determined to do feats of valor that would make him famous, but he took it for granted that his feats would be heard and live in the ears of men.

He was in the same lineage as Achilles and the other Greek heroes. And as Achilles depended on the poets to sing his undying fame, κλέος ἀθάνατον, and as the heroes of ancient India expected unfading fame, ákṣiti śrávaḥ, so also did Cú Chulainn. The Welsh poet, Phylip Brydydd, in the thirteenth century knew his duty when he told his patron,

> Gwneuthum it glot
>
> I made fame for thee.

So did one of the other Welsh court-poets when he said,

> Gwnawn glod yntau o'th draws gampau
>
> Let us fashion fame, then, of thy feats of arms.

But we must remember that the gods could deprive a man of his κλέος and that the poet could deprive a king of his honor and fame by satirizing him: indeed, it was the poet's duty to do so when the king acted against the will of the gods and strayed from the path of duty, and a satire could bring not only harm to the person satirized but also devastation to his lordship and country.

It is not surprising that, aware of those facts, classical authors took the singing of praise to be the constitutive activity of the Celtic poets. It is more surprising that we in Wales have taken the same activity as definitive for our literary tradition. We are proud of our so-called Taliesin tradition. We forget that we had at one time a Myrddin or prophetic tradition as well, and had more of our early literature survived, we would realize that our early poets sang various kinds of poems, that they celebrated the main events in the lives of their patrons up to and including their deaths, that they sang religious, admonitory and gnomic songs, that they entertained their patrons' household-soldiers and attendants, and that they sometimes used their poetic art to give expression to their personal feelings.

No one can have any doubt that the Insular Celtic poets practiced the same art as their Continental counterparts and that the earliest Welsh and Irish poets continued the traditions of their Brythonic and Goedelic predecessors.

We are told that Brythonic had developed into Welsh by about the middle of the sixth century. An early historian informs us that at that time Talhaearn Tad Awen, 'Talhaearn, the Father of the Muse', the Welsh Muse, gained renown in poetry. He mentions four other poets who gained renown at the same time in British poetry. Poems attributed to two of them, Taliesin and Aneirin, have survived. These poems were sung within a long established, not a recently begun, tradition, and like the authors of the earliest Irish poetry, Aneirin and Taliesin seem to have been trained in schools. We would call them bardic schools. There were similar schools in Ireland and there they taught not only the art of poetry but also history and law. Indeed, the late Professor Daniel Binchy was of the opinion that the collection of legal texts bearing the name of *Bretha Nemed* emanated from a school where history, law, and poetics were taught, or rather where *filidecht*, the craft of the *fili*, included history and law as well as poetics: in other words, in a school which bore marked resemblance to the druidic schools of Gaul.

finit. finit. finit.
amen.